WITHDRAWN

Theory of Population
and Economic Growth

Theory of Population and Economic Growth

Julian L. Simon

Basil Blackwell

© Julian L. Simon 1986

First published 1986

Basil Blackwell Ltd
108 Cowley Road, Oxford OX4 1JF, UK

Basil Blackwell Inc.
432 Park Avenue South, Suite 1505,
New York, NY 10016, USA

British Library Cataloguing in Publication Data
Simon, Julian L.
Theory of population and economic growth.
1. Economic development
I. Title
339.5   HD82
ISBN 0-631-14427-7

Library of Congress Cataloging in Publication Data
Simon, Julian Lincoln, 1932–
Theory of population and economic growth.
1. Population. 2. Economic development. 3. Population – Mathematical models.
4. Economic development – Mathematical models. I. Title.
HB849.41.S55   1986   338.9'00724   85-28574
ISBN 0-631-14427-7

Typeset by Unicus Graphics Ltd, Horsham, West Sussex
Printed in Great Britain by Billing and Sons Ltd, Worcester

Contents

Acknowledgements

My main debt in the preparation of this book is to Gunter Steinmann, who collaborated with me in chapters 5, 6, and 7. He found analytic solutions to propositions that I had only conjectured or simulated, solutions which make the propositions much more convincing. He also added dimensions to the work; for example, capital was not explicitly present in my sketchy treatment of the learning-by-doing model in chapter 5 when I first showed it to him. In addition, I have used various expository paragraphs from our joint papers at other places in the book. Our collaboration has borne pleasure as well as fruit.

Sanford Thatcher and René Olivieri made excellent editorial suggestions about what should and should not be included in the book. And I have benefited by conversations and correspondence about various chapters and ideas with Harold Barnett, Mark Browning, Jonathan Cave, Fritz Machlup, Leonard Mirman, Robert Pollak, William Serow, Eytan Sheshinksi, Max Singer, James Smith, and several thoughtful and open-minded referees.

Richard Sullivan and Stephen Moore were excellent research assistants, and performed a multitude of tasks well. The manuscript was originally typed by Carol Halliday's wonderful word-processing centre, much of it by Carol herself. The quality of that work execution and quick turn-around, as well as her unfailing pleasantness, will be a standard against which I will compare for a long time to come. In the final stages of preparation, Helen Demarest carried out the small but exasperating manuscript chores with unfailing hard work, good sense, and courageous good cheer; having her help on a regular basis means more to me than she believes.

I am deeply grateful for the turn of events starting in 1980 that saved my work on the economics of population from going unnoticed by the economics and demographic professions, and by the general public. Prior to that time, a positive publisher's review by Ronald Lee of my 1977 book, and courageous editorial management by Sanford Thatcher, plus later enterprise by René Olivieri, were crucial in getting my books published. Kind words by Harold Barnett, a wonderful economist and a hugely generous man from whose work I learned one of the main elements in my thinking on these subjects, plus support from my family and friends, buoyed me up when sinking seemed more reasonable. And a remarkable letter of encouragement out of the blue from Friedrich Hayek gave me new strength. But without a series of articles in general scientific journals and in the mass media, one of which publications followed the other like a set of dominos, none of which would have fallen if the first had not, my work until that time would have had no effect, and the present book would not be before you today. Hard work, yes, but luck, too, in people and events. I feel full of thanks.

Chapter 5 was published as 'The Economic Implications of Learning-by-Doing for Population Size and Growth' in *European Economic Review*, Vol. 26, 1984, pp. 167–85; chapter 6 as 'Phelps's Technical Progress Model Generalized' in *Economic Letters*, Vol. 5, 1980, pp. 177–82; chapter 7 as 'On the Optimum Theoretical Rate of Population Growth' in *Jahrbücher für Nationalökonomie und Statistik*, Vol. 200/5, pp. 508–31; chapter 8 as 'The Present Value of Population Growth in the Western World' in *Population Studies*, Vol. 37, 1983, pp. 5–21; and chapter 9 as 'The Really Important Effects of Immigrants Upon Natives' Incomes' in Barry Chiswick (ed.), *The Gateway* (Washington: American Enterprise Institute, 1981). I appreciate permission to reprint these pieces here.

Notation

Most notation used is included in this list. In a few cases, notation used only briefly in a single chapter is defined only there.

A_t = the level of technique in use, which may usually be thought of as productivity per worker as of period t

C = cost of production

D = demand for new technology, usually a superscript

E = disequilibrium gap in capital–output ratio

G = gross income

H_N = hours of work done on the output unit with serial number N

$J_{t,t}$ = a piece of knowledge existing in period t

K_t = stock of capital

L_t = population size (= labour force in most contexts) of a country (or of the more-developed world) in t

M_t = the amount of technology available as of period t

N_i = serial number for a particular unit of output of good or industry i

$P_{i,t}$ = price for good i

$Q_{i,t}$ = output of industry i or good i

R_t = potential number of ideas that might be discovered in t given a particular set of conditions

S = supply of new technology, usually a superscript

T = taxes

X = units produced of good i or by industry i

Y = total output

Z = lifetime income of natives

a, b, c, g, l, α, β, γ, Δ, ϕ, Ψ, ν, χ, ϵ = constants

f = an indefinite function, indicating that the left-hand side depends upon the right-hand side in some unspecified manner, with subscripts sometimes used to distinguish them

$g =$ a constant equilibrium value of the subscript variable, e.g.
  g_L, g_M

$h_N =$ cumulative hours of work necessary to produce units from 1
  to N

$i =$ index for an industry or a good

$\tilde{i} =$ index for industries other than i that may attract inventive
  effort from industry i

$m_t = M_t - M_{t-1}$

$r =$ rate of return on capital

$s =$ savings rate, as a proportion of output

$t =$ index for time period

$v = Y/K =$ reciprocal of capital–output ratio

$w =$ the wage rate

$x =$ superscript indicating an optimal equilibrium value, e.g. g_L^x

$y = Y/L =$ output per worker

$z =$ adjustment factor in savings function

$\cdot =$ rate of change of variable with respect to itself, e.g.

$$\dot{L} = \frac{L_t - L_{t-1}}{L_{t-1}} \text{ in continuous form}$$

Introduction

What is the effect in the long run upon the standard of living, in the more-developed world, of additional people? The aim of this book is to help answer that question. The main tool is the mathematical theory of economic growth, and the key element of the analysis is that technical change responds in various ways to population size, density and growth. That is, the book attempts to implant the central fact of economic development in the long run – productivity change – into the neo-classical growth theory, to reflect the influence of population. And it tries to do so in such a manner as will be consistent with the observed facts about the overall relationship between population and economic growth, as well as with the facts about the other linkages within the overall model.

The first purpose of the book is to serve as a practical guide to policy decisions concerning population growth – births, deaths and immigration – in a large, more-developed community such as the US or Western Europe. Growth theory may at first seem an inappropriate tool for such purposes, because it is commonly thought of (even by its practitioners) as being an art form irrelevant for policy purposes, and not a practical tool. But this separation from reality need not be so. The theory of change on the way to a steady state can have a sufficiently short time horizon to be helpful in policy discussions. And even steady-state theory can be worth developing if – as is the case here – it reaches conclusions contrary to accepted models which now influence policy even though their relevance is doubtful. That is, it requires a theory to kill a theory, as the saw has it. To reduce the influence of the existing wrong (and irrelevant) theory is the second purpose of the book.

As a rock-bottom objective, physicians are enjoined to do no harm. Economists in general, and those specializing in growth theory in particular, should take the same injunction seriously. Yet I believe that, for reasons of mathematical convenience and elegance, growth theory has mostly *not* tried hard to avoid doing harm with respect to sound understanding of the effects of population size and growth. And in some cases, deep-seated belief about the bad effects of population growth seems to have prevented some writers (e.g. Kaldor, 1957; Eltis, 1973; and Samuelson, 1975) from accepting their own sound conclusions about these matters even when such conclusions are patent in their models. This book tries to undo some of the resulting harm.

Throughout most of the book, only the underlying 'real' variables – labour, capital, technology, output, income and education – enter into the analysis. Institutional arrangements such as government regulation and transfers to dependants are not discussed, with the exception that reasonably full detail on income transfers is included in the application of the model to the assessment of immigrants as an investment for natives in chapter 9. Elsewhere, leaving out transfers should not affect the conclusions. Saving is another variable not treated in any detail, but rather is assumed to be a constant proportion of income; simulation experiments suggest that more complex treatment would not alter the conclusions, however.

Let us discuss the central question to which laypeople want an answer when they think about population policy in a more-developed country (MDC). The question refers, I believe, to the effects on living persons of adding more people (newborn or immigrants) to their country or city this year, or in a series of years starting now. Laypeople are *not* likely to be interested in a comparison of long-run growth rates with or without the additional people, analysed in a long-run equilibrium context, because they do not wish to ignore the adjustments that will be made as a result of additional people.

Laypeople, and also economists, often reach first conclusions about this question from experiences in their daily lives such as (a) an influx of people into a town such as Champaign-Urbana, Illinois, for a football game when the restaurants are jammed and the traffic is heavy, causing inconvenience for residents; (b) the camps in which refugees, for example those who came from Cuba in 1980, are kept after landing in the US, and then shortly afterwards the conditions in the cities such as Miami where the refugees concentrate; (c) the situation aboard a warship or cruise ship when, for emergency reasons, it has taken on more persons than its complement; (d) Calcutta, with many migrants from rural areas.

All these cases involve fixity of capital resources within the perceived time span, and therefore capital dilution when people are added – that is, less capital for residents to live with and work with. It is this straightforwardly Malthusian outcome that is at the root of most arguments against population growth. It is also an argument that is unassailable in its own terms. Additional people do indeed dilute capital and reduce the standard of living when they first arrive.

Other common-sense evidence, however, is confusing. There are more people alive today than in earlier epochs, and yet most people are better off in most material ways than in the past. The last 300 years, during which the Western world has had the most rapid population growth in history, has also been the period of the most rapid economic growth in history. And in the quarter century from 1950 to 1975, during which the population in less-developed countries (LDCs) has grown very rapidly, *per capita* income has also grown rapidly – at least as rapidly as in the MDC world (Morawetz, 1978). This suggests that though the Malthusian theory is logically unassailable, it is also incomplete.

The left-out element clearly is the advance of technical knowledge. New technology more than compensates for the reduction in resources caused by additional people, and therefore enables us to live better than those who came before us; there is no dispute about this. There *is* dispute, however, about the source of the technology, and the relationship of additional people to additional technology. There may also be dispute about the timing of additional technology and its benefits, concerning both the facts of the lags in adoption and the value judgement implied in the decision about how to discount those future benefits.

Bringing this previously omitted element into the model means that the level of the technology that is combined with labour and capital in the production function must be influenced by population directly or indirectly, rather than being an exogenous function of time's passage as has been traditional in growth theory. There are a variety of ways to do this, and the appropriate technical progress function is a legitimate matter for discussion. Certainly the function is a complex relationship, embodying such disparate elements as

(a) the products of 'basic' university research, which are likely to reflect the size of the research staff and other work force; and (b) the results of on-the-job improvements in production methods, which are likely to reflect the amount of output in various industries. The book concentrates on the former, formal research, whereas the latter phenomenon, 'learning-by-doing', is taken up as a secondary theme. A realistic function would embody both phenomena together, but such complexity is not likely to be worthwhile; furthermore, both elements in such a technical progress function produce similar outcomes, as shown by separate investigations of them.

In order to avoid fruitless controversy about whether a small country can ride on the technological coat-tails of other countries and therefore has no need to make advances of its own in new technology, I wish to emphasize that the context of the discussion is the more-developed world as a whole – the West plus Japan and Oceania – together with the modern enclaves in less-developed countries. This unit is broad enough to encompass the effects that would be externalities of one more-developed country with respect to another. This unit of observation also should avoid fruitless discussion of the relationship of a single country's population size to its own economic development in a cross-national context. That is, it obviates the charge that the higher income per person in Sweden than in Great Britain shows that additional people do not make for a higher standard of living in the long run. (This is not to say that important technical research is never local or domestic. It is, as is shown clearly by much agricultural research, but certainly much technology is not tied to particular geographic or cultural conditions, and it is for this reason that national borders are not the logical boundaries for the discussion in this book.) It is also well to note that with the passage of time, the poorer parts of the world surely will also come to contribute heavily to the rest of the world's technical level, rather than simply being mostly a recipient as at present.

Even though the relevant context of discussion is the more-developed world as a whole, evidence for particular countries is occasionally adduced and the relationship across countries analysed. The reason for this deviation of empirical practice from theoretical context is simply because these are the only data that exist: we do not have a set of more-developed worlds to compare at a particular moment, and there are insufficient historical data on our only more-developed world to support a time-series analysis. Cross-national analyses are likely to understate the impact of population upon technical advance, productivity and the standard of living, and therefore the results that emerge are all the more noteworthy; this also should blunt the criticism of such cross-national comparisons.

Another fundamental issue in the understanding of the effects of population growth upon and through the increase in technology is the role of social and economic institutions. This crucial issue has previously been scanted in discussion of population growth, by me as well as by others, perhaps because the issue seemed tinged heavily with ideology. But by 1985 there is objective evidence that a free-enterprise system increases economic welfare more rapidly than does a planned economy. This is most easily seen in the comparisons of North versus South Korea, East versus West Germany, and China versus Taiwan and Singapore and Hong Kong, starting after the Second World War. In all these comparisons, the birth rate was similar when the comparison begins, as were culture and language, and in each case the planned socialist economy started out with less population 'pressure' in the form of population density. Population growth under an enterprise system rather clearly poses less of a problem in the short run, and brings more benefits in the long run, than under conditions of government planning of the economy. This element is not present in the models analysed in this book, but it should be kept in mind nevertheless, and in the future the analysis should embody it explicitly.

A few definitions:[1] 'Productivity' here means the rate of change of output per person in the labour force from year to year. 'Technique' means the set of productive practices in use in the economy at a given moment. 'Technical change' means change in technique. 'Technology' means the stock of knowledge about technique that is available at a given moment, some of it already embodied in practice and some of it not. 'Knowledge' does not include anything that might not affect economic output; that is, it excludes art and mystic experience. Analytically, knowledge has the same meaning here as does technology, but its spirit is broader and relates more to basic knowledge than does the term 'technology'.

While I think the spirit of the work may properly be called 'neo-classical', the models are not closed in the sense that all resources are bought and paid for, and some quantity is subject to a conservation law. Rather, increases in technology and productivity arise without cost in these models. This is not a realistic portrayal of some situations; for example, increases in productivity due to learning-by-doing may be explicitly considered by the firm to be an intermediate good and taken into account in profit-maximizing decisions about, say, investment, pricing and output. Yet this is not done in the models, for several reasons. First, neither industry nor economic modelling has reached nearly this stage of sophistication, and to try to achieve it here would present great obstacles to getting on with the rest of the job. Second and perhaps more important, it seems to me most fruitful to consider this topic in the context of an open system in which not all the quantities of interest to us are subject to calculable conservation laws.

The extent to which technology should be thought of as a market good, or as a good that arises with little connection to the demand for it and the cost of its production, is discussed at greater length starting on pp. 48–9.

Perhaps the most general matter at issue here is what Gerald Holton calls a 'thema'. The thema underlying the thinking of most writers who have a point of view different from mine is the concept of fixity or finiteness of resources in the relevant system of discourse. This is part of Malthus' thinking, of course. But the idea probably has always been a staple of human thinking because so much of our situation must sensibly be regarded as fixed in the short run – our pay cheque, the bottles of beer in the refrigerator, the amount of energy parents have to play with their kids. But the thema underlying my thinking about resources (and the thinking of a minority of others) is that the relevant system of discourse has a long enough horizon that it makes sense to treat the system as open and not fixed, rather than finite in any operational sense. We see the resource system as being as unlimited as the number of thoughts a person might have, or the number of variations that might ultimately be produced by biological evolution. That is, a key difference between the thinking of those who worry about impending doom, and those who see the prospects of a better life for more people in the future, apparently is whether one thinks in closed-system or open-system terms. For example, those who worry that the second law of thermodynamics dooms us to eventual decline necessarily see our world as a closed system with respect to energy and entropy; those who view the relevant universe as unbounded view the second law of thermodynamics as irrelevant to this discussion. I am among those who view the relevant part of the physical and social universe as open for most purposes. Which thema is better for thinking about resources and population is not subject to scientific test. Yet it profoundly affects our thinking. I believe that this is the root of the key difference in thinking about population and resources.

Following this introduction, chapter 1 broadly reviews the relevant theory starting with Petty and Malthus. It then discusses previous work that has made technical change endogenous, especially the studies of Kaldor (1957), Arrow (1962) and Phelps (1966).

Chapter 2 presents a probabilistic model of the discovery of new ideas from the combination of existing ideas. The aim of the model is to learn about differences in the likelihood of duplication and of diminishing returns to additional researches with different sizes of population. The model suggests that duplication is of relatively little importance with a relatively fast population growth.

Chapter 3 presents a supply–demand framework for analysing the quantity of technology produced. It builds upon work by Machlup (1962), Schmookler (1966, 1973) and Rosenberg (1972), but it is cast into formal terms in such a manner that it points toward theoretical manipulations and empirical studies.

Chapter 4 presents some of the more striking empirical evidence that has bearing upon the theory discussed in chapter 1 and the supply–demand analysis discussed in chapter 3. It covers both the production of knowledge itself, as well as differences in productivity that are related to differences in population and industry size.

Part II presents the growth models; chapter 5 analyses a learning-by-doing model (joint work with Gunter Steinmann) that departs from Alchian's analysis of the learning-by-doing data and from Arrow's growth-theoretical model. It works with a function different from Arrow's that is a closer fit to the data. It shows how, when the sequence of outputs – beginning with the very first unit, a crucial assumption – is analysed in the light of various population size and growth parameters, more people imply a higher standard of living. This conclusion does not emerge from Arrow's or other steady-state analyses. A confusing apparent paradox is resolved in the course of the analysis.

Chapter 6 offers the basic model with which much of the work in the rest of the book is concerned. It is a generalization, including the economic elements suggested by the supply–demand analysis in chapter 4, of Phelps's 1966 model that was developed by him for the rather different purpose of choosing the ideal level of R&D. The steady-state solution (worked out by Steinmann) indicates that the rate of growth of consumption is a positive function of the labour force, Phelps's solution being a special case of this one.

Chapter 7 pushes the steady-state theory further, grappling with the implication of the model presented in chapter 6 (and of Phelps's model) that faster population growth has positive effects *without limit*. Steinmann and I add an adoption-of-technology function to the basic model, and the solution yields a concave-downward relationship between population growth and growth of consumption. This is more reasonable, from the point of view of economic theory and common sense, than is a linear relationship suggesting increasing benefits from population growth without limit.

Chapter 8 applies the growth theory in a context relevant to policy decisions. Rather than dealing with a very long-run steady state, this chapter considers the present values of the streams of incomes associated with various rates of population growth on a variety of assumptions. The results indicate that at reasonable discount rates, faster population growth has a higher present value than does slower population growth.

Putative limits imposed by natural resources are often cited as a constraint upon growth models, and especially in the context of population growth (e.g. Samuelson, 1975). Therefore, the appendix discusses natural resources as a possible modifier of the results yielded by the models, and offers a new analysis of why the price of natural resources relative to consumer goods falls in the very long run.

There follows a conclusion.

A word about the relationship of this book to my *The Economics of Population Growth* (1977) and *The Ultimate Resource* (1981). The 1977 book attempted to cover the entire subject described in its title, with the exception of distributional effects. The consequences of population growth within the MDCs took up only a bit more than two of its chapters, and the theory of MDC growth with endogenous technical change was covered in one of those two chapters in a rather primitive fashion. The 1981 book covered in greater depth some of the empirical material on the relationship of population to knowledge and productivity, and that new material is included here in chapter 4. The 1981 book aims at a general audience and is quite non-technical. None of the formal argument and simulation which is the backbone of this book is discussed there.

NOTE

1   This classification is intended to be in the spirit of Machlup.

PART I
Concepts and Data

1
The Theory Until Now

I. THE STATIC THEORY OF POPULATION AND INCOME

Classical economic theory apparently shows irrefutably that population growth must reduce the standard of living.[1] The heart of all economic theory of population, from Malthus to *The Limits to Growth*, can be stated in a single sentence: the more people using a stock of resources, the lower the income per person, if all else remains equal. This proposition derives from the 'law' of diminishing returns: two workers cannot use the same tool at the same time, or farm the same piece of land, without reducing the output per worker. A related idea is that two people cannot nourish themselves from a given stock of food as well as one person can. And when one considers the age distribution resulting from a higher birthrate, the effect is reinforced by a larger proportion of children, and thus a lower proportion of workers, in the larger population. Let us spell out these Malthusian ideas.

The Consumption Effect

Simply adding more people to a population affects consumption directly. If there is only one pie, the pieces will be smaller if it is divided among more eaters. This consumption effect occurs most sharply within a family. When there are more children, each one gets a smaller part of the family's earnings, if earnings remain the same.

The Production Effect

Adding people also affects consumption indirectly, through the effect on production per worker. Consider a country that possesses a given amount of land, and a given quantity of factories and other industrial capital, at a given time. If the country has a larger labour force, the production per worker will be lower because each worker has, on the average, less land or tools to work with. Hence average production per worker will be lower with a larger labour force and fixed capital. This is the classical argument of diminishing returns.

The Public Facilities Effect

If a given population is instantly enlarged by, say, 10 per cent in all age groups, there will be 10 per cent more people wanting to use the village well or the city hospital or the public beach. An increase in the demand for such freely provided public services inevitably results in an increase in the number of people who are denied service, a decrease in the amount of service per person, or an additional expenditure by the government to increase the amount of public facilities.

As a result of the increased demand, the average level of public services received is likely to be lower; the average person will receive less education and less health care than if the population remains fixed. And some tax moneys that might have gone into harbours or communication systems may go instead to the education and health care of the added people.

Age-Distribution Effects

A faster growing population implies a larger proportion of children, which means that a larger proportion of the population is too young to work. This smaller proportion of workers must mean a smaller output *per capita*, all else being equal. Therefore, the effect of sheer numbers of people, and the age distribution that occurs in the process of getting to the higher numbers, both work in the same direction, causing a smaller *per capita* product.

When one also takes women's labour into account, the effect of having a higher proportion of children is even greater. The more children that are born per woman, the less chance she has to work outside the home. There is a counter-balancing effect from the father's work, however; a wide variety of studies show that an additional child causes fathers to work additional hours, the equivalent of two to six extra weeks of work a year.

Age distribution affects income distribution, too. A larger proportion of younger persons implies that more earners will one day support each retired person, which means a better pension for each retired person and a smaller burden on each each working-age person.

Other Static Theoretical Effects

The dilution of capital through reduced saving and through reduced education per person, are other elements of the standard economic theory of population growth (though they may well be far smaller drawbacks than commonly thought, and perhaps no drawbacks at all). The only positive theoretical effect is that of larger markets and larger-scale production, that is, economies of scale.

II.   GROWTH THEORY AND POPULATION

In the simplest Harrod–Domar growth model there is no technical change at all. And the conclusion is much the same as that of Malthus, and for the same reason: with more people, more investment is necessary to maintain the same levels of capital and output per person, which implies lower consumption per person. Growth theory that introduces constant exogenous technical change leads directly to the same conclusion: faster population growth implies lower consumption.

The main corpus of growth theory with respect to population growth can fairly be summarized as a no-complications dynamization of Malthus' capital dilution with a simple conclusion: more people imply lower income. This line of thought is found both in works on population growth such as those of Phelps (1972) or Pitchford (1974), as well as in such general studies of growth as those of Solow (1970), Brems (1973) and Dixit (1976). Indeed, none mention any models of endogenous technical progress. The only exception I have found is Wan (1973), who discusses Arrow's and Phelps's models of endogenous technical progress, but does not connect them to population growth.

Furthermore, it is amply clear that this main stream of growth theory has had influence on the policies of nations and on public opinion; the former is well documented in Piotrow (1973).

Division of labour is related to the technique in practice. Petty's statement seems to be more vivid than Smith's:

> ... the Gain which is made by *Manufactures*, will be greater, as the Manufacture itself is greater and better ... each *Manufacture* will be divided into as many parts as possible, whereby the Work of each *Artisan* will be simple and easie; As for Example. In the making of a *Watch*, If one Man shall make the *Wheels*, another the *Spring*, another shall Engrave the *Dial-plate*, and another shall make the *Cases*, then the *Watch* will be better and cheaper, than if the whole Work be put upon any one Man. And we also see that in *Towns*, and in the *Streets* of a great *Town*, where all the *Inhabitants* are amost of one Trade the Commodity peculiar to those places is made better and cheaper than elswhere. .... (1682/1899, p. 473)

Taken by itself, however, division of labour seems more an issue of economies of scale than of technical *change*, because division of labour is reversible. Hence it shall not appear again in the discussion here (except as it is related to the rate of learning-by-doing; see chapter 5).

The theoretical argument that more people imply more ideas, which must eventually raise productivity and income, was stated clearly by Petty:

> As for the Arts of Delight and Ornament, they are best promoted by the greatest number of emulators. And it is more likely that one ingenious curious man may rather be found among 4 million than 400 persons.... And for the propagation and improvement of useful learning, the same may be said concerning it as above-said concerning ... the Arts of Delight and Ornament.... (1682/1899, p. 474)

More recently, Kuznets discussed this idea:

> The greatest factor in growth of output per capita is, of course, the increasing stock of tested, useful knowledge. The producers of this stock are the scientists, inventors, engineers, managers, and explorers of various description – all members of that population whose growth we are considering. Assume now that, judged by native capacities (and they do differ), 0.05 per cent of a given population are geniuses, another 2.0 per cent are possessors of gifts that may be described as talent, and another 10.0 per cent have distinctly higher than average capacity for fruitful search for facts, principles, and inventions. (The grades of native ability and percent-

ages are, of course, purely illustrative, and would probably be changed by an expert in this field.) Since we have assumed the education, training, and other capital investment necessary to assure that the additions to the population will be at least as well equipped as the population already existing, the proportion of mute Miltons and unfulfilled Newtons will be no higher than previously. Population growth, under the assumptions stated, would, therefore, produce an absolutely larger number of geniuses, talented men, and generally gifted contributors to new knowledge – whose native ability would be permitted to mature to effective levels when they join the labor force. (Kuznets, 1960), p. 328)

But many others will not say that more workers raise productivity. As Coale put it:

[T]here is no warrant for the assumption that growth and knowledge is greater with a larger population. . . .
     I think even the most cursory consideration of scientific or more general cultural history would bring to light too many counter examples to make this theory tenable. I have gifted and well-informed friends who seriously think that the intellectual heights achieved in classical Athens have never been equalled, and this was a community of a few thousand educated persons. The population of Florence at the time of the Renaissance was no greater than Trenton, New Jersey, yet Galileo was one of the key figures in the development of modern science; the Medici and their fellow bankers were pioneers in the development of modern banking, including double entry book-keeping; Dante is a figure in world literature rivalled only by Shakespeare and possibly Homer; Machiavelli is considered by some the godfather of political science, and in painting, sculpture, architecture and engineering the Florentines led the world. One could plausibly argue that this community of a hundred thousand persons did more for modern civilization in a few centuries that the U.S. has. Elizabethan London and Budapest between the two world wars (in fact, the Jewish community in Budapest) are other examples.
(Personal correspondence, 28 December 1971)

Theoretical discussion by Machlup, Schmookler and Rosenberg of the demand and supply forces affecting the flow of science and technology will be taken up in chapter 3.
     In contrast to the mainstream discussed earlier, a few growth theorists have treated the amount of technical change as endogenous.[2] In 1949 Verdoorn speculated that 'a change in the volume

of production . . . tends to be associated with an average increase in labour production' (1949/1979, p. 1), division of labour being the process he had in mind. And he showed a long-run historical relationship in various countries between the rate of increase in total product and the rate of increase in productivity. Verdoorn's technical progress function is

$$\dot{A} = a_1 \dot{Y} \tag{1.1}$$

or

$$\frac{A_t - A_{t-1}}{A_{t-1}} = a_1 \left(\frac{Y_{t-1} - Y_{t-2}}{Y_{t-1}} \right) \tag{1.1a}$$

(Notation as defined prior to chapter 1, on pp. viii–ix.)

But Verdoorn did not deal with the question of the direction of causation, that is, whether faster technical progress causes faster economic growth rather than (or in addition to) the converse. Verdoorn's function also has the unlikely property of implying that if there is zero economic growth there would be zero technical progress. In a definitional statistical sense this may well be true. But behaviourally we can be sure that some invention and innovation occur even in the absence of measured economic growth, as seen in the famous Horndal (Sweden) effect.

Kaldor (1957) picked up Verdoorn's notion, dubbed it a 'law', and introduced it into his growth theorizing. But in his writings he turned from output to capital investment as the determinant of technical progress. His original function was:

$$\dot{A} = f_1(\dot{K}) \tag{1.2}$$

and from it Kaldor concluded (incorrectly) that population growth would have a neutral or negative effect on the growth of income *per capita*. He also made no note of a possible positive effect of a larger total population through the Petty effect. And as with Verdoorn's function, if investment is zero, technical progress is zero – an unlikely outcome.

Kaldor (with Mirrlees) later worked with the function

$$\dot{A} = f_2 \left(\frac{\dot{K}}{L} \right) \tag{1.2a}$$

That is, 'the annual rate of growth of productivity per worker . . .
[is] a function of the rate of growth of investment per worker'
(Kaldor and Mirrlees, 1962/1970, p. 309). This function shows
population growth and size to be even less favourable than function
(1.2).

Eltis's technical progress function differs somewhat from Kaldor's,
being (1973, p. 151):

$$\dot{A} = f_3\left(\frac{K_t - K_{t-1}}{Y_t}\right) \tag{1.3}$$

As does Kaldor's, Eltis's function has the property that, though it
varies over the business cycle, it implies a constant long-run rate of
change of technical progress,[3] which may or may not be reasonable,
as we shall discuss later. An unrealistic feature of Eltis's model is
that it comprehends only embodied technical progress (p. 18); in
reality, disembodied technical progress must be at least as important.

Alchian took note of the fact that production of such products as
airframes improves in the course of production. He then introduced
this 'learning-by-doing' insight into economic theory, distinguishing
among various sorts of economies of scale (1959, 1963). Arrow then
built an explicit technical-progress function upon this foundation.
Like Kaldor he shifted from output to capital as the carrier (or the
proxy for the carrier) of embodied technical progress, but unlike
Kaldor's, his capital stock variable was intended to be a proxy for
cumulative output:

$$A = a_2 K^b \tag{1.4}$$

where b is a constant analogous to the coefficient of serial numbers
in learning-by-doing studies, and is of the order of 0.2. Arrow's
technical-progress function has a variety of defects for the understanding of the effects of different population sizes and growth
rates, some stemming from the inherent ambiguities in the capital
concept, some stemming from the alteration in meaning with the
shift in variables from output (the empirical basis for the learning-
by-doing phenomenon) to capital; these matters are discussed in
chapter 5. Also, as with Kaldor's model (which Arrow notes is
similar to his own), stable production implies no learning-by-doing
and no technical progress, which Arrow himself notes is contrary to
the Horndal effect and similar evidence elsewhere.

TABLE 1

Characteristics of technical-progress functions that make knowledge endogenous, together with stylized facts

	The observed historical facts in MDCs	Technical change exogenous	Ver-doorn	Kaldor (Kaldor-Mirrlees)	Arrow	Phelps	Shell	Eltis	Simon (1977)	Simon-Steinmann
Constant physical K/Y ratio?	Not likely	Yes	Yes	Yes	Yes	Yes	No	Yes	No	Yes
Technical change when $\dot{L} = 0$?	Yes	No	Yes	No	Yes	Yes	No	No	Yes	Yes
Increasing $\dot{A}$ (or $\dot{M}$)	Perhaps	No	No	No	No	Not with constant $\dot{L}$	Depends on $\dot{L}$	No	Yes	Depends on stage of development
Both disembodied and embodied knowledge?	Yes	Yes	Yes	No	No	Yes	Yes	No	Yes	Yes

Until this point in the chapter, no clear distinction has been made between the level of technique in use, A, and the level of technology available for use, M, largely because the writers under discussion have not made the distinction. Though I shall now shift to discussing M, because this seems closer to the meaning of the studies to be discussed, there is still no sharp distinction intended. That distinction must await chapters 3 and 8.

Shell (1966) wrote a function in which the *stock* of technology M is a proportional function of current output (less the decay in knowledge, which can be disregarded here).

$$M_t = a_3 Y_t \tag{1.5}$$

The constant a_3 here reflects both the R&D level and the industry success rate of inventions. This function suffers from several drawbacks, including the mutual influence of M and Y, and the implication that M will decline if Y declines and will not increase if Y is constant. Putting the absolute value of M rather than a change in M on the left side does not seem a promising way to model the invention process at the micro-level.

An attractive function is adapted from Phelps' (1966) study of R&D

$$\dot{M}_t = \frac{M_t - M_{t-1}}{M_t} = f_4\left(\frac{L_{t-1}}{M_{t-1}}\right) \tag{1.6}$$

where f_4 is concave. Set in a simple macro-model, this function has an increasing A even with a stationary population, which is realistic. It also has steady-state properties, which makes it aesthetically pleasing – constant $\dot{M}$ with constant $\dot{L}$, or decreasing $\dot{M}$ with decreasing $\dot{L}$ (the latter running contrary to Western experience in the twentieth century).

In previous work (1977, chapter 6) I made the *rate of change* of technology a function of, alternatively, the labour force and total output

$$\frac{M_t - M_{t-1}}{M_{t-1}} = a_4 Y_{t-1}^\phi \qquad \phi < 1 \tag{1.7}$$

and

$$\frac{M_t - M_{t-1}}{M_{t-1}} = a_5 L_{t-1}^{\gamma} \qquad \gamma < 1 \tag{1.8}$$

I do not any longer feel that there is evidence supporting a function that is so sensitive as to yield an increasing rate of growth of technical knowledge in response to a steady state rate of growth of population.

The difference between my function (1.8) and Phelps's formulation (1.6) is a matter of degree in the size of the impact of existing M. This may be seen by writing both functions in Cobb–Douglas production function format:

$$M_t - M_{t-1} = M_{t-1}^{0.5} L_{t-1}^{0.5} \tag{1.6a}$$

where the exponents come from the rest of Phelps's discussion, and my earlier

$$M_t - M_{t-1} = M_{t-1} L_{t-1}^{\gamma}, \qquad 0.1 < \gamma < 0.5 \tag{1.8a}$$

Phelps's function, homogeneous of degree one, yields steady-state growth (including a constant rate of change of M) whereas my function (1.7) yields an increasing rate of change of M.

From here on, following (1.6a) and (1.8a), the dependent variable on the left-hand side will generally be written as the *absolute quantity of change* in the technical level, rather than the rate of change, a form which I consider important because it is a more basic and more illuminating way to view the matter. This may be considered merely as a matter of algebraic arrangement, but the reader's interpretation may well be affected by the way the algebra is written.[4]

It is a shocking feature of all the above-mentioned growth models with technical progress endogenous that a higher rate of population growth implies a higher growth rate (and level) of consumption *without upper bound to the population growth rate*. This includes my modification of Phelps's 1966 function where, on his assumptions, the rate of growth of consumption equals twice the rate of growth of the labour force (i.e. population), or, the rate of *per capita* consumption equals the rate of growth of the labour force. The same sort of conclusion holds for Arrow's learning-by-doing function

(1962) and Kaldor's original Verdoorn's-law-based function (1957), though neither Arrow nor Kaldor stated this conclusion that is implicit in their models. Nor did Phelps (or Arrow, or anyone else, in my reading) mention the absence of a bound. (Phelps does not even mention his basic analytical proposition derived from [1.6] in his other discussions of population growth, e.g. 1968, 1972, though he does note the positive effect of more people through the creation of technology.) And nowhere in the standard literature have I found mention of the general implication of growth theory, with technical progress endogenous, that more people imply a higher standard of living, except in Eltis's discussion of his own function. Instead, the common understanding of economists is that in growth theory faster population growth implies lower growth of consumption.

NOTES

1 This section is largely drawn from previous writings.
2 I exclude from consideration the body of literature concerning the *direction* of technical change as an endogenous matter, e.g. von Weiszacker (1966) and Nordhaus (1969).
3 If profits decline, however, the rate of progress can increase, in Eltis's model.
4 Leontief argues strongly that different algebraic modes of expression of a proposition have importantly different psychological effects on the scientific reader:

[I]n the actual process of scientific investigation, which consists in its larger part of more or less successful attempts to overcome our own intellectual inertia, the problem of proper arrangement of formal analytical tools acquires fundamental importance.

... The degree of mental resistance which accompanies the use of one or another formal pattern is furthermore rather closely (although also only 'statistically') and positively correlated with the chance of committing logical mistakes. Mistakes of this kind may manifest themselves either in the inability to perceive the 'evidence' of a correct argument or in the practically much more dangerous readiness to be convinced by a false one. (Leontief, 1966, pp. 59–60)

2
A Micro-Model of Invention and its Relation to the Technical Progress Function

I. INTRODUCTION

Discussion of induced technical progress has been almost entirely at the level of the economy, the industry or the firm. That makes considerable sense because the available data are at those levels of aggregation, ranging from the Abramowitz–Solow–Denison tradition of work on the components of growth, to the Rostas–Verdoorn tradition of work on industries, to the Alchian–Arrow learning-by-doing tradition, and the industrial-organization and organizational-behaviour literatures on firms. But there has been little discussion and less formal analysis of induced technical progress at the level of the individual inventor and adapter. (I shall refer to an analysis of invention at this level as a micro-model, or a model of invention, to be distinguished from both a more aggregated analysis of technical progress, and from a macro-model of the economy as a whole that embodies a technical progress function.) Without a model of the actual actors, and their interactions with each other and with the body of existing knowledge, we are talking about a mechanism taking place in a black box, without any understanding of its mode of operation.

Therefore, it seems appropriate to offer a micro-model of invention before moving on to discuss macro-models. The little attention the topic has received has been devoted to the direction of advances in technology, whether affected by relative intensities of capital and labour, and whether influenced by demand in particular industries or autonomous (see, for example, the 1962 NBER volume edited by

Nelson). But the more important question from the point of view of both policy and growth theory concerns the determinants of the *total quantity* of technical progress and the rate of change in the level of technique.

The technical-progress functions that have been proposed in the literature – Kaldor's, Arrow's, Phelps's and others – vary greatly in their implications, and they would not be consistent with the same micro-models. Therefore, a micro-analysis can throw some light upon which of the contending technical-progress functions and accompanying macro-models is most plausible.

The aim of this chapter is to offer a model of the process of knowledge creation at the individual level, to see what it implies and how it fits with the aggregate evidence and the macro-models. Of course such a model is not likely to persuade everyone that it is reasonable, or even most people, though hopefully it will persuade *some*. And no one at all will think that by itself this model is adequate, or even more than a rough beginning. But it is hoped that this model will serve to initiate systematic discussion which will eventuate in a satisfactory micro-model of the process of technical progress, especially in relationship to population growth.

A major complication in the chain from invention to its effect on productivity and the standard of living is the relationship between invention and adoption of new techniques. At any one moment there is a large stock of useful techniques that have not been applied. But relatively few inventions ever get used – 1 in 1000, in Machlup's guesstimate. And the relationship between invention and adoption is not fixed, and there probably are diminishing returns to additional inventions in the short run. But in the long-run context of the present discussion, the number of potential appliers of knowledge should be proportional to the number of inventors, and therefore I shall assume that technical progress is a proportional function of advance in technology, without further discussion of the relationship between them.

Section II discusses the main theoretical considerations that may influence the relationship between technical progress and labour-force size and growth. Section III constructs a micro-model relating population to technical progress, and considers how it fits the various macro-models. Section IV discusses the results and qualifications of the. Section V concludes and summarizes. Afterword 2A discusses how the micro-model fits with the various macro-models. Afterword 2B discusses the prospects for continued advance in inventive activity.

This chapter may seem unfinished to the reader. Certainly, I have not found a way to make the argument as well as I would like. One source of difficulty is that the question at hand is rather different than those questions economics usually considers. Yet I think that the question is important, and the answer I suggest seems internally consistent even if the logic is not elegant. I hope, then, that you will read it in the spirit in which it is offered.

It is crucial to keep in mind that the unit to which the analysis refers is the entire human society, or at a minimum that chunk of human society which presently contributes substantially to increase in technology. In this respect, the chapter is in the same spirit as the rest of the book. Where countries are the units of analysis in empirical studies upon which I draw, that is solely because they are the best available approach to a sample of observations, in the absence of a sample of worlds.

II. ELEMENTS OF THE THEORY

Later chapters discuss technical-progress functions which contain such arguments as labour-force size, output, stock of knowledge and investment. But from the point of view of general policy questions, as well as social decisions about population growth, the key issue is not that of deciding *which* factor is the most important. Rather, the key question is whether *any* measure related to the size of the economy or the population has a strong effect on productivity. This behooves us to ask: Under which conditions might additional people *not* lead to increased productivity? These are some suggestions that have been made:

(a) Additional people dilute the stock of capital, even if they increase the stock of knowledge. Therefore, the trade-off between these two forces must be studied in the context of a full economic model, as is done in other chapters of this book.

(b) Some forces involved in technical progress are said to be 'inversely related to the rate of population growth' (Spengler, 1968, p. 115). A prominent example: faster growth and a larger population might lead to less education per person. But the data (Simon and Pilarski, 1979; Meeks, 1982; Miyata et al., 1982; Ram, 1982) suggest that this force does not operate strongly in the short run. And in the long course of history so far, it surely has not been much of a factor. Another possibility is that faster population growth reduces the rate of saving, and hence reduces the rate at which technology, embodied in capital, is brought into use. But the evidence on the population growth-saving relationship is very thin (see Simon, 1977). Therefore, neither of these matters is built into the models of this book.

(c) Another possibility is that additional people are so much like existing people that they are not likely to come up with any improvements that the existing population would not come up with. That is, people may be sufficiently homogeneous so that additional people do not produce additional variety in ideas. Evidence for similarity in people's thinking is found in the existence of independent inventions of the same idea; stochastic dominance is a recent example in finance, modelling of the consumer is an example in marketing, and DNA an example in biology; patent priority fights are additional evidence. This possibility implicitly assumes a limited base of existing knowledge which people can develop, and a limited range of other stimuli to people's imaginations.

(d) If there is a very obvious order in the value of potential projects, if people are clear-minded enough to perceive this order and if there is at least a fair amount of similarity in people's talents and interests, then there would be high duplication in work on the most important inventions.

The foregoing are arguments that have been made about why additional people might *not* lead to increased technology and productivity. Now let us add some remarks about why they *are likely* to have such effects.

Surely there is additional variety introduced by additional people. As Hayek puts it (1960, p. 29), 'the advance and even the preservation of civilization are dependent upon a maximum of opportunity for accidents to happen. These accidents occur in the combination of knowledge and attitudes, skills and habits, acquired by individual men and also when qualified men are confronted with the particular circumstances which they are equipped to deal with'. And it is clear that the more people there are, *ceteris paribus*, the

more 'accidents' that can occur. It is also true that the *'ceteris
paribus'* clause must not be ignored; the circumstances are crucial, as
for example when Hayek also notes that 'Liberty is essential in order
to leave room for the unforeseeable and predictable' (p. 29). Yet it
seems to me that the more people there are, the more accidents,
more variety, more advances in knowledge and productivity there
will be.

Even if there are diminishing returns in knowledge production, in
the very longest run an increment to knowledge now will have a
more positive effect on income than any decrement to capital per
worker due to additional people, on almost any assumptions.
The question, then, must be: how *much* additional productive
knowledge can we expect from additional people, and how long will
it take to overcome the negative effects of capital dilution?

Furthermore, there are reasons to suppose that in the long run
there are increasing returns to additional persons even in knowledge
production itself. Kuznets makes an argument for increasing returns
on two grounds: (a) the stimulating effect of a dense environment;
and (b) 'interdependence of knowledge of the various parts of the
world in which we human beings operate', (p. 328); for example,
discoveries in physics stimulate discoveries in biology, and vice versa.
And he discounts the possibility of diminishing returns because 'the
universe is far too vast relative to the size of our planet and what we
know about it' (p. 329).

Machlup suggests that 'every new invention furnishes a new idea
for potential combination with vast numbers of existing ideas...
[and] the number of possible combinations increases geometrically
with the number of elements at hand' (1962, p. 156). It is this latter
idea of an increasing number of permutations of elements of knowledge as the stock increases that seems most compelling to me, when
put together with the idea of a reduced possibility of duplicate
discoveries as the number of possibilities increases faster than the
number of potential knowledge producers. And we shall see later
that – contrary to intuition – duplication of intellectual effort is
likely to be *less and less* of a constraint with the passage of time and
with larger populations. Eventually we can expect the main constraint
to be an individual's idea-production capacity alone, while the
duplication factor will be negligible.

The divergence of views on this matter makes it important to
investigate the process at the individual level, to build a model, and

to speculate about reasonable parameters to see how they jibe with the aggregate evidence. A sound micro-model should help us decide which technical progress function is most to be preferred.

This model abstracts from the important issues of the social and economic framework within which the inventive activity is to take place, and the cost of the production of inventions. The former of these issues is discussed starting on p. 68, and the latter is discussed starting on p. 49.

III.   A MICRO-MODEL OF INVENTION

At any moment there are L_t workers in the economy, all of whom are potential creators of new knowledge. These workers differ in their propensities to invent and innovate, and one could differentiate them in the model. But that would introduce complication without changing the conclusions.

Let us first notice that no matter what assumptions one makes about the composition of the 'original' population – about the homogeneity, and about the distribution of characteristics – an increment of people similiar in composition to the original people will increase the number of ideas by that same proportion *if* the original group and the incremental group are exposed to different but equally potent stimuli. That is, if people and stimuli are all that go into idea making, the function is homogeneous of degree one. There may be individual sluggards and individual big producers, but each kind will be found in each group. Critical-minimum-size groups may be necessary to produce some kinds of ideas, but this will be true in the same way for the original as for incremental groups. In brief, the only constraint or factor that might lead to diminishing returns to additional people in idea production (leaving aside education and capital for now) is the size of the stock of knowledge that is available in common to the potential idea producers. This means – somewhat surprisingly – that we do not need to know anything about the degree of similarity of additional people to existing people in order to know how additional people will increment the flow of ideas.

New technology is built upon the stock of technology and other stimuli, that is, the number of bits of information ($\Sigma_{t-\infty}^{t} J_t$), in the environment at moment t, resulting from events in all years up to the present t. This is the key idea and the fundament of this analysis. And there are two relevant aspects of the stock of knowledge that may be used for creating new ideas. On the one hand, when an idea is created, that idea is removed from the universe of possible new ideas still to be discovered. And if ten more people come along and re-discover the idea independently, nothing is gained; here we find the operation of a process of diminishing returns to additional ideas.[1] On the other hand, newly discovered ideas also add to the stock of elements that may be combined with other elements to create still other new ideas. Surely this describes the history of human economic and intellectual growth. Newton's and Einstein's, Smith's and Malthus's and Keynes's discoveries depleted the stock of those potential ideas, but opened up vast fields of possibility for future discoveries.[2] Discoveries about indexes and national income accounts removed those fish from the pond of potential discoveries in economics, but left their eggs to spawn large numbers of new fish which could not have previously hatched. The creation of new economic data – a result of more people and more income in a country – removes the opportunity to do this for the first time, but greatly enhances the possible number of other studies a contemporary economist can do. The research that required the brilliance of Adam Smith or John Graunt or William Petty can now be done routinely by us. And an article by Arrow or Becker or Markowitz or Schultz or Stigler can – fortunately or unfortunately – spawn a career industry.

New ideas arise not only from existing ideas but also are stimulated by observations of the natural and physical world, the effective variety of which increases as economic and social development takes place and as people are more mobile and thereby come into contact with more aspects of the world around them. But for simplicity here – and, I believe, without changing the nature of the argument – the analysis will proceed as if new ideas arise only from the combination of existing ideas, without reference to observations of the world itself.

The indulgence of the reader is asked with respect to the notation that will now be used. I have not been able to find a notation that expresses the necessary concepts and yet is clear and unconfusing. This difficulty arises from the fact that an idea that is the 'output' in one period is then a potential – but not necessarily actual – input to the production of other ideas in the next period. It is therefore hoped that the reader will have patience in following the argument through the notational difficulty.

Let $J_{j\bar{j}}$ be a new idea formed of the combination of two different idea stimuli, j and $\bar{j}$, coming from the set $j = 1, 2, 3, \ldots, M_{t-1}$ of stimulus elements existing as of the end of $t - 1$. To be a new idea, this combination $j\bar{j}$ must never have occurred before, which also means that it is not itself found as an element in set $j = 1, 2, \ldots, M_{t-1}$. (A fuller treatment would also consider the higher order combinations, $J_{j\bar{j}\bar{j}}$, but here we may neglect them.)

The stock of technology M_t available at the end of any period t consists of the stock of knowledge at the beginning of the prior period M_{t-1} plus the sum of the new ideas created in that period, $\Sigma_{j\bar{j}}J_t$.

$$m_t = \sum_{t-\infty}^{t-1} \Sigma_{j\bar{j}} J_{t,j\bar{j}} + \Sigma_{j\bar{j}} J_{t,j\bar{j}} \tag{2.1}$$

And each new idea is thereby added to the stock of stimuli available as building blocks for idea creation in subsequent periods. Notationally, each $J_{j\bar{j}}$ occurring in one period becomes a j in the next period.

We shall assume that during each period, each person i among the persons in the labour force L produces exactly one combination of j and $\bar{j}$, a random drawing without replacement (for that drawing) from M_{t-1}. In reality, people differ considerably in the numbers of ideas they create, but (as discussed earlier) this will be seen not to affect the model if we notice that a partition of the labour force into the same proportional divisions each year of idea producers (one idea) and non-idea producers (zero) would not affect the model (nor would a more continuous distribution).

It would also be realistic to assume that the flow of ideas per representative person increases over the years, both because more education probably leads to more productive ideas, and also because there is, to my knowledge, no evidence that scientific production is declining in output per person.[3] And we see ever-increasing flows of new products, and of such additional carriers of new information as magazines and journals. But this matter is left aside by the model.

Our ultimate aim is to learn how the number of potential idea-producing persons (the labour force) affects the growth of the stock of knowledge. For economic purposes we will want to know whether the additional ideas produced by additional workers will be sufficient to counter-balance the negative effect of additional persons on the supply of capital per person.

The potential number of ideas that might be discovered at time t is (dropping the time subscript of M)

$$N_t = M(M-1) - \sum_{t-\infty}^{t-1} \sum_{j=1}^{j=M} J_{t,j\bar{j}} \tag{2.2}$$

that is, the total number of combinations then possible less those that have already been discovered. We assume that if a person first hits on an idea that has *previously* (not concurrently) been discovered – the negative part of the right-hand side of the above expression – the person will simply 'throw the fish back' and find another hitherto-undiscovered idea, but one which may be concurrently discovered by another person. N_t is a simplified symbol for this concept.

The probability that a combination $j\bar{j}$ is a new idea, p_{new}, is the proportion of all possible $M(M-1)$ combinations that have not previously been discovered, that is, the ratio of undiscovered combinations to all combinations.

$$p_{new} = \frac{M(M-1) - \Sigma_{t-\infty}^{t-1} \Sigma_{j=1}^{j=M} J_{t,j\bar{j}}}{M(M-1)} \tag{2.3}$$

The probability of duplication or 'overlap' – that probability that a given new $j\bar{j}$ will be discovered by more than one person in the same period – is roughly the ratio of the number of people in the 'discovery' labour force, L_t, to the total number of possible undiscovered ideas, N_t, or L_t/N_t, and the probability of non-duplication,

$$p_{nondup} \approx \left(1 - \frac{L_t}{N_t}\right) \tag{2.4}$$

That is, a larger number of potential discoverers implies more duplication and a lower probability, p_{nondup}, that a given idea will be unduplicated. Therefore the total number of new ideas that will be discovered in a given period t, not counting duplicates or higher order overlaps more than once, is the number of idea producers multiplied by the probability that any given idea has not been previously discovered multiplied by the probability that a given idea is not discovered by more than one person concurrently.

$$\sum_{j=1}^{j=M} J_{t,j\bar{j}} = L_t p_{\text{new}} \, p_{\text{nondup}} = L_t \left[\frac{M(M-1) - \Sigma_{t-\infty}^{t-1} J_t}{M(M-1)} \right]$$

$$\times \left(1 - \frac{L_t}{N_t} \right) \tag{2.5}$$

The number of new ideas discovered in t is a positive function of L_t. This may be seen by rearranging (2.5) as

$$\sum_{t=1}^{t=M} J_{t,j\bar{j}} = L_t \left(\frac{N_t - L_t}{N_t} \right) p_{\text{new}} = \left(\frac{L_t N_t - L_t^2}{N_t} \right) p_{\text{new}} \tag{2.6}$$

As long as $N_t > L_t$ (noting that p_{new} is not affected by L_t), then an increase in L_t means a larger increment to $L_t N_t$ than to L_t^2. But for two reasons this does not immediately imply that faster population growth and more people imply a higher standard of living in future years: (a) the number of people and of discoveries in t affects the stock of potential discoveries in two opposing manners – by creating more new J elements but using up more existing $j\bar{j}$ combinations. And (b), faster population growth implies less physical capital per person, *ceteris paribus*. Therefore, to understand the overall effect we must now analyse (a), and eventually take account of (b) in a complete macro-model simulation.

Intuitively we can seen that p_{nondup}, the proportion of ideas that are not duplicates, will increase each year because in successive years each new idea element can combine with an ever-larger number of existing stimuli-elements, as Machlup (1962) noticed. The number of j elements that is added to the set M each year is almost L_t, and therefore the number of new possible combinations is almost $L_t M_t$ – or better, $(L_{t-1} + \Delta L_t) M_t$, where the delta ($\Delta$) indicates the increment of population growth – whereas the number of possible duplications rises only from a bit less than L_{t-1} to a bit less than L_t, roughly ΔL_t. If ΔL_t is 2 per cent of L_t, then $L_t M_t$ is $50 M_t$ as large as ΔL_t, a very large factor of multiplication no matter what number – a million, a thousand, or a trillion – one assigns to M_t. Given this very large rise in the ratio of to-be-discovered elements relative to the number of potential duplications, in a relatively short time the number of new ideas per period will approach the number of persons, as $\Sigma_{j\bar{j}} J_{t,j\bar{j}} \rightarrow L_t$. (We know this is not quite true because people do not work on ideas across the spectrum of possibilities, but cluster where the 'action' is. But if the *size of cluster* remains the same from year to year, we can replace 'idea' with 'cluster' in our thinking without changing the results.)

To put the matter another way, an additional person in year t has a chance of L_t/N_t of producing a duplicated idea ($p_{\text{nondup}} = 1 - L_t/N_t$), which is slightly greater than the previous person added to the group, that is, diminishing returns from this factor alone. In the next period, however, the number of potential combinations $j\bar{j}$ is approximately M times what it would be otherwise, which has a relatively large impact on reducing duplication. In this fashion, the analysis implies that there are increasing returns in technology creation from additional people until the process tapers off to constant returns. This suggests that additional people imply additional knowledge, without limits. And because an increment of technology has a cumulative effect in raising income through its effect on output and capital formation, a proportional increase in technology in t comes to have a more-than-proportional positive partial effect on income in $t + x$ where $x =$ years after t.[4]

Assuredly, this analysis is far from realistically complete, but hopefully it takes the issue to a deeper level of understanding and to a higher level of precision than previously.

IV.   COUNTER-ARGUMENTS AND QUALIFICATIONS

(a) Not all ideas that might be discovered have the same potential quality and value. If people came upon ideas only by chance, this non-equality would not in any way affect the workings of the model given above. But people prefer to produce high-value ideas rather than low-value ideas. If it were also the case that people could also identify the possible high-potential ideas with perfect accuracy, then – if there were no differences among people in interests and skills – every potential knowledge-producer would be working on the same potential idea at a given moment. If there were also a reasonably high likelihood that a random person would succeed in making the discovery of this highest value idea, then diminishing returns to additional persons would be sharp.

To obtain a satisfying understanding of this mechanism would require a fuller model. Such a model would not be easy to construct. More important, however, qualitative estimates of the relevant parameters are, to my knowledge, both non-existent at present and likely to be extraordinarily difficult to produce in the future. The best that we can do at present is to discuss the matter qualitatively and to try to compare the overall results against the aggregate facts, which I will do in that order.

Diminishing returns due to concentration of efforts on the same research project requires, first of all, that all persons have the ability to work in the same general area, and that intellectual mobility is total. But this is clearly not the case. The mature individual who shifts from one major area to another (e.g. from economics to biology or psychology, or the reverse) is rare, and even shifting between minor areas (e.g. public finance and population economics) is not very common. Furthermore, there is proliferation of areas within which people study and later work, so there may not even be a greater number of effective competitors than in the past; for example, Plato and Aristotle, and Bentham and Hume and Smith, took much of human knowledge as their playground, talked to others interested in all these subjects, and made fundamental contributions in all of them; this sort of behaviour is much less likely today. It might even turn out (if one were to examine membership lists of professional organizations over hundreds of years) that one's primary professional organization has grown no bigger, for example, the American Farm Economics Association or the Population Association of America now versus the American Economic Association at the turn of the century. If the size of 'non-competing groups' has not grown over the years, this would be enough to dispatch the worry of diminishing returns from increasing concentration on the idea with the highest potential value.

Second, diminishing returns from increasing concentration of workers requires ability among workers in a given field to spot the highest-value projects. Such perfect prevision is far from the rule; even the most eminent men disagree on which areas are most worthy of attention. Furthermore, there is ample evidence that many important

ideas are not come upon even though the intellectual preconditions
and the need for the idea are present. One example is dynamic
programming, which could have been developed and used centuries
before it was invented. Another example, according to Weinberg
(1977, p. 6), is the set of 'the discoveries of the recession of distant
galaxies and of a weak radio static filling the universe. This is a rich
story for the historian of science, filled with false starts, missed opportunities, theoretical preconceptions, and the play of personalities'.

Third, people would have to be willing to practice a strategy of
working on the project with highest potential but also greatest
competition. If researchers are anything like Hotelling's spatial retail
competitors, or Downs's political competitors, or several theorists'
television-programme competitors, they will recognize that it can
make sense to move away from the highest potential area of the
market in order to face less competition. Certainly we see this in
some areas of science: India and Brazil are of greater importance on
the world scene than are Ceylon and Guyana, but some students
(even those from the US or USSR) work on the smaller rather than
on the larger of them.

With regard to the first three points above, it should be noted
that we don't know much about how people pick topics to work
upon. Some people are attracted by large concentrations of workers;
others are attracted by empty areas. Some are influenced by the
scientific literature; others – like Keynes in the 1930s – are influenced
by the news and the events of the day. Some are influenced by ideas,
others by physical objects. Some people like low-risk projects, others
are less risk averse. About all we can safely say for sure – but this is
important – is that there is great variety in people's topic-choosing
behaviour, as may be seen from the fact that seldom will two members
of an academic department be working on the same problem with
the same tools and for the same purpose.

Fourth, concentration of workers on a given problem is only a
cause of diminishing returns if the likelihood of any *one* person being
successful is great enough so that the likelihood of *more* than one
being successful is meaningfully large. And if this were really the case,
then simultaneous duplicate production of important ideas would be
seen frequently; it is not, in my observation.

Fifth, for concentration to be a cause of diminishing returns,
communication among workers in the same general areas would have
to be sufficiently slow so that a person who might work on a potential

discovery would not be warned off by the just-previous success of another. Many of us have had the experience of contemplating working on an idea, checking the literature and the field of allied workers, and finding out that in fact it has been done. This is not counter-productive duplication, because the resources devoted to the initial insight are relatively small, and can often be redeployed on the basis of the knowledge of what the other person has already discovered. Given that the speed of relevant scientific communication is almost surely increasing, there is decreasing chance of duplication of work on the highest potential ideas (as well as lower potential ideas).

We are only interested in the above set of possibilities if *all of them* are each present to a high enough degree to *together* cause increasing duplication of effort with growing numbers of people. Therefore, an aggregate test is fair: the numbers of persons eligible to make discoveries have been increasing. But the rate of duplication of discovery of the greatest ideas shows no clear direction towards greater duplication. The Leibniz–Newton conjuncture is the last great incident I know of; and, has anyone argued that the circum-stances surrounding the discovery of DNA indicate that too much talent was devoted to the task?[5] The key issue here is the concavity of $f(M)$ or $f(M,L)$ or $f(M,L,Y/L)$, upon which the number of duplications throw light, but there seems to be no increase in that concavity.

Another relevant test is the rate of investment in R&D: the very long-run trend is up rather than down, in percentage-of-GNP terms as well as in absolute terms. Of course this might reflect increasing supplies of potential investors. But it is also consistent with an increase in profitable research opportunities, and hence with decreasing duplication.

Still another line of evidence refers to the number of first-rate profitable opportunities for research, rather than to the rate of duplication itself. If the number is very large, then duplication of top possibilities is not a problem. Here are a few quotations that indicate the possibilities lying in wait for the idea producer:

> Cancer researcher Cole: 'It's not so much a question of more money to look at the problem, as a lack of people and analytical tools for the job.' (Blakeslee, 1979)

> Newton: 'I do not know what I may appear to the world; but to myself I seem to have been only like a boy, playing on the sea-shore, and diverting myself, in now and then finding a smoother

pebble or a prettier shell than ordinary, whilst the great ocean of truth lay all undiscovered before me.' (quoted by Taylor and Wheeler, 1966, p. 187)

Bethe on nuclear fusion: 'Money is not the limiting factor: the annual support in the US is well over $100 million, and it is increasing steadily. Progress is limited rather by the availability of highly trained workers, by the time required to build large machines and then by the time required to do significant experiments.' (Bethe, 1976, p. 2)

It may also be useful to examine the lengths of time between discoveries that seem to be equally important landmarks in a given field. For example, one could list and measure the times between Ptolemy, Copernicus, Newton, Lorentz and Einstein. The decreasing intervals suggest that great discoveries in physics were not becoming increasingly hard to make.

When thinking about diminishing returns in technology production, it is important to distinguish whether the subject is technology in the small or in the large – that is, advances in technology with respect to a narrowly defined topic, or technology pertaining to productivity in a wide field or in the economy as a whole. Consider the interesting data in figure 2.1. There we see that the rate of technological progress with respect to any given type of particle acceleration has been much slower than the rate of technological increase in all types of particle accelerations taken together. Clearly there would be much more sharply diminishing returns to additional researchers working on any one type of acceleration than with respect to particle generators as a set. And there would be even less diminution of returns to additional workers in nuclear physics in all its breadth.

(b) The subject of the discussion so far has been the *quantity* of knowledge production. The reader may wonder whether the *quality* may decline even if the quantity does not. This is a difficult question. A more complete discussion of this topic, which concludes that it is indeed impossible to satisfactorily compare the value of later discoveries with earlier ones, is offered elsewhere (Simon, 1984). It may even be *logically* impossible to determine the value of later discoveries relative to earlier ones, because the later discoveries depend upon the existence of the earlier ones. This implies that part of the value of

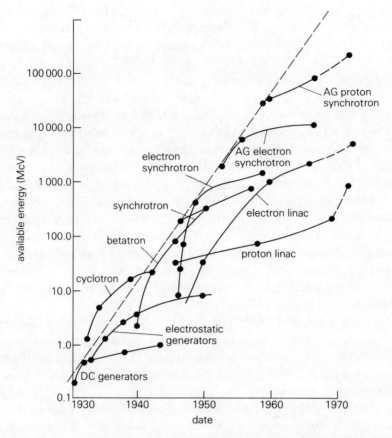

FIGURE 2.1   Energies achieved by particle accelerators from 1932 to 1968
(*Source:* Rescher, 1978, p. 177. Originally from M. Stanley Livingston, *Particle Accelerators: a Brief History*, Cambridge, 1969, p. 111.)

the later discoveries should be attributed to the earlier ones, and there is no meaningful way to make this partition. It is like the steps in a ladder: one can put a value on the benefits rendered by the first rung alone, but part of the benefit gained from the use of the second rung must be attributed to the first rung.

One possible avenue of inquiry is judgemental. We may ask questions such as: was Einstein's contribution less valuable than Newton's? Newton's less than Ptolemy's or Archimedes'? Some of this has implicitly been done in the lists that have been made of the 'great' discoveries by century (see the summary in Sorokin, 1937). But, of course, such lists are biased by difficulties in time separation between event and judges, as well as by the judges' (Western) cultural background.

A relevant fact is the relationship of the rate of knowledge accretion to the rate of productivity increases. The quantity of scientific literature has been doubling at a rate which has been fairly constant for a long time. De Solla Price (1961, p. 119) estimates that 'normal exponential growth' since 1660 has been a *constant* doubling every 30 years (whereas before that, 120 years were required for doubling). On the other hand, productivity has been increasing at an *increasing* rate, as discussed by Solow (1957) and Fellner (1970). This seems inconsistent with the idea that the 'quality' of scientific literature has been decreasing, or even remaining constant; rather, a constant doubling in the quantity of literature together with an increased rate of workplace productivity suggests an increase in economic productivity per unit of scientific literature (taking the latter as a proxy for all knowledge produced).

Of course, each and every fact and line of thought in this section is speculative at best. But this proves, more than anything, how ill-formed and uninvestigated is this topic. Under such conditions, however, any discussion, crude that it may be, may be a useful starting point.

As long as we think of knowledge as scientific knowledge in itself, we are not likely to reach a persuasive answer. But if we keep in mind that our interest here is in the output of economic welfare, we may be able to make some progress. We still will have major difficulties if we think in terms of GNP *per capita* as it is usually measured, because GNP measurement is itself affected by technological change in a variety of well-known ways. But it may be reasonable to examine the changes over time in a few key elements of economic welfare that seem reasonably comparable.

Consider grain output, for example. Its level of production technology in an economy is related to the level of other production technology, and the product is old enough so that it is not in a spectacular early-development period. Yet the rate of productivity increase has been increasing over the decades, and there seems no reason to doubt that the amount of human labour involved in grain production *per capita* will continue to diminish in the foreseeable future, and perhaps at an increasing rate (e.g. dropping 1 per cent of its manpower in the first period under discussion, 1.1 per cent in the second equal-length period, and so on – an infinitely sustainable process until the last farmer). This is at least measurable, and it is a reasonable proxy for the combined quantity and quality of technological knowledge. If the change in the level of productivity of all other products is similar to that of grain, this suggests that a given amount of product can be attained by an amount of work time that will diminish at an increasing rate, while leisure – a key element of economic welfare – will increase. There is an upper bound to the amount of leisure, of course. But if the amount of leisure is held constant and more types of goods are produced, economic welfare could continue to increase at an increasing rate.[6]

More generally, as stated earlier, it seems to me that comparative evaluation of advances in technology and productivity over the long run probably cannot be meaningful, as is discussed at length elsewhere (Simon, 1984).

(c) So far we have assumed that the rate of idea production (duplicated plus unduplicated) is the same for representative persons under all conditions. But we know – from statistical as well as casual evidence (de Solla Price, 1971; Love and Pashute, 1978) – that the production of technical-advance ideas is a positive function of *per capita* income. Including this effect of income on idea production in the model will only amplify the results shown without it.

(d) No mention has been made of the cost of producing technical knowledge. This does not imply that knowledge is costless. But the issue of the resources required is not germane here (see p. 49).

(e) There is a vast gap between the production and the application of technical knowledge, as Machlup emphasizes. But this, too, is not germane in the context of this model. The question of the extent to which knowledge should be thought of as a purchased commodity will be discussed later on pp. 48–9.

V. CONCLUSION

For hundreds of years economists and others have recognized that a denser population and faster population growth seem to be found where individual income is high and rising, though the simplest sort of theoretical reasoning suggested exactly the opposite conclusion. All the existing empirical evidence, however, is at the level of the economy or the industry. Still lacking – aside from Petty's simple suggestion – is an empirical or theoretical understanding at the micro-level of why a larger population and a bigger economy should lead to increased productivity. The task of this chapter is to propose such a theoretical model. The constituents of the model are the number of potential knowledge producers, the number of elements available in the environment to stimulate invention, and the probabilistic relationships between inventors and stimuli.

The model works out the trade-off between the forces that reduce the stock of ideas and the forces that increase the stock, under different conditions of population growth. The model shows that on assumptions that seem economically and psychologically reasonable, a larger labour force has increasing returns in knowledge production. The number of possible new combinations that result from the addition of a new idea element to the pool of knowledge is very large relative to the depletion of the pre-existing pool of knowledge by the discovery of that one idea. And the number of such possible new combinations that a representative additional person creates is very large relative to the additional possibilities of duplicated effort that result from the additional person. Hence the net result of an additional person is an increase in the total number of new ideas. And this effect will continue with the increases in total persons and total knowledge until duplication approaches zero, and unduplicated idea production for the representative person approaches the person's total capacity for idea production. Hence there are increasing returns in idea production to additional persons until convergence to constant returns.

As to the quality (or value or importance) of additional ideas with a larger rate of growth of the labour force and higher rates of increase of knowledge, there is no statistical evidence to suggest that quality is decreasing. On *a priori* grounds one might speculate, rather, that effective quality is increasing, because of the larger number of existing ideas and capital with which a new idea can interact and be fruitful. But it is logically impossible to evaluate the economic contribution of later ideas separately from the contribution of earlier ideas.

AFTERWORD 2A:
WHICH MACRO-FUNCTION DOES THE MICRO-MODEL FIT?

Which macro-models in the literature best fit the micro-model set out above? Quite obviously, there is no warrant here for technical progress being driven purely exogenously, or being considered simply a function of time. And this model does not fit Arrow's learning-by-doing model (1.4), which could be written as (see chapter 5)

$$M_t - M_{t-1} = a_6(K_t^b - K_{t-1}^b) \tag{2.7}$$

or as a more straightforward learning-by-doing model such as

$$M_t - M_{t-1} = a_7\left[\left(\sum_{t=0}^{t=\tau} Y_t\right)^b - \left(\sum_{t=0}^{t=\tau-1} Y_t\right)^b\right] \tag{2.8}$$

The micro-model views technical progress as a function of human activity together with the stock of knowledge, perhaps in conjunction with the level of education; the learning-by-doing models are purely empirical in their origin, and no knowledge-producing mechanism is suggested for them. Everything said about learning-by-doing models pertains just as well to the Verdoorn model

$$\left(\frac{M_t - M_{t-1}}{M_{t-1}}\right) = a_1\left(\frac{Y_t - Y_{t-1}}{Y_t}\right) \tag{2.9}$$

and the Kaldor model

$$\frac{M_t - M_{t-1}}{M_{t-1}} = f_1\left(\frac{K_t - K_{t-1}}{K_t}\right) \tag{2.10}$$

Furthermore, the Verdoorn, Arrow and Kaldor models have different implications than those of the micro-model, as can be seen in table 1 (p. 20).

The macro-model best fit by the micro-model seems to be the basic function 6.6 in chapter 6 with income left out and using M rather than A here, which can be written as

$$M_t - M_{t-1} = f_5(L_{t-1}^{\phi} M_{t-1}^{\psi}), \qquad \phi, \psi < 1 \tag{2.11}$$

In the limit of the micro-model this becomes

$$M_t - M_{t-1} = f_0(L_{t-1}^{\phi})$$ (2.12)

which may be viewed as equation (5.9) with $\psi \rightarrow 0$.

AFTERWORD 2B:
CAN WE BE SURE TECHNOLOGY WILL ADVANCE?

Some ask: can we know that there will be discoveries of new materials and of productivity-enhancing techniques in the future? Behind the question lies the implicit belief that the production of new technology does not follow predictable patterns of the same sort as the patterns of production of other products such as cheese and opera. But there seems to me no warrant for belief in such a difference, either in logic or in empirical experience. When we add more capital and labour, we get more cheese; we have no logical assurance of this, but such has been all our experience, and therefore we are prepared to rely upon it. The same is true concerning knowledge about how to increase the yield of grain, cows, milk and cheese from given amounts of capital and labour. If you pay engineers to find ways to solve a general enough problem – for example, how to milk cows faster, or with less labour – the engineers predictably will do so. There may well be diminishing returns to additional inventive effort spent on the same problem, just as there are diminishing returns to the use of fertilizer and labour on a given farm in a given year. But old solutions spawn new problems, and the old diminishing-returns functions then no longer apply.

The willingness of businesses to pay engineers and other inventors to look for new discoveries attests to the predictability of returns to inventive effort. To obtain a more intimate feeling for the process, one may ask a scientist or engineer whether he/she expects his/her current research project to produce results with greater probability than if she/he simply sat in the middle of the forest reading a detective novel; the trained effort the engineer applies has a much greater likelihood of producing useful information – and indeed, the very information that is expected in advance – than does untrained non-effort. This is as predictable in the aggregate as the fact that cows will produce milk, and that machines and workers will turn the milk into cheese. Therefore, to depend upon the fact that technical developments will continue to occur in the future – if we continue to devote human and other resources to research – is as reasonable as it is to depend upon any other production process in our economy or civilization. One cannot *prove* logically that technical development will continue in the future. But neither can one so prove that capital and labour and milk will continue to produce cheese, or that the sun will come up tomorrow.

As I see it, the only likely limit upon the production of new knowledge about resources is the occurrence of new problems; without unsolved problems there will be no solutions. But here we have a built-in insurance policy: if our ultimate interest is resource availability, and if availability should diminish, that automatically supplies an unsolved problem, which then leads to the production of new knowledge, not necessarily immediately or without short-run disruption, but in the long run.

I'm not saying that all problems are soluble in the forms in which they are presented. I do not claim that biologists will make us immortal in our lifetime, or even that the length of human life will be doubled or tripled in the future. On the other hand, one need not rule out that biogenetics can create an animal with most of our traits and a much longer life. But such is not the sort of knowledge we are interested in here. Rather, we are interested in knowledge of the material inputs to our economic civilization.

A sophisticated version of this argument is that the cost of additional knowledge may rise in the future. Some writers point to the large teams and large sums now involved in natural-science endeavours. Let us notice, however, how much cheaper it is to make many discoveries now than it was in the past because of the existing base of knowledge and the whole information infra-structure. Kuznets could advance further with his research on GNP estimates than could Petty. And a run-of-the-mill graduate student can now do some things that Petty could not do. Additionally, a given discovery is more valuable now than it was then; GNP measurement has more economic impact now than in Petty's day. And it seems to me that the net present value in social terms of the discovery of agriculture was less than the net present value of something even as trivial as computer games. We could try reckoning the gain in gross social product to the few million people on earth when agriculture was developed, discounted even at 2 per cent per year. That is, say, $100 per person multiplied by say 10 million people at 2 per cent, gives an estimate of $3 billion. This is peanuts compared to the gain in gross social product from the transition to nuclear fission power, or the possible value of nuclear fusion. And agriculture was the only big discovery for thousands of years, whereas we came up with the transistor and nuclear power and lots more within a few decades.

One may say: let's calculate on a per-person basis. But why? The value of no other discovery or investment is figured that way. We will not be able to thrash that one out, but at the least, it is clear that there are a lot of open questions here.

NOTES

1 Even when there is duplication, the result is not pure waste. The double exposure increases the chances of the idea being accepted and put into use. And the two discoveries are likely to reveal somewhat different aspects of the phenomenon.

2 In a recent discussion of a nuclear power plant emergency, Royster commented, 'The experience should be humbling. It should give us pause. It should remind us of an eternal truth; the more we know, the more the mystery, the more we have to learn' (*Wall Street Journal*, 11 April 1979, p. 22).

3 This does not apply to the output of a *given* person over his or her career, but rather to a comparison of similar persons at the same ages in successive cohorts. For a review of relevant data in the physical sciences, see Rescher (1978).

4 I have implicitly been assuming that knowledge is permanent and does not obsolesce. To some extent knowledge does obsolesce, as we know it does from decreases in use of journals and books with the passage of time (e.g. Fussler and Simon, 1969); but note that some old knowledge remains in use by way of being embodied in newer ideas, an effect which does not show up in readership statistics, and from the diminution of patents kept in force (Nordhaus, 1969; but notice that these patent-maintenance data also simply show patents which were finally proven to have no use and be unprofitable, and hence are dropped). To this extent, the analysis must be modified. Obsolescence would seem to make additional people relatively more valuable because the essence of knowledge production is its external effect. But this needs further study.

5 It seems as if one could profitably classify discoveries into those that were foreseen by many (e.g. DNA) and those that were not (e.g. general relativity). Whether this is so, and what it might imply, is not obvious.

6 Life expectancy is an economic good at least as valuable as leisure and GNP goods. And I see no prospect of it increasing at an increasing rate. The reader may take this as a fatal objection to the argument – or may not. I think that the better position is that though GNP *per capita* might continue to increase at an increasing rate *as measured by the conventional methods*, this does not imply that human welfare is increasing at an increasing rate, and therefore arguments about life expectancy are not crucial in this context.

3
Supply of and Demand for Inventions: Theoretical Arguments

I. GENERAL

Though economists generally begin analyses with the forces of supply and demand, it has not been so with technical change in the context of growth models.[1] Previous endogenous technical-change models have worked with only investment as a variable. And though capital investment that embodies technical change may be seen as a *carrier* of new techniques, it is identified with neither supply nor demand. (Of course cumulative capital may also be viewed as an empirical proxy for total output; see, for example, Arrow, 1962.)

This chapter discusses technology as if it is a market good which, like other market goods, is produced only on the basis of rational calculation about its economic consequences to the producer of the knowledge. But it is obviously true that not all knowledge creation is influenced by short-term or even long-term economic incentives. Economic forces do not account even for all new technical inventions. Hayek (1977, pp. 22–42) may well be right that 'Man has been impelled to scientific inquiry by wonder and by need. Of these wonder has been incomparably more fertile'. Much basic knowledge is created in universities and is influenced only distantly by economic needs and priorities. But as Hayek goes on to note, 'Where we wonder we have already a question to ask'. The need of the community, interpreted in the widest sense, often raises questions in thinkers' minds.

Other knowledge is created with the aim of increasing efficiency but yet is uninfluenced by any profit calculations, and is produced without explicit expenditure on R&D; this is the sort of improvement in production, marketing, financing or other aspects of a business that arises from an idea of a line executive about how to operate more efficiently – for example, Alfred Sloan's idea of decentralizing General Motors, or the idea of using cut-down old detergent boxes as magazine storage units, or a host of developments by ingenious farmers. As Kuznets put it when discussing 'the processes by which new knowledge and new inventions originate': '[T]he economic calculus is of limited application to a resource the returns from which are so wide-flung in space and time, and the identifiable costs of which are in such disproportion to returns when observable' (1977, p. 8). This sort of knowledge we may call 'spontaneous'.

The sort of knowledge that corresponds to the economic model may be called 'incentive-responsive'. This sort of knowledge is partly produced in universities, but to a considerable degree is the result of R&D programmes in industry. We should also take note of another class of knowledge produced in industry which is less intentional and less self-conscious than R&D. This is the applied knowledge and technical progress that is the result of casual on-the-job discovery by workers of all kinds at all levels, in response to an opportunity to make an enterprise more efficient and more profitable; it often goes under the label 'learning-by-doing'.

It should not be cause for objection that this chapter views knowledge as an economic commodity whereas chapter 2 and the formal models do not take into account the demand for knowledge and the cost of producing it. Given that both viewpoints capture part of the nature of the phenomenon, there would seem to be every reason for them both to coexist amicably, with both contributing to our broader understanding.

The absence of the cost of producing technology from the formal models in chapter 5 onwards should not be interpreted as implying that the creation of the subject knowledge is not the result of economic forces and economic calculations, but rather reflects the judgement that there is sufficiently little 'conservation' and trade-off between resources devoted to technology creation and resources devoted to other investment and to consumption to permit this simplifying choice of model.

Now may also be an appropriate place to recapitulate the characteristics of technology that distinguish it from the usual market goods in the eye of the user. The key element is that the benefits of knowledge are not fully exploited by its creators, even if it is created as an investment whose profit is realized. Advances in knowledge spill over from the individual creator to other individuals, from the firm that invests in creating new knowledge to other firms, and from one generation to another. And the firm that creates knowledge usually is not able to squeeze out from consumers all the value of the new knowledge to consumers. Of course the spillover phenomenon can also interfere with knowledge creation, because the smaller the inventor's benefits and the greater the costs to him/her alone, the less likely is the inventor (or the firm) to invest in the knowledge. To be more specific, the following are the classes of beneficiaries from knowledge creation.

The Economy as a Whole[2]

If a firm creates knowledge, invests in it and realizes profits from the project at, say, a 30 per cent yearly rate of return, whereas the economy-wide return to invested capital is 20 per cent and the break-even project returns 10 per cent, then the economy as a whole benefits from this new project paying back at 30 per cent because the resources used in it are producing returns in excess of what they would produce in alternative uses. True, the 'profit' goes to the firm, at least at first. But the owners of the firm are part of the economy, and if they are better off, *ceteris paribus*, then the society is better off. If everyone owned a firm in such circumstances, then everyone would be made better off by such profits even though the profits are 'private'.

Furthermore, the benefits from a high-return project that utilizes resources productively go to many other parties in addition to the owners of the firm – to employees as job creation and higher wages; to suppliers; and to the fisc as taxes. So again, even without externalities in the form of knowledge, a high-yielding knowledge project is good for society.

Externalities Realized by Other Firms

The benefit realized by other firms in the same industry from the knowledge created by the knowledge-producing firm is a key element of this system. And the benefits external to the innovating firm certainly must be large, even relative to the discount-factor effect mentioned above. That is, the main social benefit from profitable R&D probably derives from effects external to the firm which invests in the R&D. Firms are able to reduce costs and introduce new products more easily because of research done by others in the industry and in other industries.

Consumer Benefits from the Externalities

There is still another channel through which R&D has positive social effects: at the break-even point on the R&D opportunity ladder, the increased revenue to the firm carrying out the R&D only balances the added inputs to produce the new knowledge, so there is no net gain. But when competitors acquire some of the knowledge (almost) free, there will be a lowering of cost and then price throughout the industry, which will be a windfall gain to consumers and to society as a whole.

Furthermore, except under most unusual conditions a firm cannot charge consumers for all of the knowledge benefits they receive. So even if the firm can control its new knowledge so that competitors cannot acquire it, there will still be a net social benefit in the 'consumer surplus'.

Process and Product Research

Concerning the size of the knowledge-creation externalities: given that year-to-year growth in per-worker output as recorded in the national income accounts of MDCs has at most been something less than 3 per cent per year on the average, and given that a sizeable proportion of this growth is accounted for by inputs of labour and capital (just how sizeable depends upon the researcher and upon how you are thinking about and classifying inputs), one may wonder how much 'residual' there really is that might show the effect of increases in technical progress. But our national income accounts do not directly show the benefits of a very large part of knowledge creation – new and improved products. If a pharmaceutical firm introduces a new drug that allows people to leave mental hospitals quickly, thereby saving large sums of money and improving health and life enjoyment, the first impact on the economy is a reduction in GNP, because some hospital workers will be out of work until they find new jobs. If a firm finds a new soup recipe that increases the pleasure people get from soup, there is no effect at all on GNP unless sales of the soup change. If a firm invents a contraceptive that is more reliable and pleasant than existing products, there is no effect on GNP unless total expenditures on contraceptives change, and if the price of the new product is the same as the price of old products (per unit of use) there will be no change.

Yet such new and improved products constitute a large part of the increase in economic welfare from year to year, accounting for increases in life expectancy, physical appearance, sense of well-being, range of activities available to us and so on.

The proportion of expenditures on R&D that goes into new products is very large relative to the proportion that goes into new processes. In a survey of industrial firms, 45 per cent said that their 'main object' in R&D is to 'develop new products', and another 41 per cent said they concentrated on 'improving existing products' – a total of 86 per cent for product research – compared with 14 per cent whose R&D aims at 'finding new processes' to be used in manufacturing (*Business Week*, 7 May 1966, pp. 164–5. See also Scherer, 1970, p. 349). Of course these figures are sketchy and suggestive at best. And one firm's new products may change another firm's production process, of course. But no matter how unsatisfactory these figures may be, we can certainly rely on them to show that consumer product research is a large proportion of total research – let us say 50 per cent in subsequent work (raising process research from the observed 14 per cent all the way to 50 per cent for 'conservatism'). Even at that, there would be much more impact on consumer welfare than is shown in our audit of GNP.

Government-supported R&D is another important category of knowledge production that contributes to technical progress. But it is exceedingly difficult to make a reasonable guess about how much of the government's total expenditure on knowledge creation affects productivity. Probably we wish to exclude weapons research, though there is some by-product knowledge from it that contributes to productivity. And probably we wish to exclude 'pure' or 'basic' research, though it influences technical progress in a variety of ways. Agricultural research is the best example of the relevant sort of government-supported research. An interesting estimate of 'at least 700 per cent per year' return on investment in hybrid corn research was arrived at by Griliches (1958) and subsequent research generally supports the finding of large returns to such investment in agricultural research.

II. THE SUPPLY SIDE

The supply of technology is relatively easy to analyse. As in the quotation of Petty in chapter 1, the supply of new ideas clearly depends on the number of persons, technically trained or untrained, available to produce or adapt new ideas; this is the labour force, L. That is, if there are more potential knowledge creators and more minds at work, there will be more practical ideas created and adopted. This proposition – that, *ceteris paribus*, more people mean more inventions, faster technical change and greater productivity increase – seems as self-evident to me as any economic proposition can be. It is also so obvious to Machlup that he handles it in 12 words: 'the supply of labor – the chief input for the production of inventions' (1962, p. 143).

As noted in chapter 1, though many of the technical progress functions that we will discuss were originally written in terms of the rate of change of technology, it seems more concrete and therefore clearer and easier to think about a function that has as a dependent variable the absolute numbers of inventions and discoveries, rather than a more abstract rate of change which is itself a comparison of two magnitudes.[3] We therefore express the Petty–Kuznets idea as

$$A_t - A_{t-1} = f(L_t) \tag{3.1}$$

The supply of technology also depends upon the level of education and training of the labour force, both the amount of specific training (which could be indexed by the supply of scientists and engineers) and the unspecific general education (which can be indexed by the mean education of the society) that leads to such important innovations as new organizations. Because of the close relationship between *per capita* income and mean education, the general level of education may also be indexed by *per capita* income, Y/L.

The production of new technical knowledge requires the existence of a stock of technology. Hence the quantity of existing technology, both in storage in libraries and in action in the technical practice in the economy, constrains the amount of new technology that can be created at any moment by various numbers of persons. This implies diminishing returns to the fixed stock of technology at any moment, holding labour force constant. (This effect is not seen in a cross-national analysis because all countries have roughly the same access to the existing body of technology.) Therefore an appropriate technical-change function should contain an argument for the existing stock of technology, M_t.

The total number and variety of physical stimuli – objects and processes – that exist in a society at a given moment· must also influence the supply of inventions. *Per capita* income is one measure of this factor, but total income Y may well be another. This general argument jibes with Verdoorn's law, which makes the change in productivity a function of change in income, and with Clark's data cited in the next chapter which implicitly make the level of productivity a function of total income. It also fits the learning-by-doing data.[4] (All these data are discussed in chapter 4.)

Up to now the discussion has referred to the factors determining the supply function of a given economy at a given moment. Within such an economy, the supply of inventors and inventions clearly is a function of the expected returns in profits to the firm and payments to investors; some poets and mathematicians will temporarily turn their fine minds to productivity increases (or to writing pornographic novels) if the prize offered is large enough.[5] And more prosaically, some persons now working at non-R&D jobs – say, engineers out on the road selling existing products, and technicians working on existing electronic equipment – will move to R&D jobs and departments as the wage level rises in R&D. This effect is mostly not relevant to a study of the effect of different rates of population growth upon the rate of invention. A related idea will be explored, however, in the section on the demand side.

So far the discussion has been at the level of an economy as a whole. For some purposes, one is interested in the potential supply of inventors and inventions for a given industry. It is reasonable that, *ceteris paribus*, the larger the industry the greater the supply of inventions, due to the larger number of innovative people working in the industry, and due also to the larger quantity of capital in the industry, which influences the potential profits to invention as well as the stock of technology that already exists in the industry.[6] And the evidence in chapter 4 corroborates this supposition.

The size of the industry i may be indexed by the quantity of that good produced in the prior period, $Q_{i,t-1}$, and its price, $P_{i,t-1}$. Along the same line, we might also take into account the size of all the other major industries that might draw away potential inventors, $Q_{\tilde{i},t-1}$ (where the tilde implies that it is *not* industry i referred to) and the price of the good produced by industry i, $P_{\tilde{i},t-1}$.

The supply-of-knowledge function for a given industry may therefore be written

$$m_{i,t}^S = (M_{i,t} - M_{i,t-1})^S = f\left(L, Y, \frac{Y}{L}, M, Q_{i,t-1}, P_{i,t-1},\right.$$

$$\left. Q_{\tilde{i},t-1}, P_{\tilde{i},t-1}\right) \tag{3.2}$$

If one assumes that the mean level of education increases the average individual's technology-producing capacity, though not linearly, and if we notice that population size multiplied by *per capita* income equals total output, we can write a more explicit supply function for the economy as a whole

$$m_t^S = f(Y^\gamma M^\Delta) \tag{3.3}$$

It is important to notice that there need not be diminishing returns *over time* to additional people, because the stock of technology with which people may combine their creative talents grows with time. Kuznets makes an argument for increasing returns on two grounds: (a) the stimulative effect of a dense environment, and (b) 'interdependence of knowledge of the various parts of the world in which we human beings operate' (1960, p. 328); for example, discoveries in physics stimulate discoveries in biology, and vice versa. Kuznets discounts the possibility of diminishing returns because 'the universe is far too vast relative to the size of our planet and what we know about it' (1960, p. 329). Machlup suggests that 'every new invention furnishes a new idea for potential combination with vast numbers of existing ideas . . . [and] the number of possible combinations increases geometrically with the number of elements at hand' (1962, p. 156). It is this latter idea of an increasing number of possible permutations of the available elements of technology as the stock increases, when combined with the idea of a reduced likelihood of duplicate discoveries as the number of possibilities increases faster than the number of potential technology producers, that seems most compelling to me, and was developed in chapter 2.

III.   THE DEMAND SIDE

The expected profit to be made in producing final good i is the key factor in the demand for improvements in productivity that will cut costs in producing good i. Profit clearly depends upon product price P_i and upon the scale of the industry Q_i in which the improvements can be put to work, because price and quantity affect total expected profit from invention. We observe more total R&D in large industries than in small ones,[7] and it is reasonable to expect that a larger country will have more total R&D than will a small country, in part because of the greater scope of utilization of improvements; this receives some confirmation from the data on scientific activity in countries of various sizes discussed in chapter 4.

It may be illuminating to consider an example of how demand for R&D rises as overall product demand is expected to rise due to additional persons in the society. Imagine that your firm considers producing a new sort of reading–talking computer for the blind. Right now your financial projections are just below the break-even point. If you are suddenly informed that the population of potential users in 2, 4, 8 and 16 years from now will be 50 per cent larger than you had entered into your calculations, your present-value computation will now be positive (on any reasonable assumptions about potential competitive behaviour). You will now have a greater demand for R&D workers.

With respect to investment and productive equipment, the effective demand for new improvements is an accelerator function; if output is stable and can be supplied by existing plant and equipment, there will be little demand for the improvements that can come only with new investment. (But the experience of the Horndal factory in Sweden makes it clear that productivity change occurs even without the installation of new equipment; see Arrow, 1962, and David, 1975.) Within a given industry i, prospects also depend upon the cost of production, C_i, including the rent of capital goods and the wages of labour.

Thus, the demand for economic improvement for the economy as a whole may be seen as a function of total output, change in output and *per capita* income (or *per capita* output)

$$m_{i,t}^D = (M_t - M_{t-1})^D = f\left(Y, \dot{Y}, \frac{Y}{L}\right) \tag{3.4}$$

There is another facet of the demand side that is harder to fit with conventional economic thinking, because it requires the concepts of needs and aspirations. The concept of need is a subjective rather than objective idea, but felt need certainly can stimulate innovative activity. 'Necessity is the mother of invention' – few would be so rigid in their adherence to traditional economic categories as to deny all meaning to this notion. Implicit in this idea is that at a given moment there is a gap between the individual's rate of output and his/her stock of inputs such that the individual has a greater-than-otherwise motivation to find a new idea to increase the effective stock of inputs or to improve the manner in which the inputs can be combined, so as to increase the rate of output. Finding and developing such a new idea may require additional labour time on the part of the individual, and/or additional 'effort', whatever the meaning of the latter term.

Surely this is the process that occurs in wartime or in economic downturn or in other emergency, as a host of anecdotes show. I know of no statistical evidence linking innovation and level of 'need', but there is ample evidence, both across nations at present, and within nations over time, that lower actual average income or wages leads to more hours worked per week. There is also an observed relationship between number of children and number of hours worked (see Simon, 1977, chap. 4, and Lindert, 1978, app. B). These phenomena can be understood with the trade-off between income and leisure described for us by Hicks (1932) and in more detail for the peasant farmer by Chayanov (1966), and are consistent with Becker's theory of time allocation (1965). It seems reasonable that there should be a similar trade-off between income aspirations and leisure (in the sense

of a respite from the sort of effort required to create and develop
new innovations). The smaller the homemaker's budget, the more
ingenious one would expect her or him to be in inventing ways to
pad the hamburger with cheaper filler; and the smaller the home, the
more ideas for utilizing the space efficiently that you would expect
from the homemaker. (The ingenuity of sailors in utilizing every
nook and cranny on submarines and other small navy ships is a
marvel.)

It is also reasonable to extend this line of thought from need and
actual income to income aspirations. This effect, however, runs in
the opposite direction from actual income. The higher one's actual
past income, the higher is one's wealth and the lower is one's objective
need for present income. But the higher one's actual past income, the
higher one's aspirations for present income. It would be possible to
study the effect of aspirations econometrically by using the actual
income in a given year, or the income that the trend of past income
would lead one to expect, as an independent proxy variable.

IV.   REDUCED FORM

Next we must combine the demand and supply functions into a
reduced form. With respect to the economy as a whole (perhaps of
the entire more-developed world), the supply-side theory suggests
straightforwardly that L and M are key arguments. The demand-side
theory suggests Y as a fundamental factor, along with Y/L, ΔY and
$[(Y/L)_t - (Y/L_{t-1})]$. Considering the supply and demand arguments
together, then, we can write a reduced-form equation for the amount
of technology that will be produced as $m_t = M_t - M_{t-1} = f(L, M, Y, \dot{Y})$. For simplicity, however, we shall not include the latter two
arguments throughout the present work, though later work should
study whether the inclusion affects the results. We may also leave
aside the industry-specific variables in this work.

It is reasonable to assume that the arguments interact in a multiplicative fashion, with each of the factors subject to diminishing
returns. The reduced form function is then

$$m_t = a_8 L_{t-1}^{\gamma} M_{t-1}^{\Delta} \left(\frac{Y}{L}\right)^{\psi} Y^{\phi} \tag{3.5}$$

If we wanted to understand the dynamics of the system, we could note that the contemporary income and stock of technology (as well as other variables except perhaps for labour force) depend upon past values of these same variables. We could therefore write a set of behavioural equations for the quantities, prices, costs and incomes (and also labour force sizes, though for almost any purpose we might consider labour force exogenous). We would be able to push the system back to the point at which all variables drop out except labour force and population, because they affect each of the other variables.

If we are, however, primarily interested in determining the effect of population on variations in the rate of technology production, then we wish to evaluate the influences of the more proximate intermediate variables. And the variables in equation (3.5) are not beyond our econometric horizon, at least for the economy as a whole.[8]

Learning-by-doing does not fit well into the conventional economic analysis using the scissors of supply and demand, because the increases in productivity it induces seem to appear spontaneously as a by-product of the main work, rather than being the main product as is the case in an R&D establishment or university.[9] The factory floor and the plant engineering office are the main loci of learning-by-doing. Hence learning-by-doing complements the formal creation of technology. The framework discussed in this chapter and the model described in chapter 5 could be joined together with the model described in chapter 2. But the ensuing complexity probably would obscure the main points of both.

NOTES

1 I have benefited from discussions of this topic with Richard Sullivan.
2 The following paragraphs are drawn from Simon (1981).
3 The rate-of-change ratio involves two quantities and a comparison of them, rather than just one quantity, which is why I believe that we will make better progress if the discussion focuses on the absolute quantities. This is the spirit of the quotation from Leontief in chapter 2.
4 One may wonder how the studies showing that the rate of learning declines with output (e.g. Barkai and Levhari, 1973; Levhari and Sheshinski, 1973;

Baloff, 1966, and references cited therein) fit in here. The rate of learning in a given product situation may decrease, but there may still be changes in the processes which restart a high-rate learning process, and increase the overall rate of learning which is consistent with the envelope curve in figure 2.1 in chapter 2.

5   Machlup (1962) makes this point well.

6   This could have a negative or positive effect on future invention; the former could be due to an exhaustion of early-exploitable scientific possibilities. Kuznets has suggested that at some moment in the 1800s, the railroad industry exhausted its possibilities for big inventions, and hence inventors turned to the electrical industry. But this shift may also have been due to the completion of major railroad building projects.

7   The reason there is *some* invention in the smaller industries is the same reason there are *some* stores in small towns.

8   If we were working at the industry level, for earlier centuries we are not likely to be able to estimate $Q_{\bar{i}, t-1}$ except as a residual between total income and agriculture, and total income is likely to be a product of population and the standard of living, in which case it would probably not be a useful quantity even though calculable. But the bidding away of inventive resources from agriculture to other industries is not likely to be important here, given the inelasticity of food with respect to price and income.

9   For an interesting formalization and analysis of this joint effect, see Rosen (1972).

4
Observed Relationships of Population to Knowledge Growth

I. INTRODUCTION

Sandwiched between chapter 3 on the theoretical elements in the supply and demand of knowledge, and chapter 5 which begins the modelling of the effect of population size and growth on technology, productivity and the standard of living, would seem an appropriate position for this chapter's review of some pertinent data – the empirical relationships among technical change, economic growth and population growth. First some terminology, however.

Sometimes I shall refer to scientific knowledge, sometimes to technology and sometimes to technology that has been put into use. I shall try to keep these concepts apart, but often they are difficult to distinguish and separate. Following Machlup, the term 'technology' or the redundant 'technological knowledge' shall mean the body of existing knowledge about techniques that are useful for economic purposes. 'Technological progress' shall mean the increase in technology. 'Technical progress' shall mean improvement in techniques used, and the increase in the level of technology actually at work in the economy. I shall avoid the use of the general word 'knowledge' which, in Machlup's classification, includes both technology and all kinds of other knowledge including 'spiritual, intellectual (by which [he means] useless), practical and positive entertainment knowledge' (correspondence, 17 December 1979).

It may be appropriate at this point to remind the reader of the discussion in the introduction (pp. 4–5) of the use of cross-national evidence even though the relevant context is the more-developed world as a whole.

The most important stylized fact which the theory of population and economic growth must fit is that, throughout human history, technical progress has been faster when population size has been larger; when the population was very small 10,000 or 20,000 years ago, the amount and the rate of technical progress were small compared to later periods when population (as well as the stock of knowledge) was larger. The picture can be sharpened a bit by reducing the time scope to the last 2,500 years in the West. Population rose by a factor of perhaps 5 or 10, and the standard of living also rose,[1] by a factor of perhaps 25.

This stylized view is far from conclusive. One question it raises is whether population growth and economic growth are fortuitous fellow-travellers, with no causal relationship between them.

II. POPULATION GROWTH AND NATIONAL ECONOMIC GROWTH

This much is clear: there is no evidence that population growth is negatively associated with economic growth. One piece of historical evidence is the concurrent explosion of both population and economic development in Europe from 1650 onward. Other evidence is found in the rates of population growth and output *per capita* as compared in figure 4.1, which includes contemporary MDCs for which Kuznets could find data. No strong relationship appears. Studies of the most recent rates of population growth and economic growth are another source of evidence. Many comparisons have been made among various countries by now, and there is agreement among them that population growth does not hinder economic growth.

A summary of the evidence published until 1975 may be found in Simon, 1977, chapter 3. The following recent assessment of the evidence by Lee should help convince the reader of the clear conclusion of this body of work:

> [D]ozens of studies, starting with Kuznets' (1967), have found no association between the population growth rate (n) and per capita income growth rate (y/y), despite the obvious fact that at least since WWII, population growth rates have varied considerably (Chesnais and Sauvy, 1973; Isbister, 1975; Thirlwall, 1972; for example). These studies control for other factors such as trade, aid and investment to varying degrees. Two recent

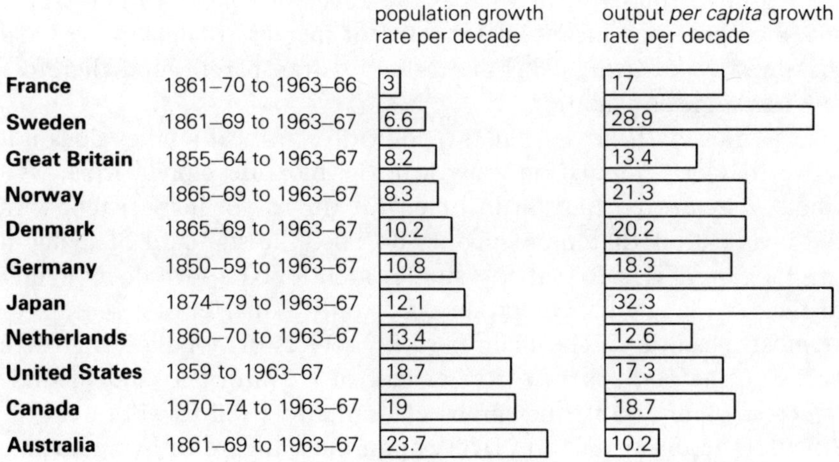

		population growth rate per decade	output *per capita* growth rate per decade
France	1861–70 to 1963–66	3	17
Sweden	1861–69 to 1963–67	6.6	28.9
Great Britain	1855–64 to 1963–67	8.2	13.4
Norway	1865–69 to 1963–67	8.3	21.3
Denmark	1865–69 to 1963–67	10.2	20.2
Germany	1850–59 to 1963–67	10.8	18.3
Japan	1874–79 to 1963–67	12.1	32.3
Netherlands	1860–70 to 1963–67	13.4	12.6
United States	1859 to 1963–67	18.7	17.3
Canada	1970–74 to 1963–67	19	18.7
Australia	1861–69 to 1963–67	23.7	10.2

FIGURE 4.1   The non-relationship between population growth and the growth of living standards

studies add historical depth to this analysis (Bairoch, 1981, and Browning, 1982); even within countries (and thus looking *only* at disequilibrium), over periods as long as a century or as short as 25 years, there is no signifi-cant association of n and $\dot{y}/y$, for either DCs or LDCs; put differently, one can't reject the hypothesis that the regression coefficient of $\dot{y}/y$ on n is unity. I know of just two exceptions to this general picture: the studies by Hazeldine and Moreland (1977) and Suits and Mason (1978), both dealing with cross-sections; both find negative effects of population growth of magnitude roughly equal to the share of non-labor inputs in production, as many theories would predict. However, data problems render these results suspect. (1983, p. 54)

This suggests that models without endogenous technical change are without value for the understanding of population growth's effects.

It has been suggested in conversations that the studies showing the absence of a relationship between the population growth rate and the economic growth rate also demonstrate that additional people do not imply a higher standard of living in the long run. That is, it has been asserted that because these studies do not show a *positive* relationship, I am making claims beyond the evidence when I say that over the very long sweep of human history a larger population in the world (or perhaps, in what is the developed part of the world at any moment) has meant faster rates of increase of technology and the standard of living. This matter is not transparent, and therefore requires some explanation.

It is indeed the case that the body of empirical studies does not prove that fast population growth in the more-developed world as a whole *increases* per person income. But this is not inconsistent with the proposition that more people do raise the standard of living in the long run. Recall that the studies mentioned above do not refer to the *very* long run, but rather cover only a quarter of a century or at most a century. The main *negative* effects of population growth occur during perhaps a quarter or half of a century so that, if these effects *are* important, the empirical studies referred to will reveal the effects. These shorter run effects upon the standard of living include the public costs of raising children – schools and hospitals are the main examples – and the costs of providing additional production capital for the additional persons in the work force. The absence of an observed negative effect upon economic growth in the statistical measures therefore is enough to imply that in the very long run more people have a *positive* net effect. This is because the most important positive effects of additional people – improvement of productivity through both the contribution of new ideas, and also the learning-by-doing consequent upon increased production volume – happen in the long run, and are cumulative. To put it differently, the statistical measurements of the relationship of population growth to economic growth are biased in favour of showing the shorter run effects, which tend to be negative, and not showing the longer run effects, which tend to be positive. If such negative effects do not appear, one may assume that an unbiased measure of the total effect would reveal a positive effect of population growth upon economic growth.

There is still another reason why the studies mentioned above do not imply an absence of positive effect in the long run. Those studies focus on the *process* of population *growth*. If we look at the *attained level* of population – that is, the population density as measured by the number of persons per square mile, say – we see a somewhat different result. Studies of MDCs are lacking. But in LDCs, Hagen (1975) and Kindleberger (1965) show visually, and Simon and Gobin (1979) show in multivariate regressions, that higher population density is associated with *higher* rates of economic growth; this effect may be strongest at low densities, but there is no evidence that the effect reverses at high densities. Strycker shows a similar effect for agricultural productivity (1976). And the data showing a positive effect of density upon economic growth constitute indirect proof of a positive long-run effect of population *growth* upon economic growth, because density changes occur very slowly, and therefore they pick up the very long-run effects as well as the short-run effects.

It may at first seem unbelievable that greater population density leads to better economic results. This is the equivalent of saying that if all Americans moved east of the Mississippi, we would all be better off. Upon reflection, this proposition is not as unlikely as it sounds. The main loss involved in such a move would be large amounts of farmland, and though the United States is a massive producer and exporter of farm goods, agriculture is not crucial to the economy. Less than 3 per cent of US income comes from agriculture, and less than 3 per cent of the US working population is engaged in that industry. The capitalized value of all US farmland is just a bit more than a tenth of only one year's national income, so even if the US were to lose all of it, the loss would equal only about one year's expenditures upon liquor, cigarettes and the like. On the other hand, such a change would bring about major benefits in shortening transportation and communication distances, a factor which has been important in Japan's ability to closely coordinate its industrial operations in such a fashion as to reduce costs of inventory and transportation. Additionally, greater population concentration forces social changes in the direction of a greater degree of organization, changes which may be costly in the short run but in the long run increase a society's ability to reach its economic and social objectives. If we were still living at the population density that people achieved say 10,000 years ago, we would have none of the vital complex social and economic apparatus that provides the backbone of our society.

III.   HISTORICAL EVIDENCE ON POPULATION AND TECHNOLOGY

Figures 4.2 and 4.3 for Greece and Rome suggest some coincidence in rises and falls of population and of invention; those figures also suggest that the *rate of growth* of population, as well as the total

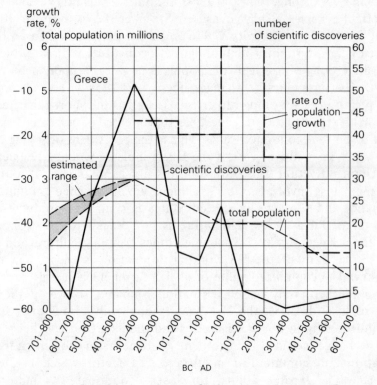

FIGURE 4.2   Population and scientific discoveries in Ancient Greece

population size, may be an important determinant of the rate of invention.

One might reasonably wonder whether the fecundity in terms of both invention and children coincident in Greece and Rome early in their peak periods were both reflections of some other underlying force. But whether or not this is true – and I believe that it probably is true – it does not refute the idea that there is a causal connection between population *size* and invention, which is the main visible correlation.

Slicher van Bath observed that the European publication of scientific writings on agriculture waxed greatly during periods of population increase and higher food prices, and then waned when population growth declined (1963). And Sullivan and I have explored the influences of population size, food prices, wage rate and quantity

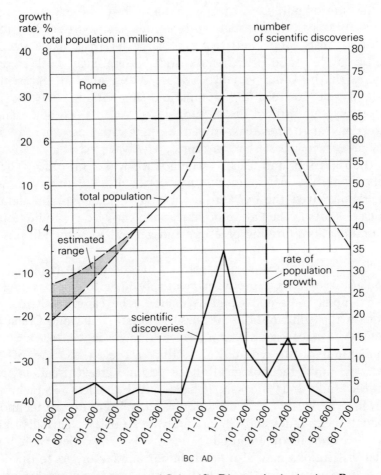

FIGURE 4.3   Population and Scientific Discoveries in Ancient Rome

of existing knowledge upon the rate of production of agricultural book titles and of patents in England from 1541 to 1850 (1985). (Only the analysis of such a long period can reveal whether as slow-moving a variable as population size has an effect on the creation of knowledge, and only the pre-modern period is likely to show the variations in population that enable the analysis to be made success-fully.) We found that all the variables had the effects predicted for them in chapter 3, though the strength of the effects differs. Both population size and the amount of cumulative knowledge (measured by the sum of published titles or patents from the beginning of the period, plus a fitted constant in some runs) show strongly significant statistical tests, and coefficients of large but reasonable size. The coefficient for food prices is statistically significant both in regressions with the other variables (where it operates to represent the demand side so that the population size variable may be more reasonably interpreted as a supply-of-inventors variable) and in regressions of the residuals from the other variables, where its independent effect is easiest to interpret. The wage variable consistently has the right sign and usually attains statistical significance. The fact that the results are so nicely in accord with the theory is rather remarkable given the extraordinarily rough quality of the data and the large shifts in the nature of education, knowledge production and communication, farming practices and general social conditions over such a long period of time.

There often arises a question about countries that have large populations but have produced relatively little technology recently, for example, India and China. We should be careful not to underestimate the contributions of these nations – India and China were the most advanced countries in the world in earlier centuries. Starting a millenium or so ago, however, Europe began to take off with relatively rapid technological and economic growth, and in recent centuries India and China clearly have contributed less new technology than has the West. The explanation of the present rate of technology production in India and China surely lies (at least partially) in the low *per capita* income and education of these societies, though their social institutions may also be an important factor. As to the differential development in the past, the historians offer many hypotheses for the rise of the West, mostly based (here I follow McNeill, 1963) on the fairly loose social system and the general lack of stability in the West. But no explanation of the West's and East's differential development is nearly conclusive.

Most (if not all) historians of the period (e.g. Nef, 1958, 1960; Gimpel, 1976) agree that the period of rapid population growth from before AD 1000 to the beginning of the middle of the 1300s was a period of extraordinary intellectual fecundity. It was also a period of great dynamism generally, as seen in the extraordinary cathedral building boom. But during the period of depopulation due to the plague (starting with the Black Death cataclysm) and perhaps to climatic changes from the middle 1300s (though the change apparently began earlier at the time of major famines around 1315–17, and perhaps even earlier, when there also was a slowing or cessation of population growth due to other factors) until perhaps the 1500s, historians agree that intellectual and social vitality waned.

Pirenne's magisterial analysis (1925/1969) of this period depends heavily upon population growth and size. Larger absolute numbers were the basis for increased trade and consequent growth in cities, which in turn strongly influenced the creation of a more articulated exchange economy in place of the subsistence economy of the manor. And according to Pirenne, growth in population also loosened the bonds of the serf in the city and thereby contributed to an increase in human liberty (though the causes of the end of serfdom are a subject of much controversy).[2]

The development of cities also boded well for the creation of new knowledge by way of what might be called the 'culture of cities'. Kuznets asserts that 'creative effort flourishes in a dense intellectual atmosphere, and it is hardly an accident that the locus of intellectual progress (including that of the arts) has been preponderantly in the larger cities', and there is some statistical verification for this assertion in contemporary data. Kelley (1972) examined Higgs's (1971) data on inventions from 1870 to 1920, and found that the elasticity of the number of inventions with respect to city size in the US was more than unity, even when urbanization is controlled. Kelley suggests it is unlikely that education or another variable accounts for the apparent relationship. And he finds some indication that the elasticity has declined somewhat over time. It should be noted, however, that an elasticity of unity for knowledge with respect to population growth is very high from the point of view of progress in economy and civilization, and an elasticity of much less than unity (in fact, any elasticity greater than zero) is compatible with a rise in population having an overall positive effect on per-worker income in the long run.[3]

IV. CONTEMPORARY EVIDENCE ON POPULATION AND TECHNOLOGY

A comparison of the cross-national distribution of scientists and scientific activity provides interesting evidence on the relationship between population and technology. Though scentific knowledge is not, by any means, the same as technology, it is a key precursor of it, and of both 'spontaneous' and 'induced' technical change. Hence, the evidence that, in a cross-section of countries, population size and *per capita* income together are an excellent explanation of the amount of scientific activity (as measured by the number of published scientists), is relevant and important (de Solla Price, 1967, 1971, 1975; Love and Pashute, 1978). This is, if output per scientist is the same from place to place, holding *per capita* income constant, the quantity of scientific output is proportional to the size of the country. Or, doubling the labour force implies doubling the rate of scentific output, *ceteris paribus*, as figure 4.4 shows. This diagram illustrates the close relationship between the total amount of scentific activity (as measured by the number of authors of scientific publications) and the population of countries, after *per capita* income is allowed for. This fits with the idea that more people imply faster increases in technology and economic growth. Technically, this is a plot of log population versus the residuals of the model log (authors in country) = a + b log (*per capita* income) – see footnote 4. The US is much larger than Sweden, and it produces much more scientific knowledge. Sweden benefits from the larger US population because it 'imports'

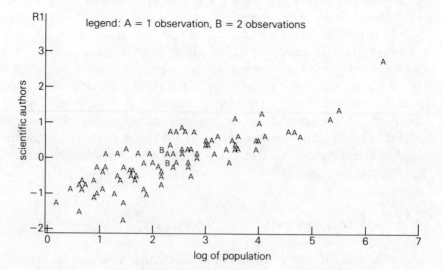

FIGURE 4.4   The relationship of scientific activity to population size

much more knowledge from the US than the US imports from Sweden; this can be seen in the references used in Swedish and US scientific writings, and in the number of patented processes licensed from each other.[4]

Please keep in mind that our interest here is the more-developed world as a whole, within which technology passes back and forth; data for countries are used in these discussions only because there are enough countries to constitute a sample, whereas we have only one set of MDCs as a whole. And one cannot directly deduce from this evidence that if the number of people were doubled in the more-developed world as a whole, scientific output would double. If there were no national or cultural or spatial barriers to knowledge, one would expect to find scientific output proportional to the labour force in each place even if additional workers were highly redundant and produced much less than the proportional increment. But there are, in fact, important barriers to the free flow of knowledge and persons from place to place, as well as differences in the kind of scientific knowledge needed in various places. Hence, the scientific establishments in various countries are self-contained to at least some degree. And the fact that scientific output is nevertheless proportional to labour-force inputs suggests that additional labour force might well contribute proportionally to scientific output.[5]

V. EVIDENCE ON PRODUCTIVITY

Given the very close relationship between productivity and technology, data on the relationship of productivity to population size are obviously relevant. Let us begin the discussion with an estimate of the overall effects of population size on productivity in less-developed countries (LDCs). Chenery (1960) compared the manufacturing sectors in a variety of countries and found that, all else being equal, if one country is twice as populous as another, output per worker is 20 per cent larger. This is a very large positive effect of population size no matter how you look at it.

Now let us move from the national level down to the industry level, and let us shift from LDCs to MDCs because most of the available information pertains to MDCs.

In every industry, there is some minimum size of factor that must be attained to reach a reasonable operating efficiency. But though this is the sort of economy of scale that has been most studied in the past (because of its industrial applications), it is not the economy of scale that is most relevant to population questions.

More relevant are studies of industries as wholes. As mentioned above, it is an important and well-established phenomenon that the faster an industry grows, the faster its efficiency increases – even compared with the same industry in other countries. In figures 4.5 and 4.6 we see comparisons of the productivity of US industries in 1950 and 1963, and of UK industries in 1963, with UK industries in 1950, and also comparisons of US industries in 1963 with those of Canada in the same year. The larger the industry relative to the UK or Canada base, the higher its productivity. This effect is very large: productivity goes up roughly with the square root of output. That is, if you quadruple the size of an industry, you may expect to double the output per worker and per unit of capital employed.[6]

The effect Chenery saw in economies as wholes, together with the effects seen in individual industries, constitutes strong evidence that a larger and faster growing population produces a greater rate of increase in economic efficiency.

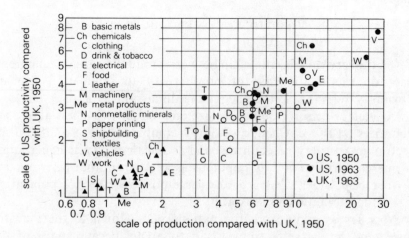

FIGURE 4.5   The effect of industrial scale upon productivity, US v. UK

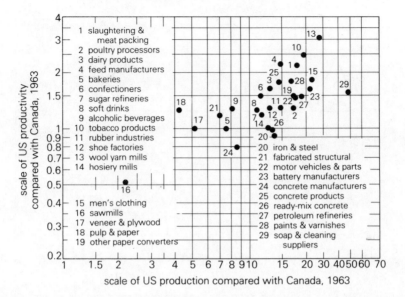

FIGURE 4.6   The effect of industrial scale upon productivity, Canada v. the US

The phenomenon called learning-by-doing[7] is surely a key factor in the improvement of productivity in particular industries and in the economy as a whole. The idea is a simple one: the more units produced in a plant or an industry, the more efficiently they are produced, as people learn and develop better methods. Industrial engineers have understood learning-by-doing for many decades, but economists first grasped its importance in the production of airplanes in the Second World War, when it was referred to as the '80 per cent curve': a doubling in the cumulative production of a particular airplane led to a 20 per cent reduction in labour per plane. That is, if the first airplane required 1,000 units of labour, the second would require 80 per cent of 1,000, or 800 units, the fourth would require 80 per cent of 800, or 640 units and so on, though after some time the rate of learning probably slows. Similar 'progress ratios' have been found for lathes, machine tools, textile machines and ships. The economic importance of learning-by-doing clearly is great.

The effect of learning-by-doing can also be seen in the progressive reduction in price of new consumer devices in the years following their

FIGURE 4.7   Sales prices of room air conditioners and colour television sets

introduction to the market. The examples of room air conditioners and colour television sets are shown in figure 4.7.

Modern data with which to relate population size and technical change are scarce and not very meaningful. The population is larger in the later decades of the twentieth century in the US than it was in the earlier decades. And Solow (1957) calculated that the yearly rate of change of the technological coefficient in his model went from 1 per cent to 2 per cent over the 20 years from the (median of the) first half of his study period to the (median of the) second half of his period (1909–49). Fellner computed rates of growth of productivity of 1.8 per cent for 1900–29, 2.3 per cent for 1929–48 and 2.8 per cent for 1948–66 (1970, p. 11–12). And the Kendrick–NBER data show that the rate of growth of output per unit of labour input rose 0.012 per cent per year from 1890 to 1957, which means a rise from 1.62 per cent yearly at the starting point to 2.38 per cent at the endpoint.

Since 1973 there has been a fall in the rate of growth of productivity in the US. This may indicate a lack of relationship of the sort suggested by the above-cited data. But the fall also may be simply a historical blip lasting one or two decades, after which the long-term trends may continue. It is seldom sensible to read changes in long-run secular trends from a few years' data; doing so has produced more wrong predictions than any other single bad practice in social science (e.g. the predictions of shortages and scarcities starting in 1973).

There are at least some writers on the physical sciences (see Rescher, 1978 and citations therein) who argue that a given quantity of resources brings decreasing amounts of knowledge as time progresses. Whether or not this is true for the physical sciences – and there are vast and perhaps insuperable problems in comparing the values of different discoveries, as well as strong philosophical arguments both against and for this position – there is no analogy to the rate of technical progress as measured by various proxies for national income. And even if there is a limit to the number of 'laws' that can be discovered in the physical sciences, there is certainly no such limit in the social and economic sciences, because increasing institutional complexity creates new material for study and understanding.

VI.   THE EFFECT THROUGH EDUCATION

So far we have dealt with the relationship of population size to the rate of knowledge output. But a word about the relationship of population size to education – a key input into knowledge creation – may not be amiss here. Taxpayers might not wish to provide (or authorities might not demand) enough additional tax revenues to maintain an equivalent level of schooling in the face of population growth. If so, a larger population, with its larger proportion of children, might lead to less education on the average, and thus less potential to increase the stock of knowledge, than a smaller population.

The conventional theory of population growth's effect upon the amount of education per child is straightforward first-edition Malthus: a fixed educational budget of money and resources divided among more students implies less education per student. But as we know from a host of evidence, people and institutions often respond to population growth by altering the apparently fixed conditions. In agricultural countries, for example, having more children causes parents to increase their labour on the land. And in industrial countries, when there are additional profitable opportunities for investment, people will shift some resources from consumption to investment; additional children constitute such an opportunity. Therefore, we must allow for responses contrary to the simple Malthusian pie-sharing theory.

There is no way of knowing from theory alone which of the two effects – dilution of resources or increase of work – will dominate. Therefore we must turn to empirical data. In general there seems no reason to believe that larger community size is associated with less education; historically, the association seems to have been positive. And comparison of rates of population growth in LDCs with the amounts of education given to children shows that an increase in the birth rate somewhat reduces educational expenditures per child and secondary enrolment, but not primary or postsecondary enrolment.[8] Perhaps the most meaningful finding is that the negative effect is nowhere near as great as the simple Malthusian theory would suggest, and in general the effect does not seem to be large.

VII. SUMMARY

At the least, the evidence cited in this chapter should make it clear that the growth of technology must be treated as endogenous in any sensible model of the effect of population growth upon the standard of living. The data show that the number of people, and the consequent size of demand for given products, affect the stock of knowledge through the main channels that the theory in the previous chapter suggests they should – the supply of inventive minds, the effect on productivity through learning-by-doing (probably compounded with the quickening effect of greater competition) and perhaps the effect through total demand upon the adoption of new ideas through increased investment. But the empirical study of these topics is still a painfully underdeveloped field.

NOTES

1 This observation about change in the standard of living is based simply on the agricultural labour force in the US as a proportion of the population at

present being 1/25 of its proportion in 1800 – say 2.7 per cent versus 73 per cent. The labour time that bought one bushel of wheat then will now buy that bushel of wheat, plus what you can get in trade for 24 bushels of wheat. This does not adjust downwards for sectoral shifts in classification, but it also does not allow upwards for new products and for extension of life, and the latter set of forces must vastly dominate the former. The estimate of an increase by a factor of 25 therefore is a modest estimate, as I see it.

2 'It was in the course of the tenth century that there reappeared in continental Europe a class of professional merchants whose progress, very slow at first, gathered speed as the following century moved forward. The increase in population, which began to manifest at the same era, is certainly in direct relation to this phenomenon. It had as a result the detaching from the land of an increasingly important number of individuals and committing them to that roving hazardous existence which, in every agricultural civilization, is the lot of those who no longer find themselves with their roots in the soil. It multiplied the crowd of vagabonds drifting about all through society, living from day to day by alms from the monasteries, hiring themselves out at harvest-time, enlisting in the armies in time of war and holding back from neither rapine nor pillage when occasion presented. It is among this crowd of foot-loose adventurers that the first adepts of trade must, without any doubt, be looked for' (Pirenne, p. 114).

3 The subject of this chapter is the relationship of population size to knowledge. But this paragraph's discussion of city size and invention may seem one-sided without at least some mention of a possible countervailing effect of city congestion, because it will not be mentioned elsewhere in the book. If there really are important congestion problems in bigger cities, for example, one would expect them to be reflected in the cost-of-living data for cities of different sizes. But no strong relationship between size of city and cost of living is apparent. More detailed statistical studies of this evidence reveal that at most there is a tiny effect. The largest estimate is a 1 per cent increase in the cost of living for each additional million people, for people living on a high budget; other estimates range downward to no effect at all (Sheffer, 1970; Alonso and Fajans, 1970; Haworth and Rasmussen, 1973).

A study of the relationship of city size to the prices of over 200 individual goods and services found that although more prices increase with increasing city size than decrease, for almost every good or service workers are more productive in the larger cities after the higher wage in bigger cities is allowed for. And the higher incomes in larger cities more than make up for the higher prices, so that the overall purchasing power of a person's labour is greater in the bigger cities (Love, 1978). This suggests that the disadvantages of congestion are less than the positive effects of greater population, including better communications and more competition, on the standard of living in larger cities.

4 The results of a key regression are as follows:

$$\log \text{AUTHORS}_i = -2.767 + 1.110 \log \text{POP}_i - 0.598 \log \text{URBAN}_i$$
$$\quad\quad\quad (-6.62)\quad (14.01)\quad\quad\quad\quad (-2.74)$$

$$+ 1.90 \log \frac{\text{GNP}}{\text{POP}}_i - 0.282 \log \text{CHILD}_i$$
$$\quad (12.62)\quad\quad\quad\quad (-1.51)$$

where AUTHORS_i is the arithmetic mean number of scientific authors from country i, DENSITY_i is the population per square kilometer of country i, CHILD_i is the percentage of the population of country i that is under age 15 and the numbers in brackets are t statistics.

5 Implicit in the previous discussion is that the genetic potential for knowledge creation is, on the average, the same among people in larger and smaller populations. That is, it is assumed that a larger population is not larger just because the least gifted people are having more children; if in fact it were true that the difference in growth is made up only of those who will not contribute to knowledge, the total stock of potential knowledge-producers might be no higher with the larger population than with the smaller. But in the United States, most children are born to the middle class, and it is variations in the middle-class birth rate that have largely accounted for the post-World War II variations in the aggregate birth rate. Hence, the assumption about equal average genetic potential in various size populations seems reasonable in the United States context. Furthermore, I have seen no convincing evidence for genetic transmission of intellectual ability among humans, and if there is no such evidence after all the study of the matter that has been done, the entire issue is nugatory.

6 The inter-country comparisons in the same year are relatively free of the potential bias arising from the fact that those industries where world technology grew faster exogenously were also those whose scale of production therefore expanded faster, a bias which afflicts analogous time-series studies within a single country. A particularly strong piece of evidence that there is no confusion about the direction of the causality is the behaviour of the forest-products industries in Canada and the US. It is quite clear that Canada did not come to have large forests because it had antecedently developed a high level of productivity in those industries, and therefore it stands to reason that the high achieved level of productivity in those industries must now be due to the large forests that Canada began with. Further discussion of the nature of the causal relationship may be found in Simon (1981, chapter 14).

7 The basic paper on learning-by-doing by an economist is that of Alchian (1963). In it he refers to the Rand study he did just after the Second World

War, and to the earlier engineering literature. More general data and discussion are found in Hirsch, 1956. Since then the theoretical and empirical literature on the subject has greatly increased, but to my knowledge has not been well summarized.

8 Winegarden, 1975; Simon and Pilarski, 1979; Meeks, 1982; Miyashita *et al.*, 1982.

PART II
The Growth Models and Applications

5
The Effects of Population Size and Growth through Learning-by-Doing

Julian L. Simon and Gunter Steinmann

I. INTRODUCTION

Following on the empirical studies of learning-by-doing by Wright (1936), Asher (1956) and others, and the summary and interpretation by Hirsch (1956) and Alchian (1963), Arrow combined the effect of experience with a macro-model to study the economic implications of the phenomenon. Arrow's model followed Kaldor's in making technical progress endogenous, though Kaldor's point of departure was Verdoorn's macro and industry data (1949), rather than the firm-level data on which Arrow built and which lend themselves more obviously to a learning interpretation than do Verdoorn's data.

The conclusion which this chapter reaches, working with a model like Arrow's, is that population growth, and even more importantly, population size, may well have positive effects upon the rate of economic growth through their positive effects on the rate of technical progress, with reasonable assumptions about the likely capital–output ratios with different demographic structure, though the model produces negative effects with other less-reasonable assumptions about the capital–output ratio. This positive conclusion could have considerable implications for the understanding of population size and growth, and for the formation of social policy with respect to these forces.

Section II gives an intuitive explanation of the implications of learning-by-doing for evaluation of different *sizes* of population. This requires the unravelling of an apparent paradox in Arrow's analysis which can lead to incorrect conclusions about this matter. Section III builds a learning-by-doing model at the micro-level referring to continuous processes such as shipbuilding. It then determines under which capital-dilution conditions a large population and faster population growth have positive and negative effects upon the standard of living. Section IV offers some discussion, and section V summarizes the work and the conclusions. The appendix criticizes the concept of experience Arrow used, to make clear the reasons for the choice of concept used here.

A brief historical digression before beginning work: for Adam Smith, the source of technical progress was the division of labour accompanying increases in population and demand. (Petty was just as clear on the division of labour, and he also took into account the invention of new ideas which Smith did not, to any significant degree.) Perhaps because of modern evidence on the cessation of economies of scale at moderate outputs in most industries, interest in division of labour seems to have waned. But it is worth noting that along with the increased manipulative skill that occurs in workers with increased division of labour, there is likely to be more learning-by-doing because some workers are paying more attention to each aspect of the operation (though of course this can have negative effects, too). Everett saw this clearly in 1826:

> It is sufficiently notorious, that an increase of population on a given territory is followed immediately by a division of labor; which produces in its turn the invention of new machines, an improvement of methods in all the departments of industry, and a rapid progress in the various branches of art and science. (1826/1970, p. 26)

II. FOUNDATIONS OF THE ANALYSIS

All the emprical studies on which Arrow relied, and also most of those that have come afterwards (with exceptions to be noted below) correlated measures such as 'the amount of direct labor required to produce an airframe and the [cumulative] number of airframes produced' (Alchian, 1963, p. 680).[1]

$$H_N = H_1 N^{-b} = H_1 - H_1(1 - N^{-b}) \tag{5.1}$$

where N = serial number of a particular unit of output
    H_N = hours of work per unit of output for serial number N
    b = constant.

Arrow is very clear on this: 'The economic examples given above suggest the possibility of using cumulative output (the total output from the beginning of time) as an index of experience' (p. 157). We shall work with this concept rather than with cumulative gross experience with which Arrow worked. Our reasons for this choice, and the unfortunate results of the choice Arrow made, are described in the afterword to this chapter.

We begin our intuitive description of the process at work by noting that a key difference between our models and that of Arrow boils down to a distinction between equilibrium and non-equilibrium analyses; the latter is appropriate for the issue under discussion here, which is analysis of the effects of population size rather than of steady-state growth patterns. This point may immediately be obvious to the reader; if so, please skip to the formal and more general analyses in section III. But experience has shown that this argument usually must be made at length for it to have a chance to persuade the reader. This is partly because there is an apparent paradox here. It is also because the main body of growth theory is framed in equilibrium terms, and therefore the reader is likely to come to this book with a predilection to view the matter in a growth-equilibrium context. We hope that you the reader will accept that, though equilibrium growth theory may be appropriate in some contexts, for most population-policy questions one wishes to either compare economies of different initial population sizes with the same rates of population growth, or economies of the same initial size with different rates of growth (or economies that differ in both size and growth rates). Such non-equilibrium analysis (akin to comparative statistics) leads to entirely different conclusions than does growth-equilibrium analysis, as we shall see.

We must be crystal clear about the nature of the empirical process on which the function is based, because a subtle shift in interpretation cause a fundamental misinterpretation. It is all-important not to skim over the fundamentals of the process and rush into the formal model and manipulation in section III, otherwise the value we think lies in our analysis, as distinguished from Arrow's, will be lost.

For the first unit made, the measured number of work hours spent on it is equal to H_1 in equation (5.1), which is one of the two key values in the system. The process is assumed to start at this point, with H_1 given exogenously as a result of a variety of specified previous experiences. Successive units produced require amounts of labour equal to the amount needed for the initial unit less a proportion of that initial amount, the proportion depending on the serial number of the successive unit. To portray a learning-by-doing process one must therefore either know (or be able to estimate from later data) the original level of skill at which this particular process begins.

Assume that the good i, whose cumulative quantity produced up to period t is indexed by serial number $N_{t,\,i}$, is a normal good. It is reasonable to assume that the output of i in any period t is a proportional function of total income

$$N_t - N_{t-1} = gY \tag{5.2}$$

and that total income is a proportional function of labour force size

$$Y = \lambda L \tag{5.3}$$

where g and λ are constants. (Date subscripts for income and labour force will be added later when necessary.) The volume $N_t - N_{t-1} = g\lambda L$ produced in t therefore is an increasing function of the population size. (It is all-important here to distinguish between, on the one hand, the volume produced in a given period t, and, on the other hand, the serial number N, which might be produced in any period t.)

Consider the moment when a given production process N begins with serial number $N = 1$. For convenience, this takes place on 1 January of year $t = 1$ in country Alpha. Assume population size is $P_{t=1}$, labour force size is $L_{t=1}$ and total national output for that year is $Y_{t=1}$. For those conditions, there will be X units of good i produced, so at the end of the first year the serial number is $N_{t=2}^{\alpha} = X$.

Now assume instead that we are in country Beta and population size instead is $2P_{t=1}$, labour-force size is $2L_{t=1}$ and consequently total national output is $2Y_{t=1}$. (Furthermore, the population and output have *always* been twice as large in Beta as in Alpha.) From equations (5.1) and (5.2) we can expect that the end-of-year serial number will be $N_{t=2}^{\beta} = 2X$ rather than $N_{t=2}^{\alpha} = X$. Hence $N_{t=2}^{\alpha} - N_{t=1}^{\alpha} = X$ for $L_{t=1}$ and $2X$ for $2L_{t=1}$.

Next consider the rate of change of productivity A over the first period. Whatever the percentage change $(A_{t=2} - A_{t=1})/A_{t=1}$, the rate will be roughly twice as large for $2L_{t=1}$ as for $L_{t=1}$ (assuming that the change is small relative to the initial value, which one can ensure by making the period short, say a day rather than a year).

To elucidate this point, let us write out the learning-by-doing concept in the greatest possible detail. Defining the level of productivity A as the inverse of work time per unit, and using equation (5.1)

$$A_N = \frac{A_{N=1}}{N^{-b}} = A_{N=1} N^b = A_{N=1} + A_{N=1} (N^b - 1) \qquad (5.4)$$

From (5.4) it is quite clear that for two firms or economies α and β that produce, up to the same date, N^α and $N^\beta > N^\alpha$ units, the rate of change of productivity from the beginning to that date is greater for β than for α,

$$\frac{A_{N^\beta > N^\alpha} - A_{N=1}}{A_{N=1}} > \frac{A_{N^\alpha} - A_{N=1}}{A_{N=1}} \qquad (5.5)$$

In Arrow's model, which works with cumulative investment rather than cumulative output, we do *not* find that the rate of change of productivity is a function of output or labour force in anywhere near the same way, because it is in the nature of any capital stock that it does not correspond in any simple additive way to all the capital produced since the beginning of time. (For more details, see the appendix.) And this is even more true in Arrow's model which includes obsolescence.[2]

Yet more importantly, Arrow's model invites one to write an experience function such as

$$\frac{A_{t+1} - A_t}{A_t} = \frac{aK_{t+1}^b - aK_t^b}{aK_t^b} \qquad (5.6)$$

where the dates include any given period rather than one of the dates being the first period. Though Arrow does not write this function explicitly, he likens his model to Kaldor's, who writes the similar function

$$\frac{A_{t+1} - A_t}{A_t} = c \left(\frac{K_t - K_{t-1}}{K_{t-1}} \right) \qquad (5.7)$$

In Arrow's words, 'The production assumptions of this section are designed to play the role assigned by Kaldor to his "technical progress function", which relates the rate of growth of output per worker to the rate of growth of capital per worker. I prefer to think of relations between rates of growth as themselves derived from more fundamental relations between the magnitudes involved' (p. 160). He also says that 'Verdoorn had also developed a similar simple model' (p. 160); Verdoorn differs in using output per year, but his independent variable is also a rate of change of the *current* magnitude. So there is little doubt that (5.6) is a fair representation of Arrow's model. In his empirical 'Tests of the "Learning By Doing" Hypothesis', Sheshinski (1967) estimated exactly this model where 'the increase in experience . . . is attributed to current gross investment' (that is, the rate of change of productivity = investment/capital stock),[3] or in an alternative model, 'the change in experience is attributed to the rate of output' (that is, the rate of change of productivity = output/ 'cumulated gross output', where Sheshinski's empirical referent of the latter concept is unclear but is certainly not cumulated gross output since the beginning of the process, as is required for a reasonable portrayal of the learning-by-doing process).

Given that a country's situation at any given date is compared to *its own* situation at some slightly earlier date, the rate of change of the capital stock may be expected to be the *same* for larger country Beta as for smaller country Alpha, *ceteris paribus*. Hence in Arrow's model the rate of increase of productivity is essentially independent of the scale of the economy and of the population, though it will reflect short-run changes in output (through differences in investment and the capital stock). That is, though this model may lend itself to estimating the rate for a given process, it does not enable one to compare the results for two entities of different sizes.

To make the point as graphic as possible: if fathers cut their male offspring's hair monthly, a father with twin sons will get twice as much practice in any period, and his skill at any date will be higher than that of a father with only one son (assuming equal beginning skill). This does not imply that in each period the twins' father's *rate of increase* of skill will be higher than that of the father of only one son; if the learning curve has the same exponent at all points, the rates will be the same in each period after the first. But the rate of increase of productivity *from the beginning* to any given later date will be greater for the father with twins than for the father with one son.[4]

There is an apparent paradox here: if two countries with different sizes of population and output are compared for a period starting *after* a process has begun, between the same dates in both, the rates of change of productivity over the period can be the same even though if the period begins *at the beginning* of the process, the rate of change of productivity of the larger country will be greater. For example, assume that Alpha produces one unit per period, and Beta produces two units per period. Between periods four and five, Alpha goes from serial 4 to serial 5, whereas Beta goes from 8 to 10. If A_1 – the level of technology of the first unit, the inverse of the numbers of hours required to make the first unit – is equal to 10, if b = 0.5 and hence if $A_N = 10N^{0.5}$, then for Alpha

$$\frac{A_{t=5} - A_{t=4}}{A_{t=4}} = \frac{A_{N=5} - A_{N=4}}{A_{N=4}} = \frac{10\sqrt{5} - 10\sqrt{4}}{10\sqrt{4}} \cong 0.414 \quad (5.8)$$

and also for Beta

$$\frac{A_{t=5} - A_{t=4}}{A_{t=4}} = \frac{A_{N=10} - A_{N=8}}{A_{N=8}} = \frac{10\sqrt{10} - 10\sqrt{8}}{10\sqrt{8}} \cong 0.414 \quad (5.9)$$

But from the beginning of the process to the end of period 5, the calculations are, for Alpha

$$\frac{A_{t=5} - A_{t=1}}{A_{t=1}} = \frac{10\sqrt{5} - 10\sqrt{1}}{10\sqrt{1}} \cong 1.236 \quad (5.10)$$

and for Beta

$$\frac{A_{t=5} - A_{N=1}}{A_{N=1}} = \frac{10\sqrt{10} - 10\sqrt{1}}{10\sqrt{1}} \cong 2.162 \quad (5.11)$$

So Beta's rate of increase of productivity is faster than Alpha's when calculated from the beginning of the process.

III.   FORMAL ANALYSIS OF POPULATION EFFECTS
THROUGH LEARNING-BY-DOING

We shall work with a production process that refers to a continuously changing process such as airframe construction or ship building, from which the learning-by-doing data originate. An alternative production process would be a batch process that changes technique more intermittently, such as car manufacturing. The conclusions are found to be the same in an analysis not shown here.

We define

H_N = work hours necessary to produce the Nth unit of a given type with serial number N

h_N = cumulative work hours necessary to produce the series of units from 1 to N

$$h_N = \sum_1^N H_N \tag{5.12}$$

or in continuous form

$$h_N = \int_0^N N_N \cdot \mathrm{d}N \tag{5.13}$$

We exclude from our model any transfer of technical knowledge from other industries.

It is reasonable to assume that capital and labour force should remain the same throughout the production of a given product type, and this realistic assumption makes the analysis tractable.

$$K_{t=x} = K_{t=1}, \; L_{t=x} = L_{t=1} \tag{5.14}$$

According to the learning-by-doing process modelled in (5.1), an industry can produce the Nth serial-number unit faster than the $(N-1)^{\text{th}}$ serial-number unit because of the increasing experience with the production of the good. The standard assumption for describing this process of experiencing and learning is

$$H_N = (H_{N-1})^\gamma \qquad 0 < \gamma < 1, \text{ and } \gamma = -b \tag{5.15}$$

As in the previous literature, H_N here is a function only of H_{N-1} and of the learning-by-doing parameter γ, which implicitly assumes a given labour force and stock of capital. But because we wish to compare worlds in which the industries or plants under discussion differ in these respects, we must broaden the H_N function. We do so as follows:

$$H_N = \frac{1}{A(N)^\gamma K^\alpha L^{1-\alpha}} \tag{5.16}$$

or for $N = 1$

$$H_1 = \frac{1}{A(1)^\gamma K^\alpha L^{1-\alpha}} \tag{5.16a}$$

and therefore

$$A = \frac{1}{H_1 K^\alpha L^{1-\alpha}} \tag{5.16b}$$

When K and L are ignored, as in the standard literature, this reduces to

$$A = \frac{1}{H_1} \tag{5.16c}$$

and

$$H_N = H_1 N^{-\gamma} = H_1 - H_1(1 - N^{-\gamma}) \tag{5.16d}$$

That is, A is the level of technique in effect at the time of production of the first unit.

The Cobb–Douglas function with exponents adding to unity implies that in this model there are no diminishing returns to production of the first unit. (In another model there may be.) This assumes that the generalized skills brought to the plant by workers and engineers are the same in both cases, and that management chooses a satisfactory plant size (though not 'optimum' size, which would be a more complex inter-temporal concept including differential learning speeds with different numbers of plants).

Next we calculate the cumulative time necessary to produce the first N units by substituting (5.16) into (5.13):

$$h_N = \frac{1}{AK^\alpha L^{1-\alpha}} \int_0^N \frac{1}{N^\gamma} \, dN \tag{5.17}$$

or

$$h_N = \frac{N^{1-\gamma}}{(1-\gamma)AK^\alpha L^{1-\alpha}} \tag{5.18}$$

We then ask how many units are produced in various equal-in-length periods of time: $1, 2, \ldots t$.

$$h_N = t$$

We obtain from (5.18) the serial number at the end of period t (i.e., the cumulative output within all past periods $1, 2, \ldots t$).

$$N_t = [(1-\gamma)At]^{1/1-\gamma} K^{\alpha/1-\gamma} L^{1-\alpha/1-\gamma} \tag{5.19}$$

In the same way we can calculate the serial number at the end of period $(t-1)$ as

$$N_{t-1} = [(1-\gamma)A(t-1)]^{1/1-\gamma} K^{\alpha/1-\gamma} L^{1-\alpha/1-\gamma} \tag{5.19a}$$

From (5.19) and (5.19a) we can calculate the output produced within period t by simply subtracting N_{t-1} from N_t

$$Y_t = N_t - N_{t-1} = [(1-\gamma)A]^{1/1-\gamma} K^{\alpha/1-\gamma} L^{1-\alpha/1-\gamma}$$

$$[t^{1/1-\gamma} - (t-1)^{1/1-\gamma}] \tag{5.20}$$

Dividing the output by the labour force we obtain the output per worker y_t in period t

$$y_t = \frac{Y_t}{L} = [(1-\gamma)A]^{1/1-\gamma} K^{\alpha/1-\gamma} L^{\gamma-\alpha/1-\gamma}$$

$$[(t)^{1/1-\gamma} - (t-1)^{1/1-\gamma}] \tag{5.21}$$

Now we are ready to compare this industry's output per worker in two closed worlds, I and II, with different sizes of population but the same parameter values of A, α and γ. We shall first examine the case in which capital per worker is the same in the two worlds

$$L_I > L_{II} \tag{5.22}$$

and

$$\frac{K_I}{L_I} = \frac{K_{II}}{L_{II}} \tag{5.23}$$

By substituting (5.22) and (5.23) into (5.21) we get

$$\frac{y_{t,I}}{y_{t,II}} = \left(\frac{L_I}{L_{II}}\right)^{\gamma/1-\gamma} > 1 \text{ if } 1 > \gamma > 0$$

This says that output per worker is higher in each period when population size is larger, if capital per worker is the same in each world. This proposition is not surprising when we reflect that the larger population has no drawbacks in this model. Yet the conclusion is useful as a precise statement of an observation which is elusive in the sort of verbal statement found in section II above.

An increase in population can (at least temporarily) induce a fall in capital per worker. Let us therefore consider the case where the capital–labour ratio is lower in world I, to the extent that capital is no larger in total than in world II.

$$K_I = K_{II} \tag{5.24}$$

By substituting (5.22) and (5.24) into (5.21) we get

$$\frac{y_{t,\text{I}}}{y_{t,\text{II}}} = \left(\frac{L_\text{I}}{L_\text{II}}\right)^{\gamma - \alpha/1 - \gamma} \quad \begin{aligned} &> 1 \text{ if } \gamma > \alpha \\ &= 1 \text{ if } \gamma = \alpha \\ &< 1 \text{ if } \gamma < \alpha. \end{aligned}$$

That is, if the learning-by-doing exponent is larger than the capital exponent, the larger population has a higher output per worker in each period; if not, not. And with representative parameters of 0.2–0.3 for learning-by-doing and 0.33 for capital, the smaller population would do better under this regime.

These two polar cases – full capital adjustment for additional persons, and no capital adjustment for additional persons – lead one to ask about *how much* capital adjustment would be needed, with representative parameters, for the larger population to do better. We can calculate from (5.21) that the break-even point, $y_{t,\text{I}} = y_{t,\text{II}}$ is where

$$\frac{K_\text{I}}{K_\text{II}} = \left(\frac{L_\text{I}}{L_\text{II}}\right)^{\alpha - \gamma/\alpha}$$

At that point the incomes per worker in worlds I and II will be the same in each period.

Other interesting questions may be raised about this model. For example, what if there are decreasing returns to labour in the first unit produced in larger plants, due to more confusion? One answer to this question is that management in the bigger world I would use plants the same size as in world II, but more of them. There might be less learning-by-doing in smaller plants, but this would leave the bigger world at least as well off as the smaller world, with some additional learning-by-doing produced in the additional plants and communicated among the plants.

IV. DISCUSSION

The model developed in this chapter implies that the rate of growth of productivity increases with time, rather than being characterized by steady-state growth as Arrow concluded that it is. To show that this is so, we must return our thinking to the firm and industry level at which the learning-by-doing phenomenon actually takes place, rather than move directly to the macro-level by simple analogy to the firm, as Arrow did.

Once a given learning-by-doing process begins, the rate of learning may indeed be constant with continued production.[5] But another process that is identical in all economic details with the one previously under discussion, except that it comes along later in production, will operate in an environment of a bigger total market and total output (due in part to the earlier innovation) even if population size remains constant. Furthermore, price will be lower due to improved productivity. Therefore sales will be greater than before if the good is a normal one, and the rate of learning per unit of time will be faster for the later innovation than for the earlier one. To the extent that these innovations are representative of the economy as a whole, the rate of increase of productivity for the economy as a whole will therefore be increasing over time.

An increasing rate of growth of productivity implies that there is not a constant capital–output ratio, as may be deduced immediately from the well known

$$s = v(\dot{L} + \dot{A}) \qquad\qquad (5.25)$$

where s = savings ratio
   v = capital–output ratio.

But this is in no way inconsistent with observed reality nor is it a ground for theoretical concern, despite the supposed 'stylized fact' of an observed constant K/Y ratio, because the monetary estimates of the capital–output ratio tell nothing about the physical capital–output ratio, as is shown elsewhere (see Appendix A). The observed constant K/Y ratio in value terms is simply an inevitable price response of competitive markets and has no significance for long-run production relationships.[6] The relevant K/Y ratio – the physical ratio – probably is not constant in MDCs but rather secularly falling, through this proposition cannot ever be examined rigorously in its aggregate form.

One might wonder why larger economies do not grow faster than smaller economies, in light of the above analysis. In fact, Chenery and associates (e.g. Chenery and Syrquin, 1975) *do* observe economies of size in cross-national comparisons of growth rates in LDCs. And the Rostas-tradition data discussed in chapter 4 show a strong effect of scale in individual industries. But additionally, to the extent that economies are open, there are forces that reduce the observed differences in growth among countries. Specialization (e.g. Sweden in cars, Holland in communications) can lead to larger markets than the national economy provides. And a considerable proportion of technical progress is not locally tied, but rather moves across national boundaries, and therefore the relevant conceptual unit for analysis of the sort given here is the Western industrialized world as a whole, with the relevant comparison being between imagined larger and smaller sizes of it. Hence there is no inconsistency between the observed data and the analysis given here.

V.   SUMMARY AND CONCLUSIONS

We have shown that in a comparison of two worlds that have different population sizes, but that are otherwise alike (including their capital/labour ratios and the initial per worker outputs) the larger world will come to have a higher per worker output. This was demonstrated for continuous processes such as shipbuilding but is true as well for batch processes such as car and shirt production. This conclusion is unlike the conclusion implicit in Arrow's model, because Arrow looked at steady-state rates of growth rather than changes in the level of income from the starting point. (Arrow's analysis also is damaged by the use of capital stock rather than cumulative output as the measure of experience, though output is the variable used in the empirical analyses that are the basis of this line of work. This assertion is argued in the afterword to this chapter.)

If the *total* capital is the same for the two worlds, the larger world probably will have a lower output per worker than the bigger world, given likely parameters. But a capital–labour ratio so much smaller in the larger world is not a likely condition in any scenario. We have therefore figured the break-even point of capital–labour ratios.

There are no obvious pitfalls in moving from the industry level micro-economics of the data and of the present analysis to an economy as a whole.

In brief, given likely conditions and parameters, the chapter suggests that large populations will have faster economic growth and a higher standard of living, *ceteris paribus.*

AFTERWORD:
CRITICISM OF ARROW'S MEASURE OF EXPERIENCE

As noted in section II of the chapter, all the empirical studies that Arrow or we have found measure experience with the cumulative number of units produced. But because Arrow doubted the psychological generalization implicit in that concept (a concept which also avoids the necessity of having a measurement for cumulated output since the beginning of time), he shifted to a very different concept, with entirely different implications. 'I therefore take instead cumulative gross investment [the capital stock] (cumulative production of capital goods) as an index of experience' (p. 157). That is,

$$A_t = \frac{1}{H_t} = f(K_t) = \mathrm{d}K_t^{\mathrm{b}} \tag{5.26}$$

where A_t = level of technique
K_t = capital stock.

He also shifted from a serial-number concept to a time-period concept.

This afterword is more critical of the work of another writer than is usual for us. We are writing in this fashion for two reasons. First, if one is to be critical, it seems appropriate to challenge those who are most worthy of it and who will be least injured by it, the best workers in the field; Arrow certainly falls into that category, as his Nobel prize attests. Second, because of Arrow's stature, there is a presumption on the part of many that he is likely to be right where there is a difference in views, and therefore a more complete criticism of his work is required to establish the validity of one's own view than would be the case with a lesser writer.

Arrow was aware of some of the limitations of the way that he constructed the model, and he described it as applicable only to the capital-goods industry. And other writers such as Wan have criticized Arrow's model on much the same grounds that we do.[7]

Arrow's... assumption is somewhat at variance with empirical studies where unit labor requirement is shown as inversely related to the cumulative output in a loglinear equation. Moreover, such studies are conducted on a plant basis. Arrow argued that cumulative output *should* be less suitable than cumulative investment as an index of experience, since the appearance of new machines *should* provide more stimulation for innovation while the cumulation of outputs (say, at a constant rate per unit time) appears to be a rather uninspiring environment. One may take issue with Arrow on two counts: (a) repetitive operation leads to familiarity and expertise; hence, constant output rate is by no means an unfavorable situation for cost reduction, and (b) cumulated output as an index for experience is supported by observed evidence, whereas there is no empirical evidence of a similar dependency on cumulative investment. (Wan, 1971, pp. 226-7)

Our aim here is to show the confusion that is caused – both in general, and also more specifically for the understanding of the effects of different population sizes – by taking the capital stock rather than cumulative gross output as the index of experience. One such confusion is that, even using Arrow's own assumptions, cumulative capital and cumulated output yield different conclusions, as may be seen in the following argument. In monetary terms, the capital-output ratio may be taken (and is so assumed by Arrow) to be roughly constant in this context. Hence the capital stock and *one* year's production are roughly proportional. So the capital stock can be considered as a proxy for *incremental* output rather than *cumulated* output. And incremental output is generally *not* proportional to cumulated output; if production in t and $t + 1$ are equal, cumulative output is higher in $t + 1$ than in t even though capital is constant.

Formally,

$$A = \left(a \sum_{i=-\infty}^{t} Y \right)_i^b \tag{5.27}$$

where Y_t = output in period t which can be rewritten

$$\frac{A_t - A_{t-1}}{A_{t-1}} = \frac{\left(\sum_{i=-\infty}^{t} Y \right)_i^b - \left(\sum_{i=-\infty}^{t-1} Y \right)_i^b}{\left(\sum_{t=-\infty}^{t-1} Y \right)_i^b} \tag{5.28}$$

where the right-hand side is always positive.

Now consider Arrow's function (5.26) from which can be written

$$\frac{A_t - A_{t-1}}{A_{t-1}} = \frac{K_t^b - K_{t-1}^b}{K_{t-1}^b} \tag{5.29}$$

If the capital–output ratio is a constant c, as Arrow assumes it is, then (5.29) can be rewritten

$$\frac{A_t - A_{t-1}}{A_{t-1}} = \frac{(cY)_t^b - (cY)_{t-1}^b}{(cY)_{t-1}^b} = \frac{Y_t^b - Y_{t-1}^b}{Y_{t-1}^b} \tag{5.30}$$

This is unequal to (5.28), as can be seen from the fact that if $Y_{t-1} = Y_t$, (5.28) will be positive but (5.30) will be zero. And (5.18) corresponds to the facts that Arrow cites, including the Horndal effect, whereas (5.30) does not.

Even worse are all the difficulties that flow from that most troublesome of all economic concepts to conceptualize and measure satisfactorily – capital. Most fundamental here is that the capital concept used in the Arrow model is physical, whereas the observed capital–output ratio that Arrow builds on is a monetary notion, and there is no necessary or likely correspondence between the two.

Arrow's definition of the capital stock also is not analogous to cumulated output in that it excludes old capital that has already obsolesced. This is important because it means that Arrow's model does not sum up experience since the *very beginning* of the learning process, which causes the paradox in interpretation of rates of productivity change discussed in section II.[8]

In brief, the use of capital rather than cumulated output is a source of erroneous interpretation of the implications of learning-by-doing. When discussing the effects of population size, cumulated output leads to quite different conclusions than does the capital stock.

NOTES

1 Here we should note that the empirical basis for the learning-by-doing function mostly comes from industry rather than economy-wide studies (Sheshinski's 1967 study is the exception). And this is as it should be, because the specific learning mostly takes place within firms, and across firms within the same industry. But an economy is an aggregate of industries. And unless there is

reason to believe that the industries not yet studied follow entirely different processes than the industries that have been studied, or unless there is reason to believe that the economy is not essentially additive in this respect – and we know of no such persuasive reason to believe so – then it seems legitimate and reasonable to extrapolate from the industry level of analysis to the economy as a whole. This is what Arrow has done implicitly. And it is what must be done here if the issue is to be joined with Arrow, and if we are to go forward from his model rather than being locked into a wrong conclusion about the effects of population size and growth.

As to whether the nation is too small to be the appropriate unit of analysis: the more-developed world as a whole, within which advanced technology and production methods are developed and applied, is the appropriate unit of analysis, and the model discussed here should be thought of as applying to that multi-country aggregate; individual countries are used in the empirical studies we refer to only because of their convenience as research observations and for thought experiments. We do not mean to imply that simply erasing the boundary lines between two nations would give rise to the processes modelled here (though in some industries such simple expansion could effect considerable increases in technique, for example in electricity and railroad networks).

2 The possibility of obsolescence does not cause difficulties in this chapter's formulation, on reasonable assumptions.

3 Actually, Sheshinski estimated Kaldor's model in which the right-hand side is

$$\left(\frac{K_t - K_{t-1}}{K_{t-1}}\right)$$

rather than Arrow's model in which the right-hand side would be

$$\frac{K_t^b - K_{t-1}^b}{K_{t-1}^b}$$

though Sheshinski said that he was testing the learning-by-doing model.

4 If one worries about the inequality in total employment of the two fathers, the example could be changed to a society with one father-barber versus a society with two father-barbers, all with one child each. In the economy with two fathers, they exchange information on what they learn, and hence increase the rate of their learning; this is quite realistic.

5 Or it may decline with output (e.g. Barkai and Levhari, 1973; Levhari and Sheshinski, 1973; Baloff, 1966, and references cited therein). Though the rate of learning in a given product situation may decrease, there may still be changes in the processes which restart a high-rate learning process, and increase the overall rate of learning.

6 It is still another problem with Arrow's model that despite its real-resource nature, he bases it upon the assumption of a constant K/Y ratio, despite the meaninglessness of the monetary K/Y ratio to describe the physical K/Y ratio in the long run and the likelihood that the physical K/Y ratio is falling in the long run. But all this is not a central issue here.

7 Though it seems clear that output rather than capital is the appropriate measure of learning-by-doing, it is less obvious than output *alone* as the appropriate measure. More specifically, by analogy with Alchian's (1959) distinction between the rate of output and the quantity of output, Pollak (1980) suggested that not only may the serial numbers of the units produced at time t in countries α and β affect the relative productivities in t within α and β but also the time profiles of past production, because the learning acquired in earlier periods may have partially obsolesced. Though this may well be the case (it makes sense on some assumptions about worker retirement and replacement of older processes but not on the assumption that the learning-by-doing is embodied in accumulative step-by-step knowledge), this phenomenon would not change the results obtained later as long as the two economies are of the same proportional size in each period. This can be shown as follows. If the output history in country A is $\ldots + Y_{t-3}, Y_{t-2}, Y_{t-1}, Y_t$, and the output history of country B is $\ldots 2Y_{t-3}, 2Y_{t-2}, 2Y_{t-1}, 2Y_t$, then if the obsolescence rate is r per year, the obsolescence-weighted sum of output for the two countries is

$$\sum_{i=-\infty}^{t} Y_i = \ldots r^3 Y_{t-3} + r^2 Y_{t-2} + rY_{t-1} + Y_t$$

and

$$\sum_{i=-\infty}^{t} Y_i = \ldots r^3 2Y_{t-3} + r^2 2Y_{t-2} + rY_{t-1} + Y_t$$

It is clear that the ratio of the r-weighted sums is the same as if $r = 1$ and there is no obsolescence. We may therefore disregard this matter in further discussion, because there is no reason to make an assumption other than proportional size of the economies in each period.

8 Even cumulative output would have to be defined carefully because of the difficulty of estimating it for an economy or society as a whole. The entire transposition from, on the one hand, the firm or industry level with technical measurements to, on the other hand, the national economy value measurements can – and in this case does – cause the argument to lose its way, and later to be misinterpreted in empirical work by others.

6

A Model of Supply, Demand and Technical Progress

Julian L. Simon and Gunter Steinmann

I. INTRODUCTION

The aim of this chapter[1] is to build a steady-state[2] model of the relationship of population and labour-force growth to the level and rate of growth of consumption, taking into account the arguments identified in the analysis of supply and demand in chapter 4. This model does not include the effects of learning-by-doing upon productivity, a matter dealt with in a separate model in chapter 5.

A function that Phelps used in his search for 'The Golden Rule of Research' – the amount of its resources that a society should devote to research, and the allocation of the labour force to research and to non-research activities – can be adapted to provide a foundation for our work.

Phelps (1966) proposed the technical progress function

$$\frac{A_t - A_{t-1}}{A_{t-1}} = \left(\frac{A_{t-w-1}}{A_{t-1}}\right) h \left(\frac{R_t}{A_{t-w-1}}\right) \tag{6.1}$$

where

A = level of technology
R = number of researchers

and later

g = equilibrium growth rate of a subscripted variable
K = the stock of capital

L = labour force
w = retardation factor
Y = total output

Phelps makes $h(R_t/A_{t-w-1})$ a concave function[3] because, he says, this assumption is necessary if 'an exponential growth of researchers will produce an exponential increase of the level of technology' (p. 134). The number of research workers, R, may be considered proportional to the labour force for the special purposes of this chapter on population effects, and w is a 'retardation factor' to represent the delay in adoption of newly produced knowledge.

This function has the realistic properties that (a) more persons imply more knowledge, (b) there are diminishing returns at a given moment and (c) a larger stock of knowledge leads to a larger increment of knowledge. Furthermore, it has the attractive theoretical characteristic that an exponential growth of researchers (or more simply for our purposes here, exponential growth of the labour force) produces an exponential increase in technical progress, and hence is consistent with the standard growth-theoretic notion of a steady state.

Phelps (1966) deduced from his model the golden-age equilibrium that 'consumption will grow at the rate $2\dot{L}$' where $\dot{L}$ is the rate of growth of the labour force; that is, *per capita* output (just as *per capita* consumption) will grow at the rate of growth of the labour force. He then goes on to derive an interesting golden rule for the amount of research, together with the amount of accumulation.

What is not mentioned by Phelps in that article is the implication that – contrary to the implications of standard growth theory, and also contrary to the conventional wisdom – a higher rate of population growth leads to a higher rate of economic growth. Furthermore, this has not been suggested by anyone else, before or afterwards, anywhere in the literature of population economics or of growth theory, except by Eltis (1973). Also implicit in Phelps's model is that a population which is larger in absolute size will, *ceteris paribus*, have faster technical progress. Even Phelps himself, when discussing population growth and in a general way observing that more people mean more inventions (1967; 1972), did not draw upon his 1966 model for a formal demonstration of the proposition.[4]

Aside from the variables not present in Phelps's function – to which we shall turn immediately – there are two important loose ends in Phelps's work: (a) There is no upper bound to the optimal population growth rate in Phelps's model (except, implicitly, fecundity). Economists are usually uncomfortable with such a theoretical outcome. But it is not obvious which reasonable economic force, if any, might be included in such a model that would yield a concave rather than a monotonic function for consumption level as a function of population growth. Chapter 7 deals with this matter. (b) Phelps's function indicates that technical progress should have become slower as population growth has declined in the twentieth century in the US and in the Western world generally. In fact, technical progress has apparently been higher in the more recent decades than in the early decades of this century (Solow, 1957; Fellner, 1970), except for the 1970s.[5] This empirical observation is consistent with technical progress being a function of the *total size* of the labour force (or R&D force). This dependence is not indicated in Phelps's equilibrium analysis. But as we shall see in chapter 7, a non-equilibrium analysis with Phelps's function shows that, in two populations of different sizes but growing at the same rate, the larger population will have a higher technological level even though the rate of productivity increase will be the same for the two populations. And higher population growth leads to a larger total population, *ceteris paribus*. Hence Phelps's function understates the contribution of population size and growth to the advance of economic welfare.

II.   A FULLER MODEL

Before constructing a fuller model embodying the necessary elements, let us manipulate Phelps's model a bit. In order to make it analogous to a production function,[6] Phelps's function may be written as

$$A(t) - A(t-1) = A(t-w) \, h\left(\frac{R(t)}{A(t-w)}\right) \qquad (6.2)$$

The factor $A(t-w)$ is reasonably equal to $A(t-1)$ at all times. Hence the function boils down to (shifting to labour force, L, in place of R)

$$A(t) - A(t-1) = A(t-1) \, h\left(\frac{L(t)}{A(t-1)}\right) \qquad (6.3)$$

or

$$A_t - A_{t-1} = A_{t-1} h \left(\frac{L_t}{A_{t-1}} \right)$$ (6.3a)

This may be rewritten in the Cobb–Douglas form as

$$A_t - A_{t-1} = a A_{t-1}^{\Delta} L_{t-1}^{\gamma}$$ (6.4)

where $\Delta < 1, \gamma < 1$.

Implicit in Phelps's discussion is that $\Delta + \gamma = 1$ in equation (6.4), as seen in Phelps's requirement that the function be homogeneous of degree one, and his statement that 'if the technology level should double we would require exactly twice the amount of research to double the absolute time rate of increase of the technology' (p. 135).

Phelps's function is far more restrictive than it need be, however, even to satisfy his objective of golden-age steady growth. There are two directions in which this general framework will be extended.

(a) There is no need to assume that the function is homogeneous of degree one. As long as Δ is even slightly below unity, the result is the constant golden-age rate of growth of A and of consumption *per capita* that Phelps sought – even if there are increasing returns rather than the function being homogeneous of degree one that Phelps assumed was necessary. The reason for this interesting result can be seen intuitively as follows. Rewrite (6.4) as

$$\frac{A_t - A_{t-1}}{A_{t-1}} = \frac{a A_{t-1}^{\Delta} L_{t-1}^{\gamma}}{A_{t-1}}$$ (6.4b)

where $\Delta, \gamma < 1$. If A rises at a rate greater than L, then A will grow large relative to L. As this happens, the denominator A_{t-1} on the right-hand side grows faster than the term A_{t-1}^{Δ} in the right-hand side numerator, and hence tends to choke off the growth of the right-hand side, and at some point a balance is reached at which the right-hand side is pushed downward by this force as hard as it is pushed upward by the sum of coefficients Δ and γ being greater than unity. So here we have a considerable generalization of Phelps's result which allows us to get closer to the observed empirical data mentioned earlier. A formal proof of this proposition emerges as a special result from our analysis of a technical progress function with additional arguments as discussed below.

(b) In Phelps's function there is no purely economic argument, and hence technical progress proceeds without depending upon capital or output.

On the basis of earlier discussion in chapter 3, let us write the more general function

$$A_t - A_{t-1} = bL_{t-1}^\gamma A_{t-1}^\Delta Y_{t-1}^\phi \left(\frac{Y}{L}\right)_{t-1}^\psi \qquad (6.5)$$

or

$$A_t - A_{t-1} = bL^\mu A^\Delta Y^\epsilon \qquad (6.5a)$$

where $\mu = \gamma - \psi \lessgtr 0$ and $\epsilon = \phi + \psi > 0$. The implications of this function will now be explored with a simple model composed of the following output and savings equations

$$Y_t = K_t^\alpha (A_t L_t)^\beta \qquad (6.6)$$

where α and β are constants

$$S_t = sY_{t-1} \qquad (6.7)$$

$$K_t = sY_{t-1} + K_{t-1} \qquad (6.8)$$

where $1 > s > 0$. Implicitly we have the short-run equilibrium condition that investment equals savings. Next, the exogenous labour-force growth

$$L_t = L_{t-1} + dL_{t-1} \qquad (6.9)$$

where d is a control variable in the analysis. The long-run equilibrium conditions are standard:

$$\frac{A_t - A_{t-1}}{A_{t-1}} \simeq \frac{1}{A} \cdot \frac{dA}{dt} = \dot{A} = g_A \qquad (6.10)$$

which is a constant in equilibrium.

$$\frac{Y_t - Y_{t-1}}{Y_{t-1}} \simeq \frac{1}{Y} \cdot \frac{\mathrm{d}Y}{\mathrm{d}t} = \dot{Y} = g_Y \tag{6.11}$$

which is a constant in equilibrium.

$$\frac{K_t - K_{t-1}}{K_{t-1}} \simeq \frac{1}{K} \cdot \frac{\mathrm{d}K}{\mathrm{d}t} = \dot{K} = g_K \tag{6.12}$$

which is a constant in equilibrium.

We began by rewriting (6.5a) as

$$\dot{A} = bL^\mu A^{\Delta-1} Y^\epsilon \tag{6.13}$$

Taking logs and differentiating we get

$$\frac{1}{\dot{A}} \frac{\mathrm{d}\dot{A}}{\mathrm{d}t} = \mu \dot{L} + (\Delta - 1) \dot{A} + \epsilon \dot{Y} \tag{6.14}$$

Using (6.10) we get

$$\frac{1}{\dot{A}} \frac{\mathrm{d}\dot{A}}{\mathrm{d}t} = 0 \tag{6.15}$$

This with (6.14) yields the following relation between the equilibrium values of g_Y, g_A and g_L.

$$g_A = \frac{\epsilon}{1 - \Delta} g_Y + \frac{\mu}{1 - \Delta} g_L \tag{6.16}$$

The equations (6.6), (6.7), (6.9), (6.10), (6.11), (6.12) plus the short-run equilibrium savings-equals-investment condition can be transformed and reduced into the well known

$$g_A = \frac{1 - \alpha}{\beta} g_Y - g_L \tag{6.17}$$

Equations (6.16) and (6.17) contain only the arguments g_A, g_Y and g_L plus constants. Therefore we can determine the equilibrium values of g_Y and g_A as follows:

$$g_Y = \frac{1 - \Delta + \mu}{\dfrac{1 - \alpha}{\beta}(1 - \Delta) - \epsilon} \, g_L \tag{6.18}$$

$$g_A = \frac{\left(\dfrac{1 - \alpha}{\beta}\right)\mu + \epsilon}{\dfrac{1 - \alpha}{\beta}(1 - \Delta) - \epsilon} \, g_L \tag{6.19}$$

For the special case of constant returns to scale in the production function (6.6), $\alpha + \beta = 1$, and we get the special results

$$g_Y = \frac{1 - \Delta + \mu}{1 - \Delta - \epsilon} \, g_L \tag{6.18a}$$

and

$$g_A = \frac{\mu + \epsilon}{1 - \Delta - \epsilon} \, g_L \tag{6.19a}$$

In this special case, the equilibrium value of the growth rate of per-worker income is

$$g_{(Y/L)} = g_Y - g_L \; (= g_{(Y/P)} \text{ if } g_P = g_L,$$

$$\text{where } Y/P \text{ is } per \; capita \text{ income})$$

or

$$g_{(Y/L)} = \frac{\mu + \epsilon}{1 - \Delta - \epsilon} \, g_L = g_A{}^7 \tag{6.20}$$

Let us see what values of the parameters are possible, and acceptable for equation (6.20) to be consistent with our equilibrium conditions. First, we know that the numerator, $\mu + \epsilon$, must be positive because $\gamma + \phi > 0$, and $\mu + \epsilon = \gamma + \phi$. Next, the denominator must also be positive, or else there could be no equilibrium with positive growth rates of L, A and Y. We can see in (6.5a) that $\Delta < 1$ or else A would increase with time, which violates an equilibrium condition. Furthermore, from (6.18a) and (6.19a) we know that $\Delta + \epsilon > 1$ implies $g_A < 0$ and $g_Y < 0$ for $g_L > 0$. This solution is not only economically meaningless, but some simulation calculations also show that, for all initial values $\dot{A}$, $\dot{Y} > 0$, the condition $\Delta + \epsilon > 1$ causes the system to explode because dA/dt and dY/dt are positive. Hence for positive population growth a reasonable equilibrium exists only for $\Delta + \epsilon < 1$. What is most important, however, is that under these conditions there is an equilibrium.

Now to interpret our results. Given that both the numerator and demoninator in equation (6.20) are positive, a higher rate of labour-force growth implies a faster equilibrium rate of growth of *per capita* income. And the mechanism is clear: we see in equation (6.19a) that a higher rate of growth of the labour force implies a faster equilibrium rate of growth of technology, and the multiplier is the same as in equation (6.20). That is, more workers imply more technical change, and an increased rate of technical changes translates into growth of *per capita* income that is faster to the same extent. Phelps's model yields the same result because it is a special case of this model.

If, as Phelps assumed, $\gamma = 1/2$, $\Delta = 1/2$, $\phi = 0$ and $\psi = 0$ (the latter two being the exponents of variables not in his function) then (6.20) reduces to Phelps's conclusion that the equilibrium rate of growth of per-worker income equals the rate of growth of the labour force. If $\gamma > 1/2$, $1/2 \leqslant \Delta \leqslant 1$ and/or ϕ or $\psi > 0$, the equilibrium rate of growth of per-worker income is faster than the rate of growth of the labour force, to the extent which is easy to figure from (6.20) for any set of exponents. The same is true if $1/2 < \Delta < 1$ and $\gamma \geqslant 1/2$. If ϕ and/or $\psi > 0$, the positive effect of labour-force growth is intensified, *ceteris paribus*.

The extent to which an increment of population growth raises the equilibrium growth rate depends on the exponents (the 'population elasticities') of the technical-progress function in the linear function shown in figure 6.1. This continues until $\Delta + \epsilon$ increases to unity, at which point the equilibrium system explodes, and the rate of techni-cal progress increases with time rather than remaining constant; this is by no means implausible economically, however.

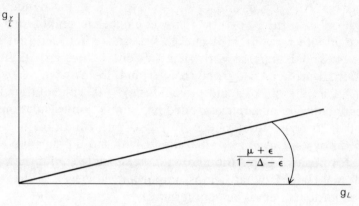

FIGURE 6.1

It seems remarkable that the elasticity of the labour force can be large without limit without causing the equilibrium system to explode, though continuing to raise the equilibrium rate of growth of *per capita* income. This is because the relationship between $\dot{L}$ and $\dot{Y}$ is unidirectional, whereas $\dot{A}$ and $\dot{Y}$ influence each other in a mutually reinforcing feedback relationship.

In brief, the macro-model with either Phelps's function or our more general function has the important implication – which is exactly the opposite of the implication of conventional growth theory with technical progress exogenous – that faster population growth implies a faster equilibrium rate of growth of the standard of living. It also has the pleasant property for theory and theorists that a realistic model of technical change, and of the effect of population size and growth upon technical change, may be comfortably embodied in growth theoretical models without upsetting the basic structure of that theory.

III. HISTORICAL MODIFICATION

Phelps's function, and the generalized function described above, do not differ for different historical ages. But the parameters of the technical-progress function clearly change as economic development proceeds. Consider the situation in 6000 BC. There were relatively few new ideas for which both the intellectual basis and the need then existed. Agriculture obviously was such an idea. And agriculture was independently invented in many different places, which suggests that an even larger number of potential inventors would not have increased the rate of knowledge creation. Of course this invention repeatedly had to be made independently because of the lack of communication among groups, and because of the lack of means to 'store' the idea in writing. But these conditions are key characteristics of that earlier time when the stock of knowledge was much lower than now. Therefore we can say that Δ was large relative to γ at that time, perhaps approaching unity.

Now consider a moment such as the present. It would seem reasonable that the coefficients Δ and γ sum to at least unity; if we took the people and literature in half of the intellectual disciplines and industries on an odd–even random basis – chemistry but not physics, sociology but not psychology, French but not German, desks but not chairs, tyres but not engines and so on – and moved them to another planet, the sum of knowledge produced on this planet should diminish by half, and should double when they return to this planet. If we assume for the moment that all ideas created in a given year are of equal value,[8] and if we assume that each new idea creates a much larger number of possible new ideas by combination with existing ideas than the number by which it reduces the pool of potential ideas when it is discovered,[9] then we can easily show that the pool of potential new ideas is increasing relative to the number of idea producers. The relative increase continues until the likelihood of duplicated inventions reaches zero. At that time there are no longer diminishing returns to more researchers, and the operative constraint is only the idea-creating capacity of the individual. At that moment Δ approaches unity and γ approaches zero.

To make the function better fit the flow of history we should also take into account the capacities of people to contribute as researchers, which includes education and the tools of research. After we pass into the time of writing, and until the amount of education that people receive is as much as they can profitably use, the effect of such an education-and-tools factor – which we may index with *per capita* income – will be positive; that is, ψ, ϕ and ϵ will be greater than zero. But at some time in the future, assuming income rises, the effect of this factor will approach maximum.

The courses of these three factors may be viewed as functions of time, or of the level of knowledge, or – most reasonable – of *per capita* income.

The effect of total resources, as indexed by ϕ, may continue to be positive indefinitely, however, and we are agnostic as to whether this exponent will rise or fall with the level of living.

IV. SUMMARY

A faster rate of growth of labour force produces higher steady-state consumption *per capita* then does slower labour-force growth, with all functions which are similar to the one we adapt from Phelps and realistic in the sense of making the absolute amount of change in technical knowledge a function of the total size of the labour force and the technical level, and perhaps of the level of income as well. As long as the exponents on the level of technique and total income sum to less than one in a Cobb–Douglas technical-progress-function formulation, constant exponential growth will appear – a much more general result than is implicit in Phelps' work. And if the exponent on technical change is unity or above – as is suggested by the data on comparisons of markets of different sizes in various countries – the rates of change of technique and of consumption will increase rather than be constant.

We shall see later that the same conclusion – higher population growth and larger population size imply faster growth of the standard of living – emerges from even richer models along this line, as it also does from the learning-by-doing model presented in chapter 5.[10]

NOTES

1 Steinmann developed the analytic proof in this chapter. This material earlier appeared in Simon and Steinmann (1981) and Steinmann and Simon (1980).

2 The comparison of golden-age growth paths is not the relevant comparison for a given society's policy choice at a given moment. Rather, the society wishes to evaluate its future streams of costs and benefits with different rates of population growth, *given* its present endowment of capital and level of income. That comparison is the subject of chapter 8.

3 In Phelps's continuous notation, the function is

$$\frac{\dot{A}(t)}{A(t)} = \left(\frac{A(t-w)}{A(t)}\right) h\left(\frac{R(t)}{A(t-w)}\right)$$

where $\dot{A}(t)$ = time rate of change of A.

4 In his discussions of the general topic in 1967 and 1972, Phelps restates what may be called the Petty–Kuznets effect that a larger population implies more 'ingenious men' who create economic progress, but he does not connect this up to his model.

5 This is written in awareness of the productivity slowdown in the 1970s and 1980s so far. The remark refers mostly to the decades studied by Solow and Fellner, but recent experience does not vitiate this general observation, in my view.

6 Leontief's point is particularly relevant here: '[I]n the actual process of scientific investigation, which consists in its larger part of more or less successful attempts to overcome our own intellectual inertia, the problem of proper arrangement of formal analytical tools acquires fundamental importance' (1966, p. 59).

7 The general solution is

$$g_{(Y/L)} = \frac{(1-\Delta)\dfrac{\alpha+\beta-1}{\beta}+\mu+\epsilon}{(1-\Delta)\dfrac{1-\alpha}{\beta}-\epsilon}\; g_L \tag{6.20a}$$

8 The fact that some ideas are of much higher value than others will not disturb this analysis as long as we observe that people differ considerably in their interests and capacities so that they will work on different ideas, and also that people have far less than perfect foresight about which projects will turn out to be the most valuable. The details of this argument are given in chapter 11.

9 Machlup (1962) mentions this mechanism.

10 In fact, it is reasonably easy to show that in a comparison of two populations with different rates of labour-force growth (with optimum savings ratios) that are already on the equilibrium growth path, faster labour-force growth implies higher consumption – as along as technical progress is a function of the size of the labour force or of total output, even to the slightest degree. Consider a situation in which technical progress does not depend upon either labour force or total output; if so, technical progress will be the same, and the rate of growth of *per capita* output will also be

the *same*, for every rate of population (labour force) growth, though consumption will be lower with higher population growth due to the higher warranted savings rate. But if technical progress *is* faster with a higher population growth rate – as it is with function (6.5a) because faster population growth implies faster increase in aggregate income and hence income per person – then the rate of growth of per-person output must be faster with higher population growth. And this must therefore eventually (no matter how slight the dependence of technical progress on population or output) lead to higher levels of per-person output and consumption.

7
The Optimum Rate of Population Growth

Gunter Steinmann and Julian L. Simon

I. INTRODUCTION

Chapter 6 noted an uncomfortable – perhaps 'shocking' would be the better term – loose end (literally) in our model, as well as in Phelps's model: higher labour force growth implies higher consumption *without limit*.[1] Economic theorists cannot be happy with such an outcome because it seems unaesthetic. And demographers and lay-persons feel intuitively that there must be some bound to the process. The aim of this chapter is to tie up this loose end, to produce a more general and realistic model of population growth and technical progress, and thereby to analyse the optimum rate of population growth.

The reasons why higher population growth implies a higher level of consumption without limit in Phelps's model, and in our extension of it, is that the only counter-balancing force – capital dilution – operates in the same fashion no matter what the rate of population growth. But if there is to be any 'optimum' rate of population growth, a counter-balancing negative force must act differently at different rates of population growth. And indeed, popular perception of the growth process – correct or incorrect – is that beyond some point additional increments of population growth are more burdensome and less productive than were 'previous' increments. There is also at least one scrap of evidence that suggests a bow-shaped relationship, although it refers to LDCs rather than MDCs – Browning's examination (1981), following a suggestion by Clark of the relationship between the population growth rate and the rate of growth of productivity in LDCs. The middle rates of growth of the labour force show faster growth of product per head than do both lower and higher rates of growth of the labour force.

The only theoretical ways in which a bow-function might appear are if (a) some factor of production were to operate in some manner different than suggested by standard production functions, or (b) the production of technical knowledge does not increase monotonically with the size of population, *ceteris paribus*, or (c) the rate of adoption of technology is, beyond some point, negatively influenced by population size or the rate of population growth. Possibility (c) makes the most sense to us, which we shall now explain.

It is well accepted that in MDCs the innovation process is influenced by the relative price of 'efficiency' labour. If labour is more plentiful, less new capital will be purchased, *ceteris paribus*; less new embodied knowledge will be put to work, and there will be less demand for new discoveries. On the other hand, if both labour and demand do not grow at all, the acceleration concept suggests that there will also be no new capital produced. Taken together, these analyses suggest a concave-downward function relating change in technical practice to labour-force growth. Along with these solid micro-economic ideas is the vague psychological notion that *some* amount of challenge increases people's physical and intellectual energies, but *too much* challenge makes them feel helpless and lethargic.

In ending this introduction perhaps we should mention that there is little relevant literature. Samuelson labelled a paper 'The Optimum Growth Rate for Population' (1975), but it deals mainly with savings and transfer payments. Starting around the turn of the century there was discussion for three decades about the optimum *size* of population, but only in a static context. And recent models following on Coale and Hoover (158) have dealt only with LDCs, and have concentrated on the effects of various dependency rates.

II.   THE MODEL

The model begins with either Phelps's production function for technology, rewritten for our purposes here as

$$M_t - M_{t-1} = aL_{t-1}^\gamma M_{t-1}^\Delta \tag{7.1}$$

or the more general Simon–Steinmann function

$$M_t - M_{t-1} = bL_{t-1}^\gamma M_{t-1}^\Delta Y_{t-1}^\phi \left(\frac{Y}{L}\right)_{t-1}^\psi \tag{7.2}$$

The key issue in the modelling to come is the technology-adoption function, that is, the function which describes the relationship of $(A_t - A_{t-1})$ to changes in M. We desire a function which both represents a theoretically satisfying relationship as well as one which has the technical property of yielding a curvilinear relationship between $g_{Y/L}$ and g_L.

Variant One

Our first model simply makes the rate of change of technique g_A a direct function of g_M and a concave-downward function of g_L, or for example

$$\dot{A} = \dot{M} - a_1(\dot{L} - a_2)^2 \qquad a_1, a_2 > 0 \tag{7.3}$$

$\dot{L} = a_2$ is the rate of population growth at which existing knowledge is applied fastest, at which point $\dot{A} = \dot{M}$. Equation (7.3) has the reasonable properties that (a) the growth rate of M is equal to or greater than that of A, and (b) the technology that is applied always equals or is less than the existing technology[2]

$$\dot{M} \geqslant \dot{A}, \; M_t \geqslant A_t$$

Now the rest of the model:

$$M_t - M_{t-1} = bL_{t-1}^\mu M_{t-1}^\Delta Y_{t-1}^\epsilon \tag{7.4}$$

with $\mu = \gamma - \psi$ and $\epsilon = \phi + \psi$

$$Y_t = K_t^\alpha (A_t L_t)^\beta \tag{7.5}$$

$$S_t = sY_{t-1} \tag{7.6}$$

$$K_t = sY_{t-1} + K_{t-1} \tag{7.7}$$

The long-run equilibrium conditions are

$$g_A = \text{constant}, \ g_M = \text{constant}, \ g_K = g_Y = \text{constant} \tag{7.8}$$

Taking logs and differentiating (7.4) and combining (7.8) we get (as in the earlier model)

$$g_M = \frac{\epsilon}{1 - \Delta} g_Y + \frac{\mu}{1 - \Delta} g_L \tag{7.9}$$

In the same way equations (7.5), (7.6), (7.7) and (7.8) lead to

$$g_A = \frac{1 - \alpha}{\beta} g_Y - g_L \tag{7.10}$$

which is similar to the earlier model. But we now have on the left side of the two equations (7.9) and (7.10) two different variables: g_M and g_A. Previously we did not distinguish between A and M, that is, our production function (7.5) of the present model contains the *applied* technology as a determinant of Y, whereas the technology-creation (7.4) explains only the creation of *potential* technology which – contrary to the previous model – is not assumed to be fully applied.

We link the variables g_M and g_A with equation (7.3). Equations (7.3), (7.9) and (7.10) contain only the arguments g_M, g_A, g_K and g_L plus constants. Therefore we can determine the equilibrium values of

g_Y, g_A, g_M and $g_{Y/L} = g_Y - g_L$. For the special case of constant returns to scale in the production function (7.5), $\alpha + \beta = 1$, and we get:

$$g_Y = \frac{1 - \Delta + \mu}{1 - \Delta - \epsilon} g_L - \frac{a_1(1 - \Delta)}{1 - \Delta - \epsilon} (g_L - a_2)^2 \qquad (7.11)$$

$$g_M = \frac{\mu + \epsilon}{1 - \Delta - \epsilon} g_L - \frac{\epsilon a_1}{1 - \Delta - \epsilon} (g_L - a_2)^2 \qquad (7.12)$$

$$g_A = \frac{\mu + \epsilon}{1 - \Delta - \epsilon} g_L - \frac{a_1(1 - \Delta)}{1 - \Delta - \epsilon} (g_L - a_2)^2 \qquad (7.13)$$

$$g_{Y/L} = g_A \qquad (7.14)$$

We now obtain the optimal rate of population growth g_L^x, that is, that population growth rate which results in the fastest equilibrium rate of *per capita* income ($dg_{Y/L}/dg_L = 0$).[3]

$$g_L^x = \frac{\mu + \epsilon}{2a_1(1 - \Delta)} + a_2 \qquad (7.15)$$

The optimum rate is positively related to μ, ϵ, Δ (elasticities of production of technology) and a_2 (population growth rate which produces the fastest application of technology) and negatively related to a_1. We may also note that g_A is lower than g_M in the optimum situation $g_A < g_M$. That follows because $g_L^x > a_2$. This is perhaps the most interesting aspect of the solution. *The optimal rate of population growth is higher than the rate which produces the fastest application of new technology.* This important idea (which also applies to our other and very different models to be discussed below) may be understood intuitively as follows.

Imagine that technology creation were exogenous instead of endogenous. The optimum rate of population growth would then be the rate at which adoption of new technology would be at the fastest possible rate, because that would be the highest rate of technical change, which in such a world equals the rate of growth of consumption *per capita*. But when technology creation is endogenous, additional people yield an additional benefit and therefore a somewhat higher rate of population growth must be better than otherwise. And this rate, therefore, must be faster than the optimum rate of application of technology when technology creation is exogenous.

There are, however, questions about the adoption function (7.3) which qualify enthusiasm about this model. First, let us rewrite (7.3) in production function format, because there is no reasonable economic interpretation of one rate influencing another here; rather it is reasonable to think of various influences affecting the absolute amount of technology newly adopted.

$$A_t - A_{t-1} = \left(\frac{M_t}{M_{t-1}} - 1 - a_1(\dot{L} - a_2)^2 \right) A_{t-1} \tag{7.16}$$

$$= \frac{M_t}{M_{t-1}} A_{t-1} - A_{t-1} - a_1(\dot{L} - a_2)^2 A_{t-1}$$

The product of A_{t-1} and M_t/M_{t-1} on the right-hand side does not suggest a reasonable economic interpretation, which we regard as a drawback. Furthermore, the following implication of (7.16) seems difficult to square with reality when one considers a system not in equilibrium but rather a one-period *ceteris paribus* situation: imagine any M_{t-1} – add to it a single given invention. The larger is the M_{t-1}, the less effect there is of this additional invention upon A_t. To be more specific, this says that if someone invented the computer in 1500, the effects upon A_t would be greater than if the computer were invented in 1940. That does not seem reasonable. Rather, it would seem that the computer added more to productivity or at least as much in 1940 than it would have added earlier.

Variant Two

The adoption function in our second variant is

$$A_t - A_{t-1} = b_1 M_{t-1}^v A_{t-1}^x \dot{L} - b_2 M_{t-1}^v A_{t-1}^x \dot{L}^2 \tag{7.17}$$

with

$$\dot{L} = \frac{L_t - L_{t-1}}{L_{t-1}} \cdot 100$$

This function straightforwardly makes the absolute amount of technology adopted in any period a quadratic function of the rate of growth of the labour force, as well as depending monotonically upon M_{t-1} and A_{t-1}. Now we may transform (7.17) (neglecting the indices) into the following

$$\dot{A} = \frac{A_t - A_{t-1}}{A_{t-1}} = M^v A^{x-1} \dot{L} (b_1 - b_2 \dot{L}) \qquad (7.17a)$$

Only the positive solutions of $\dot{A} = g_A$ are reasonable. And from (7.17a) we know $\dot{A} > 0$ if and only if $(b_1 - b_2 \dot{L}) > 0$ (if $\dot{L} > 0$), or

$$\dot{L} = g_L < \frac{b_1}{b_2} \qquad (7.18)$$

Next take the logs of (7.17a) and differentiate by time

$$\frac{d \log \dot{A}}{dt} = v \cdot \dot{M} + (x - 1) \dot{A} + \frac{d \log \dot{L}}{dt} + \frac{d \log (b_1 - b_2 \dot{L})}{dt}$$
$$(7.17b)$$

In equilibrium

$$\frac{d \log g_A}{dt} = 0$$

Furthermore, if the rate of population growth $\dot{L}$ and b_1 and b_2 are constant, then (7.17b) can be rewritten as

$$g_A = \frac{v}{1 - x} g_M \qquad (7.19)$$

This, together with (7.9) and (7.10), determines g_Y, g_M and g_A as functions of g_L. For the special case of constant returns to scale in the production function $\alpha + \beta = 1$, we get the special results[4]

$$g_Y = \frac{\dfrac{x-1}{v} - \dfrac{\mu}{1 - \Delta}}{\dfrac{\epsilon}{1 - \Delta} - \dfrac{1 - x}{v}} g_L \qquad (7.20)$$

and

$$g_{Y/L} = g_Y - g_L = \frac{\mu + \epsilon}{\dfrac{1-\chi}{\nu}(1-\Delta) - \epsilon}\, g_L \qquad\qquad (7.20a)$$

Equation (7.20a) is very similar to the solution of $g_{Y/L}$ in our earlier chapter, which was

$$g_{Y/L} = \frac{\mu + \epsilon}{1 - \Delta - \epsilon}\, g_L$$

We know from that model that $\mu + \epsilon$ and $(1 - \Delta - \epsilon)$ have to be greater than zero, to avoid the explosion of the model. If $\nu = 1 - \chi$ we now get the same results. As to the values of ν and $1 - \chi$, we know from (7.19) that $\nu/(1-\chi) \leqslant 1$ or else g_A would exceed g_M, which is impossible in the long run ($\to A$ cannot exceed M). Therefore $(1 - \chi/\nu) \geqslant 1$, that is, the numerator and denominator of equation (7.20a) are positive. $g_{Y/L}$ increases with g_L until $g_L \to (b_1/b_2)$ at which point g_L becomes too high to imply a positive g_A (equation 7.18). Figure 7.1 illustrates this result. The final results:

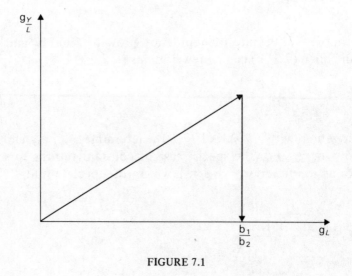

FIGURE 7.1

(a) For constant returns in the A function [e.g. (7.17) with $\nu + \chi = 1$] the model yields results identical to our old model as long as g_L is lower than b_1/b_2.

(b) The sum of ν and χ must not exceed 1, that is, there are neither constant or decreasing returns to scale in the adoption function.

(c) The saving rate has again no influence to our results.

(d) The optimal rate of population growth depends only on b_1 and b_2 and is independent of the production elasticities α, β, μ, ϵ, χ, ν, Δ.

Variant two also is less than completely satisfactory, however. Though the adoption function itself seems to be reasonable, the results of the model as a whole are not quite reasonable, in that increasing labour force has monotonically positive effects until it suddenly goes negative; this does not fit our curvilinear vision of this phenomenon, and the sudden discontinuity does not make economic sense.

The reason why this result occurs is of some importance. The exponential growth of technology creation (the M function), depending in a positive fashion on $\dot{L}$, is sufficiently powerful that it continues to overmaster the constant-proportion choice value in the adoption function.

Variant Three

In our third variant we make the exponents in the adoption function depend upon labour-force growth.

$$A_t - A_{t-1} = aM_{t-1}^{z_1} A_{t-1}^{z_2} \tag{7.21}$$

with $z_1 = z_1(\dot{L})$ and $z_2 = z_2(\dot{L})$. For simplicity we assume

$$z_1 = z_2 = z = z(\dot{L})$$

Simplifying (7.21) to

$$A_t - A_{t-1} = a(M_{t-1} \cdot A_{t-1})^z \tag{7.21a}$$

Now dividing through by A_{t-1}, taking the logs, and differentiating by time (neglecting the indices)

$$\frac{d \log g_A}{dt} = z g_M + (z - 1) g_A = 0 \text{ in equilibrium}$$

or

$$g_A = \frac{z}{1 - z} g_M \tag{7.22}$$

Again, g_A must not exceed g_M in equilibrium ($A \leqslant M$). To ensure this condition we must restrict the z values. From (7.22) we get

$$\text{If} \quad g_A \leqslant g_M \quad \text{then} \quad \frac{z}{1 - z} \leqslant 1 \quad \text{or} \quad z \leqslant \tfrac{1}{2} \tag{7.23}$$

where z is a function of $\dot{L} \{z = z(\dot{L})\}$. We shall specify this relationship by two alternative functions

$$z = f_1(\dot{L}) = b\dot{L} - c\dot{L}^2 \tag{7.24}$$

with $b > c > 0$; or alternatively

$$z = f_2(\dot{L}) = \frac{m g_L}{(\dot{L} + n)^2} \tag{7.24a}$$

$m, n > 0$. Under the first alternative (7.24) z can take both positive and negative values depending on $\dot{L}$ (see figure 7.2):

$$z = 0 \quad \text{if} \quad \dot{L} = 0 \quad \text{or} \quad \dot{L} = \frac{b}{c}$$

$$z > 0 \quad \text{if} \quad 0 < \dot{L} < \frac{b}{c}$$

with maximum $z_{\max} = b^2/4c$ for $\dot{L} = b/2c$

$$z < 0 \quad \text{if} \quad \dot{L} > \frac{b}{c}$$

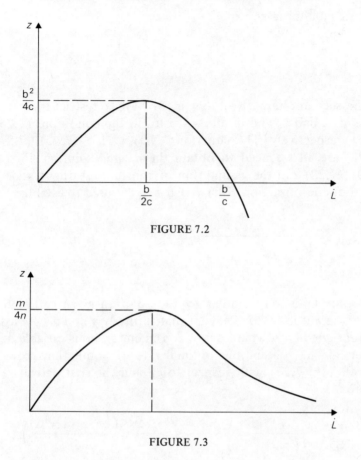

FIGURE 7.2

FIGURE 7.3

Under the second alternative (7.24b) z cannot adopt negative values for non-negative population growth (see figure 7.3).

$$z = 0 \quad \text{if} \quad \dot{L} = 0 \quad \text{or} \quad \dot{L} \to \infty$$

$$z > 0 \quad \text{if} \quad 0 < \dot{L} < \infty$$

with maximum $z_{max} = m/4n$ for $\dot{L} = n$.

The condition (7.23) $\leqslant \frac{1}{2}$ is true for all positive $\dot{L}$ if and only if

$$c \geqslant \frac{b^2}{2} \tag{7.25}$$

for the first alternative[5] and

$$n \geqslant \frac{m}{2} \qquad (7.26)$$

for the second alternative;[6] that is, we have to restrict the parameter values of c and b, and m and n, to fulfill the conditions (7.25) and (7.26), respectively. The equations (7.9), (7.10), (7.22), (7.24) and (7.24a) are all we need to obtain the desired solution. First (7.9), (7.10), (7.22) and the assumption of constant returns to scale in the the production function (7.5), $\alpha + \beta = 1$, are used to establish[7]

$$g_{Y/L} = \frac{\mu + \epsilon}{\dfrac{1-z}{z}(1-\Delta) - \epsilon} g_L \qquad (7.27)$$

This solution is very similar to the solution given earlier for our second variant in (7.20a), except that formerly χ and ν were assumed as *given parameters* whereas now z is an endogenous variable dependent on g_L. To obtain the optimal rate of population growth, we differentiate (7.27) with respect to g_L and the first derivative must be zero

$$\frac{dg_{Y/L}}{dg_L} = \frac{\mu + \epsilon}{\left\{ \dfrac{1-z}{z}(1-\Delta) - \epsilon \right\}^2} \left(\frac{1-\Delta}{z} + \frac{(1-z)(1-\Delta)}{z^2} \right) g_L$$

$$\times \frac{dz}{dg_L} + \frac{\mu + \epsilon}{\dfrac{1-z}{z}(1-\Delta) - \epsilon} = 0 \qquad (7.28)$$

or

$$g_L^x \cdot \frac{dz}{dg_L^x} + z - z^2 \frac{1-\Delta+\epsilon}{1-\Delta} = 0 \qquad (7.28a)$$

The solution of (7.28) depends on the assumed z function.

Alternative A for Model Three

Substituting (7.24) in (7.28) and using (7.25) we get

$$g_L^3 - \frac{2b}{c} g_L^2 + \left(\frac{3}{c} \frac{1-\Delta}{1-\Delta+\epsilon} + \frac{b^2}{c^2}\right) g_L - \frac{2b}{c^2} \frac{1-\Delta}{1-\Delta+\epsilon} = 0 \quad (7.29)$$

The solution (7.29) is a third-order-equation in g_L. To solve equation (7.29) for the optimal rate of population growth g_L^x we try

$$g_L^x = \frac{xb}{2c} \quad (7.30)$$

with x an unknown positive variable. Substituting (7.30) in (7.29):

$$x(x-2)^2 = \frac{2c/b^2}{1 + \dfrac{\epsilon}{1-\Delta}} (8 - 6x) \quad (7.31)$$

The left side $g(x) = x(x-2)^2$ and the right side

$$h(x) = \frac{2c/b^2}{1 + \dfrac{\epsilon}{1-\Delta}} (8 - 6x)$$

of equation (7.31) are drawn in figure 7.4.

The $g(x)$ function has a maximum at $x = \frac{2}{3}$ and a minimum at $x = 2$. Its values for $x = 0, 1, \frac{4}{3}, 2$ are $g(0) = 0, g(1) = 1, g(\frac{4}{3}) \approx 0.59$, $g(2) = 0$. The $h(x)$ function is linear with

$$h(\tfrac{4}{3}) = 0, \quad h(1) = \frac{4c/b^2}{1 + \dfrac{\epsilon}{1-\Delta}}$$

We know from the earlier models that to establish an equilibrium solution, $\epsilon + \Delta$ must be smaller than 1 and from this model (equation

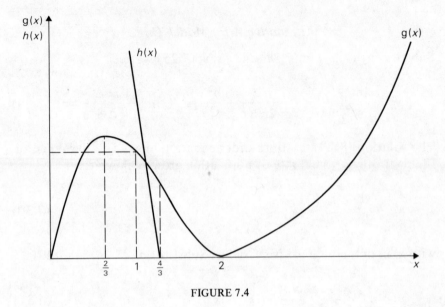

FIGURE 7.4

7.25) we know that $4c/b^2$ must be greater than or equal to 2. Therefore $h(1) > 1$ and we have

$$h(1) > g(1) \quad \text{and} \quad h(\tfrac{4}{3}) < g(\tfrac{4}{3})$$

From this we can conclude that the intersection of the $g(x)$ and the $h(x)$ function is at

$$1 < x = x(b, c, \epsilon, \Delta) < \tfrac{4}{3} \tag{7.32}$$

The higher is x, the lower are the values of b, ϵ, Δ and the higher is the value of c [i.e. the $h(x)$ function becomes steeper for lower b, ϵ, Δ and for higher c].

But at any rate $1 < x < \tfrac{4}{3}$ and the influence of b, c, ϵ and Δ on x is weak

$$0 \leqslant \frac{\partial x/x}{\partial c/c} < 1, \ 0 \geqslant \frac{\partial x/x}{\partial b/b}, \ \frac{\partial x/x}{\partial \epsilon/\epsilon}, \ \frac{\partial x/x}{\partial \Delta/\Delta} > -1$$

and vanishes when b, c, ϵ and Δ approach their limiting values.[8] The solution for g_L^x is then (7.32) in (7.30)

$$g_L^x = \frac{xb}{2c} \quad \text{with } 1 < x = x(b, c, \epsilon, \Delta) < \tfrac{4}{3} \tag{7.33}$$

and

$$\frac{\partial g_L^x}{\partial b} = \frac{x}{2c} \left(\frac{\partial x/x}{\partial b/b} + 1 \right) > 0$$

$$\frac{\partial g_L^x}{\partial c} = \frac{xb}{2c} \left(\frac{\partial x/x}{\partial c/c} - 1 \right) < 0$$

$$\frac{\partial g_L^x}{\partial \epsilon} = \frac{b}{2c} \frac{\partial x}{\partial \epsilon} < 0$$

$$\frac{\partial g_L^x}{\partial \Delta} = \frac{b}{2c} \frac{\partial x}{\partial \Delta} < 0$$

The lowest possible $g_L^x(\min) = 0$ which is realized if $b \to 0$ or $c \to \infty$. The highest possible $g_L^x(\max) < 4/3b$ because $x \leqslant \tfrac{4}{3}$ and the condition $c \geqslant b^2/2$ has to be fulfilled. It may be surprising that g_L^x is independent of μ and negatively related to ϵ and Δ. To interpret this result we have drawn the $g_{Y/L}$ function (7.27) for alternative values of Δ and ϵ (see figure 7.5).

In figure 7.5 we see that though the peak rate of growth of consumption is at lower rates of population growth when Δ and ϵ are higher, higher Δ and ϵ nevertheless imply higher peak rates of consumption growth than do lower Δ and ϵ. And at any given g_L, $g_{Y/L}$ is higher with higher Δ and ϵ. So in that basic sense, an increase in Δ and ϵ increases consumption.

The case $(\epsilon + \Delta = 1)$ is more complex but illuminating. For $\epsilon + \Delta = 1$ and $g_L > 0$ the growth rate of the level of technique would simply accelerate if there were no further complications with respect to adopting new technological knowledge (see our earlier chapters with the solution $g_{Y/L} = \infty$ for $\epsilon + \Delta = 1$ and $g_L > 0$). But in this model population growth also influences the adoption of new

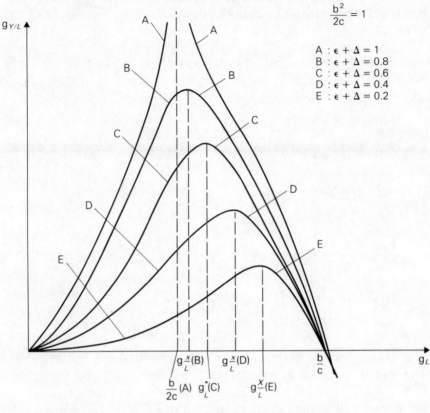

FIGURE 7.5

technical knowledge ($g_A = 0$ for $z = 0$, that if, for $g_L = 0$). Therefore the growth rate of *per capita* income is positive and finite, and as long as higher population growth promotes the adoption of new technical knowledge ($0 < g_L < b/2c$), higher population growth increases the growth rate of *per capita* income. Population growth $g_L = b/2c$ guarantees the fastest adoption of new technical knowledge, and it is only at this rate that the system can explode (when $b^2/2c = 1$ and therefore $z = \frac{1}{2}$ as assumed in figure 7.5). For still higher population growth rates ($b/c > g_L > b/2c$) the growth rate of *per capita* income is finite again but negatively related to the population growth rate because of the increasing difficulties in adopting the new technical knowledge. At $g_L \geqslant b/c$ population growth is too great to allow adopting any new technical knowledge, and consequently *per capita* income is then stationary or even shrinking.

The analysis of the case $(\epsilon + \Delta = 1)$ helps us understand why the optimal rate of population growth is negatively related to $(\epsilon + \Delta)$. We know that for smaller values of $(\epsilon + \Delta)$ the rate of population growth has monotonically increasing importance for the *creation* of new technical knowledge. And up to $g_L = b/2c$ a higher rate of population growth always facilitates the adoption of new technical knowledge, too. Therefore the optimal population growth is at least

$$g_L^x \geqslant \frac{b}{2c} \quad \text{for } \epsilon + \Delta \leqslant 1$$

For population growth rates $g_L > b/2c$ faster population growth is still favourable to the creation of new technical knowledge but unfavourable to its adoption. If $(\epsilon + \Delta)$ is relatively high the positive knowledge-creation effect has relatively smaller importance because the high $(\epsilon + \Delta)$ guarantees a fast growth rate of new technical knowledge even for small g_L. In this case the negative impact of high population growth on the adoption of the new technical knowledge is therefore more important, and the optimal rate of population growth is consequently less than it is for low $(\epsilon + \Delta)$. With low $(\epsilon + \Delta)$ population growth is more essential for knowledge creation, and the creation of new knowledge becomes relatively more important than the adoption of new knowledge. Therefore the optimal rate of population growth g_L^x and the elasticities ϵ and Δ are negatively related to each other.

Now let us summarize the results of this model:

(a) The optimal population growth rate depends both on b and c, which are the parameters in the adoption function, and on ϵ and Δ, which are the production elasticities of M and Y in the technology-production function.

(b) The optimal population rate is higher the lower are c, ϵ and Δ and the higher is b.

(c) If $(\epsilon + \Delta < 1)$ then g_L^x is greater than b/2c which is the g_L value at which the z function reaches its peak. For this reason in the optimum it is true that $g_A < g_M$ (even if $z_{max} = \frac{1}{2}$) just as in Model One.

(d)   The parameter μ, the production elasticity of L in the technology-production function, influences the $g_{Y/L}^x$ corresponding to the optimal g_L^x but has no impact on the optimal population growth rate ($\partial g_{Y/L}^x / \partial \mu > 0$, $\partial g_L^x / \partial \mu = 0$).

Alternative B for Model Three

The assumed z function of alternative A which underlies the results discussed above allows positive, zero and negative z values for $g_L > 0$. The latter is not reasonable, because a negative z would imply a negative relationship between $(A_t - A_{t-1})$ on the one side and M_{t-1} and A_{t-1} on the other side [see equation (7.21)]. It does not make sense that – *ceteris paribus* (i.e. for a given population growth rate) – firms apply less technical knowledge if the stock of available and known technical knowledge (M_{t-1}) and the stock of applied technical knowledge (A_{t-1}) are higher than before. Therefore we prefer a z function that excludes negative z values for positive g_L rates. With function (7.24a) high growth rates of population $g_L > n$ delay the adoption of new technical knowledge but only negate the positive relationship between the change of A $(A_t - A_{t-1})$ and the stocks of M_{t-1} and A_{t-1} when $g_L \to \infty$.

$$z = \frac{m\dot{L}}{(\dot{L} + n)^2}, \quad m, n > 0 .\tag{7.34}$$

and

$$n \geqslant \frac{m}{2} \tag{7.35}$$

Substituting (7.34) in (7.28) we get

$$g_L^x = \frac{n}{\dfrac{m}{2n} \dfrac{1 - \Delta + \epsilon}{1 - \Delta} - 1} \tag{7.36}$$

A positive and finite optimum rate of population growth exists if and only if

$$n < \frac{m}{2} \frac{1 - \Delta + \epsilon}{1 - \Delta}$$

In this case the result is very similar to the result of Alternative A. Again in the optimum $g_L^x > n$ and therefore $g_A < g_M$ because of the conditions

$$\frac{m}{2n} \leqslant 1$$

and

$$\frac{1 - \Delta + \epsilon}{1 - \Delta} < 2$$

The cases

$$n \geqslant \frac{m}{2} \frac{1 - \Delta + \epsilon}{1 - \Delta}$$

do not produce an optimal solution[9] but generate a positive relationship between $g_{Y/L}$ and g_L for all $g_L \geqslant 0$. To interpret our results graphically let us substitute (7.34) in (7.27)

$$g_{Y/L} = \frac{(\mu + \epsilon)\, m g_L^2}{(1 - \Delta)\left\{ (g_L + n)^2 - m \left(1 + \dfrac{\epsilon}{1 - \Delta)} \right) g_L \right\}} \tag{7.37}$$

with

$$g_{Y/L} = \frac{\mu + \epsilon}{1 - \Delta + \epsilon} \frac{n}{1 - \dfrac{m}{4n} \dfrac{1 - \Delta + \epsilon}{1 - \Delta}} \quad \text{for } g_L = g_L^x \tag{7.37a}$$

and

$$g_{Y/L} = \frac{\mu + \epsilon}{1 - \Delta} m \quad \text{for } g_L \to \infty \tag{7.37b}$$

Equation (7.37) is drawn in figure 7.6 for given values of μ, ϵ, Δ, m but different values of n to distinguish the three cases

$$n \lessgtr \frac{m}{2} \frac{1 - \Delta + \epsilon}{1 - \Delta}, \left(n_1 < n_2 < n_3,\ n_2 = \frac{m}{2} \frac{1 - \Delta + \epsilon}{1 - \Delta} \right)$$

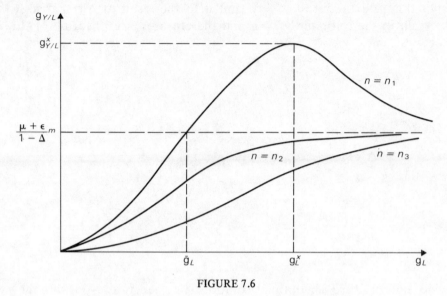

FIGURE 7.6

(The three cases are explicated in the numerical example presented in table 7.1.) In all three cases

$$g_{Y/L} \to \frac{\mu + \epsilon}{1 - \Delta} m \quad \text{if } g_L \to \infty$$

But while in the first case $(n = n_1) g_{Y/L}$ is still higher as long as $\bar{g}_L < g_L < \infty$, in the other two cases $(n = n_2 \text{ or } n = n_3) g_{Y/L}$ is always lower as long as $g_L < \infty$.

III. SUMMARY AND CONCLUSIONS

The aim of this chapter is to examine formulations within the spirit of steady-state growth theory that will lead to an intuitively satisfying model for the optimum rate of population growth.

We build upon the foundation of Phelps's model of exogenous technical progress, plus the Simon–Steinmann extension of it, both of which yield the result that the rate of growth of consumption per head is a positive linear function of the rate of growth of population, and without bound. We consider possible economic forces that might

TABLE 7.1
Simulations of variant three alternative B

Assumed parameter values: $\epsilon = \frac{1}{3}$, $\Delta = \frac{1}{3}$, $\mu = \frac{1}{6}$, $m = 4$.
We know from (7.37b) that for those parameter values

$$g_{Y/L} = \frac{\mu + \epsilon}{1 - \Delta} \, m = \frac{\frac{1}{6} + \frac{1}{3}}{1 - \frac{1}{3}} \, 4 = 3 \quad \text{for } g_L \to \infty$$

Furthermore

$$\frac{m}{2} \frac{1 - \Delta + \epsilon}{1 - \Delta} = 3$$

We can therefore distinguish the three cases $n \gtrless 3$.

(a) case: $n = 4$ (no optimum solution g_L^x)
(b) case: $n = 3$ (no optimum solution g_L^x)
(c) case: $n = 2$ [optimum solution according equation (7.36) $g_L^x = 4$].

	$g_{Y/L}$		
g_L	case 1: $n = 4$	case 2: $n = 3$	case 4: $n = 2$
0	0.000	0.000	0.000
1	0.158	0.300	1.000
2	0.500	0.923	3.000
3	0.871	1.500	3.857
4	1.200	1.920	4.000[a]
5	1.471	2.201	3.947
6	1.688	2.400	3.857
7	1.861	2.534	3.769
8	2.000	2.630	3.692
9	2.113	2.700	3.627
10	2.201	2.752	3.571
⋮	⋮	⋮	⋮
100	2.937	2.997	3.060
⋮	⋮	⋮	⋮
1000	2.999	3.000	3.006
⋮	⋮	⋮	⋮
∞	3.000	3.000	3.000

[a] Maximum value.

cause the rate of consumption ultimately to turn downwards with additional population growth, and we conclude that the likeliest force is the decrease in the adoption of available technology as labour becomes cheap relative to capital, and as very high population growth overtaxes people's will and ability to respond. We therefore added an adoption-of-technology function to our previous model. The nature of this function is the crucial issue in this chapter.

Our first variant simply makes the rate of growth of adoption equal to the rate of growth of technology less a factor which depends curvilinearly upon labour-force growth. The steady-state solution of this model has the property that the relationship of $g_{Y/L}$ to g_L is curvilinear, as intended. And it yields the insight that the optimum rate of growth of population g_L, is higher than the g_L which maximizes the rate of adoption of technology, a_2. But this model also has disadvantages:

(a) The relationship of g_A to g_M is rather mechanical and lacks theoretical or intuitive appeal, largely because it is framed in terms of growth rates rather than in absolute changes in technology or adoption of technique.

(b) Viewed not in equilibrium, this function has the rather perverse property that, in a single-period non-equilibrium context, a given increment of newly adopted technology has a more positive effect in an earlier year, when development was at an earlier stage, than in a later year at a more developed stage.

Our second variant applies a quadratic multiplier to the other arguments in the adoption function, so that the *ceteris paribus* amount of available technology adopted in any given year is a curvilinear function of labour-force growth. This function portrays the absolute amount of change in technical level in a period as depending upon the existing technical level, and upon the amount of technology that stands ready to be adopted. The relationship between g_L and $g_{Y/L}$ resulting from this adoption function is not curvilinear even though the adoption function is. Rather, it has the same positive linear shape as the Phelps and Simon–Steinmann functions until a point of discontinuity at which the relationship suddenly goes negative. Certainly this does not fit our intuitive notions. But upon reflection, one sees that *any* adoption function that contains the multiplicative elements $M^\nu A^\chi$ will have this property in equilibrium, because of the awesome properties of exponential growth.

Another candidate function is something like the second variant except that the exponents of M and A depend upon the rate of growth of the labour force (population). The resulting steady-state relationship between g_L and $g_{Y/L}$ has the curvilinear relationship that fits our intuition, and it follows for intuitively satisfying adoption and technology-production functions. It agrees with the Phelps and Simon–Steinmann models in that the standard of living and its growth are higher at substantial positive rates of population growth than they are at negative, zero or very low rates, but at some point even higher population growth slows the growth rate of consumption.

It should be noted, however, that higher rates of population growth in years prior to t would result in higher levels of consumption starting in some year following t for any *given* rate of population growth in the years after t. This is because the higher accumulated stock of unadopted technology due to the bigger populations earlier would eventually be turned into more adopted knowledge, at that time raising the standard of living higher than otherwise.

All our functions show that there are some rates of labour-force growth that yield a higher rate of per-person consumption growth than do rates either lower or higher. This accords with general intuitive notions, and jibes better with the spirit of economic theory than does a monotonically increasing function as seen in Phelps and Simon–Steinmann earlier.

As to the practical outcome of this work – a question that generally does not seem in good taste to raise in discussion of growth theory – perhaps most important is that this work calls into question the easy generalization drawn for growth theory with technical progress exogenous that population growth is negatively related to the growth of consumption per head. And the chapter does so in a manner consistent with our general intuition that the relationship is not monotonic. Also, this work points us to use this theoretical framework in a disequilibrium framework, to assess the present-value effects of differing rates of labour-force growth beginning from a common beginning economy, or of different sizes of population with the same growth rates, as in chapter 8.

NOTES

1 In a policy context, the highest rate of population growth clearly is *not* demonstrably optimal. If one starts with a given endowment of people and

capital, a rate of population growth takes time to overcome its capital dilution disadvantage through its creation of additional technology. Hence the best choice of population growth rate depends on the social discount rate chosen; at a low discount rate, the higher population growth rate is better without bound: at a high discount rate, low or zero or even negative population growth is best; and at some intermediate discount rates a population growth rate of 1 per cent leads to a higher per cent value of future consumption than does either a higher or lower population growth rate.

2   In Phelps's and our earlier models $\dot{M} \equiv \dot{A}$, $M_t \equiv A_t$.

3   For decreasing returns to scale $\alpha + \beta < 1$, in the production function (7.5) we get

$$g_{Y/L} = \frac{\mu + \epsilon + \dfrac{1 - \alpha - \beta}{\beta}(1 - \Delta)}{\dfrac{1 - \alpha}{\beta}(1 - \Delta) - \epsilon} g_L - \frac{a_1(1 - \Delta)}{\dfrac{1 - \alpha}{\beta}(1 - \Delta) - \epsilon}(g_L - a_2)^2 \tag{7.14a}$$

and

$$g_L^x = \frac{\mu + \epsilon + (1 - \Delta)\dfrac{1 - \alpha - \beta}{\beta}}{2a_1(1 - \Delta)} + a_2 \tag{7.15a}$$

Notice that it is not only true for constant returns to scale, but also true for decreasing returns to scale, that a growing population is more favourable than a stationary or shrinking population with respect to the equilibrium rate of *per capita* income, given a positive relationship between population growth and technical progress.

4   For the case of decreasing returns to scale the results are

$$g_Y = \frac{\dfrac{\chi - 1}{\nu} - \dfrac{\mu}{1 - \Delta}}{\dfrac{\epsilon}{1 - \Delta} - \dfrac{1 - \chi}{\nu}\dfrac{1 - \alpha}{\beta}} g_L \tag{7.20b}$$

and

$$g_{Y/L} = \frac{\mu + \epsilon - \dfrac{1 - \alpha - \beta}{\beta}\dfrac{1 - \chi}{\nu}(1 - \Delta)}{(1 - \Delta)\dfrac{1 - \chi}{\nu}\dfrac{1 - \alpha}{\beta} - \epsilon} g_L \tag{7.20c}$$

The denominator in (7.20c) is always positive, because

$$\frac{1-\chi}{\nu} \geqslant 1, \quad \frac{1-\alpha}{\beta} > 1 \quad \text{and} \quad (1-\Delta) > \epsilon$$

For this reason $dg_{Y/L}/dg_L > 0$ if the numerator in (7.20c) is positive, that is, if

$$\mu + \epsilon > \frac{1-\alpha-\beta}{\beta} \frac{1-\chi}{\nu}(1-\Delta)$$

5 $\quad z_{max} = \dfrac{b^2}{4c} \leqslant \dfrac{1}{2}$

6 $\quad z_{max} = \dfrac{m}{4n} \leqslant \dfrac{1}{2}$

7 In the case of decreasing returns to scale we obtain

$$g_{Y/L} = \frac{\mu + \epsilon - \dfrac{1-\alpha-\beta}{\beta} \dfrac{1-z}{z}(1-\Delta)}{\dfrac{1-z}{z} \dfrac{1-\alpha}{\beta}(1-\Delta) - \epsilon} \, g_L \qquad (7.27a)$$

We will omit the case of decreasing returns to scale in the analysis, because the resulting equations are very complex and difficult to handle.

8 $\quad \dfrac{\partial x/x}{\partial c/c}, \dfrac{\partial x/x}{\partial b/b}, \dfrac{\partial x/x}{\partial \epsilon/\epsilon}, \dfrac{\partial x}{\partial \Delta/\Delta} \to 0 \quad \text{for} \quad \epsilon \to 0, \ \Delta \to 0, \ (\epsilon + \Delta) \to 1, \ c \to \dfrac{b^2}{2}$

9 The solution

$$g_L^x < 0 \quad \text{for} \quad n < \frac{m}{2} \frac{1-\Delta-\epsilon}{1-\Delta}$$

is economically unreasonable, because it would imply a negative z. But our z function (7.34) is chosen only to exclude negative z values and is therefore defined for $g_L \geqslant 0$.

8

The Present Value of Population Growth in the Western World

I. INTRODUCTION

The context of the models discussed so far has mostly been the very long run, when equilibrium is reached. From a policy point of view, however, the comparison of alternatives in long-run equilibrium is quite unrealistic.

Whether additional people are judged good or bad, from an economic point of view, depends entirely upon whether people's welfare in the near future is taken mostly into account, or whether the long-run future also is allowed to weigh heavily in the judgement. With the concept of discounting one can compare offsetting events that will occur at separate moments, and arrive at a single-valued judgement about the net value in the present of that stream of future events. But this powerful tool has not hitherto been put to work in the evaluation of long-run population growth, a situation where evaluation over time is particularly crucial.[1] To put this tool to work, and thereby to arrive at some overall judgements about the social value of population growth within models that appropriately embody the most important impact of population growth and size – the effect of a larger population and a larger market upon technical change – is the aim of this chapter.

The main arguments may be summarized briefly as follows:

(a) At a very high discount rate – that is, where only the present and the near future matter – the value of an additional person is negative, because there are some short-run negative externalities for those already alive resulting from (i) transfer payments for social services, and (ii) reduction in output per worker caused by dilution of capital.

Argument (ii) is central to the entire corpus of Malthus' reasoning: diminishing returns to fixed capital. The effect of the rate of population growth on these factors is, however, small.

(b) Conventional growth theory introduces dynamic factors into the Malthusian system, but the conclusion remains the same: a higher rate of population growth implies lower consumption per person in all circumstances, because a greater proportion of output must go into investment to maintain an equilibrium growth rate; a negative rate of population growth is best, all the way to zero births.

(c) Any growth model in which the amount of technical change is regarded as a function of absolute population size, market size or capital stock will *eventually* have higher consumption with faster than with slower population growth, because of the cumulative nature of knowledge;[2] this is also true of most models in which the rate of technical progress is made a function of the rate of change of capital or output (but these models are less germane theoretically). The date at which consumption becomes higher with faster population growth varies depending on the model and the parameters.

(d) Simulations with a variety of parameters of the various models of absolute size show that faster population growth almost always results in a higher present value of future consumption at real inflation-adjusted discount rates below 4 to 10 per cent; at higher real discount rates, lower (or negative) population growth generally results in a higher present value. This suggests a much higher return to additional population than the long-run private riskless real market rate of between 2 and 3 per cent.

At the centre of any analysis of the effect of additional population on income through the production of technical knowledge is this indigestible kernel: no matter how small the contribution to technology of the additional individual, that contribution will some day – though perhaps a long time ahead – inevitably lead to income per head being higher than it would otherwise have been, *ceteris paribus*.

There is also a sub-plot to the story. In a modern society such as the US (other countries such as Germany differ somewhat), workers' transfers of income to retired persons are large in comparison to transfers to children (outside of their own families). This means that any given individual benefits if some other individual has more children, *ceteris paribus*; this effect raises the discount rate at which the present value of population growth is positive above what it would otherwise be in any given model. This chapter concentrates on the main argument, however. The calculations disregard transfers to retired persons and for child services, negative environmental adjustment costs, positive environmental externalities of all sorts (especially those that decrease the entropy of the earth) and changes in work and savings patterns due to larger numbers of dependants.

In order to compare the present values of different population growth rates, I simulated on a computer the model described in chapter 6.

II.   RESULTS

Runs were made with a variety of parameters in the production function, adding alternatively to less than unity, unity and more than unity. L and M are given much larger exponents than (Y/L) and Y in most cases. I also ran a variety of functions without one, two or three of the variables in equation (6.9) (noting that Y/L can be reduced to Y and L when both the latter are also in the equation). The results of various simulation runs are shown in table 8.2. They yield the present values of the stream of consumption at different discount rates. An example of the underlying data, year by year for ten years, and then at 10- and 50-year intervals is shown in table 8.1.

Present values were calculated at the end of 300 years, by which time the present value has virtually ceased to grow with the addition of more periods, except at a zero discount rate. For those runs in which the computer ceased functioning short of 300 years because some variable in the simulation became too large (usually M, though sometimes C), present values were compared for all $\dot{L}$ at the highest of 250, or 200, or 150 years for which the calculations are complete. For some runs in which it was interesting to look for convergences and golden-age paths, the model was run for 600 years (results not shown here).

Findings

The general picture for any particular model is that the yearly consumption level starts out lower with a higher rate of population growth than with a lower, but becomes higher somewhere around the

TABLE 8.1
Results for sample trial with Phelps's parameters $M_t - M_{t-1} = aL_{t-1}^{0.5}M_{t-1}^{0.5}$

Year	L	K	$\dot{K}$	Y	$\dot{Y}$	Y/L	K/y	M	$\dot{M}$	C/L
0	1 000	1 000	0.0200	500	0.0270	0.500	2.00	1.00	–	0.500
1	1 020	1 020	0.0205	514	0.0270	0.503	1.99	1.01	0.0100	0.483
2	1 040	1 040	0.0207	527	0.0271	0.507	1.98	1.02	0.0100	0.487
3	1 060	1 060	0.0208	542	0.0272	0.510	1.96	1.03	0.0101	0.490
4	1 080	1 090	0.0209	556	0.0272	0.514	1.95	1.04	0.0101	0.494
5	1 100	1 110	0.0211	572	0.0273	0.518	1.94	1.05	0.0102	0.497
6	1 130	1 130	0.0212	587	0.0274	0.522	1.93	1.06	0.0102	0.501
7	1 150	1 160	0.0213	603	0.0295	0.525	1.92	1.07	0.0103	0.504
8	1 170	1 180	0.0215	620	0.0275	0.529	1.90	1.08	0.0103	0.508
9	1 200	1 210	0.0216	637	0.0276	0.533	1.89	1.10	0.0104	0.512
10	1 220	1 230	0.0217	655	0.0277	0.537	1.88	1.11	0.0104	0.516
20	1 490	1 540	0.0230	864	0.0284	0.581	1.78	1.23	0.0109	0.558
30	1 810	1 940	0.0242	1 150	0.0292	0.634	1.69	1.38	0.0114	0.609
40	2 210	2 480	0.0254	1 540	0.0299	0.696	1.62	1.55	0.0119	0.668
50	2 690	3 210	0.0265	2 070	0.0306	0.770	1.55	1.75	0.0124	0.739
60	3 200	4 190	0.0275	2 810	0.0313	0.856	1.49	1.98	0.0128	0.822
70	4 000	5 530	0.0285	3 840	0.0319	0.959	1.44	2.25	0.0133	0.921
80	4 880	7 360	0.0294	5 270	0.0325	1.080	1.40	2.58	0.0137	1.040
90	5 940	9 890	0.0303	7 270	0.0331	1.220	1.36	2.96	0.0141	1.170
100	7 240	13 400	0.0311	10 100	0.0336	1.390	1.33	3.41	0.0145	1.340
110	8 830	18 300	0.0318	14 100	0.0341	1.600	1.30	3.95	0.0149	1.530
120	10 800	25 100	0.0325	19 700	0.0346	1.830	1.27	4.59	0.0153	1.760
130	13 100	34 600	0.0332	27 800	0.0350	2.120	1.25	5.35	0.0156	2.030
140	16 000	48 200	0.0338	39 300	0.0354	2.460	1.22	6.26	0.0160	2.360
150	19 500	67 300	0.0343	55 800	0.0358	2.860	1.21	7.35	0.0163	2.750
200	52 500	385 000	0.0365	338 000	0.0374	6.440	1.14	17.00	0.0175	6.190
250	141 000	2 390 000	0.0379	2 180 000	0.0385	15.500	1.10	41.60	0.0184	14.800
300	380 000	15 700 000	0.0388	14 700 000	0.0392	38.600	1.07	105.00	0.0190	37.100
350	1 020 000	107 000 000	0.0394	102 000 000	0.0396	99.300	1.05	272.00	0.0194	95.400
400	2 750 000	748 000 000	0.0398	716 000 000	0.0399	260.000	1.04	716.00	0.0196	249.000
450	7 410 000	5 290 000 000	0.0400	5 100 000 000	0.0401	687 000	1.04	1 900.00	0.0198	660.000
500	20 000 000	37 800 000 000	0.0402	36 500 000 000	0.0402	1 830 000	1.04	5 060.00	0.0199	1 760 000
550	53 700 000	272 000 000 000	0.0403	263 000 000 000	0.0403	4 890 000	1.03	13 500.00	0.0199	4 700 000
600	145 000 000	1 960 000 000 000	0.0403	1 900 000 000 000	0.0403	12 100 000	1.03	36 300.00	0.0199	12 600 000

TABLE 8.2

$PV_{t=300}$ for the equation $M_t - M_{t-1} = aL_{t-1}^\gamma M_{t-1}^{\hat{\Delta}}(Y/L)_{t-1}^{\psi} Y_{t-1}^{\phi}$

Run no.	Exponents for[a]						Discount rate[b]						$\dot{M}$
	L	M	Y/L	Y	$\dot{L}$	S	0.00	0.02	0.04	0.06	0.08	0.10	
1.1	0.5	0.5	NA	NA	0.01	0.02	696	39.2	14.9	9.20	6.67	5.24	—
1.2	0.5	0.5	NA	NA	0.02	0.04	2 110	52.3	15.4	9.20	6.61	5.17	⌒
1.3	0.5	0.5	NA	NA	0.01	0.04	917	45.1	15.8	9.52	6.81	5.30	—
2.1	0.3	0.3	NA	NA	0.01	0.02	451	35.6	14.6	9.13	6.65	5.23	/
2.2	0.3	0.3	NA	NA	0.02	0.04	666	38.8	14.7	9.07	6.57	5.15	/
2.3	0.3	0.3	NA	NA	0.01	0.04	585	40.5	15.5	8.44	6.78	5.29	/
3.1	0.7	0.7	NA	NA	0.01	0.02	1 740	48.5	15.3	9.29	6.70	5.25	⌒
3.2	0.7	0.7	NA	NA	0.02	0.04	480E + 4	261	17.7	9.41	6.67	5.20	⌒
3.3	0.7	0.7	NA	NA	0.01	0.04	2 350	57.5	16.4	8.62	6.84	5.31	⌒
4.1	0.9	0.9	NA	NA	0.01	0.02	37 000	193	16.7	9.42	6.74	5.27	⌒
4.2	0.9	0.9	NA	NA	0.02	0.04	6.58E + 10	1.74E + 8	4.18E + 6	9.26	8.65	5.23	⌒
4.3	0.9	0.9	NA	NA	0.01	0.04	51 900	256	18.2	9.77	6.88	5.33	⌒
5.1	0.5	0.9	NA	NA	0.01	0.02	2 360	51.8	15.4	9.30	6.70	5.25	⌒
5.2	0.5	0.9	NA	NA	0.02	0.04	1.30E + 8	514	18.2	9.36	6.66	5.19	⌒
5.3	0.5	0.9	NA	NA	0.01	0.04	3 190	62.0	16.5	9.63	6.84	5.31	⌒
6.1	0.4	0.6	NA	NA	0.01	0.02	696	39.2	14.9	9.20	6.67	5.24	—
6.2	0.4	0.6	NA	NA	0.02	0.04	1 790	49.6	15.3	9.18	6.60	5.17	⌒
6.3	0.4	0.6	NA	NA	0.01	0.04	917	45.1	15.8	9.52	6.81	5.30	—

7.1	0.6	0.4	NA	NA	0.01	0.02	696	39.2	14.9	9.20	6.67	5.24	—
7.2	0.6	0.4	NA	NA	0.02	0.04	2 420	55.0	15.5	9.22	6.62	5.18	⟨
7.3	0.6	0.4	NA	NA	0.01	0.04	917	45.1	15.8	9.52	6.81	5.30	—
8.1	0.5	1.0	NA	NA	0.01	0.02	6 170	69.6	15.6	9.33	6.71	5.26	⟨
8.2	0.5	1.0	NA	NA	0.02	0.04	5 500	1 470	375	10.2	6.67	5.19	⟨
8.3	0.5	1.0	NA	NA	0.01	0.04	8 430	86.4	16.8	9.66	6.85	5.32	⟨
9.1	0.5	1.1	NA	NA	0.01	0.02	1 140	397	16.9	9.36	6.72	5.26	⟨
9.2	0.5	1.1	NA	NA	0.02	0.04	1.08E+13	6.98E+10	4.07E+8	2.13E+6	9 950	446	⟨
9.3	0.5	1.1	NA	NA	0.01	0.04	157 000	538	18.5	9.71	6.86	5.32	⟨
10.1	0.5	0.5	NA	0.5	0.01	0.02	397 000	1 270	20.1	9.45	6.75	5.27	⟨
10.2	0.5	0.5	NA	0.5	0.02	0.04	2.31E+29	5.47E+26	1.14E+24	2.09E+21	3.36E+18	4.68E+15	⟨
10.3	0.5	0.5	NA	0.5	0.01	0.04	2.23E+6	6 560	36.6	9.92	6.91	5.34	⟨
11.1	0.5	0.48	NA	NA	0.01	0.02	171 000	607	18.1	9.43	6.74	5.27	(
11.2	0.5	0.48	NA	NA	0.02	0.04	5.51E+20	1.33E+18	2.83E+14	5.31E+12	8.72E+9	1.25E+7	(
11.3	0.5	0.48	NA	NA	0.01	0.04	746 000	2 370	25.2	9.87	6.90	5.34	(
12.1	0.8	0.5	NA	NA	0.01	0.02	3.09E+7	83 900	227	10.1	6.78	5.28	(
12.2	0.8	0.5	NA	NA	0.02	0.04	2.00E+38	4.74E+35	9.90E+32	1.82E+30	2.92E+27	4.07E+24	(
12.3	0.8	0.5	NA	NA	0.01	0.04	2.46E+8	65 560	1 610	13.6	6.95	5.35	(
13.1	0.5	0.5	0.5	NA	0.01	0.02	2 710	52.8	15.3	9.28	6.70	5.25	⟨
13.2	0.5	0.5	0.5	NA	0.02	0.04	1.23E+6	3 680	27.0	9.38	6.65	5.19	⟨
13.3	0.5	0.5	0.5	NA	0.01	0.04	5 980	76.1	16.7	9.66	6.85	5.32	⟨

^{a} NA = not applicable.

^{b} E + n indicates the entry must be multiplied by 10 raised to the nth power.

25th year after the entry of the additional persons into the labour force. For purposes of decision about population policy, however, we must know the trade-off between present and future consumption. An appropriate way to think about this problem is to examine the present values of the alternatives at a discount rate deemed reasonable, and select the alternative with the highest present value. The present values for the alternatives of $\dot{L}$ in the various models with various parameters, are, therefore, shown at a range of discount factors that span all conceivable choices.

Unlike the mathematician, however, the economist may not simply present the entire range of logical possibilities and leave it at that. For one thing, the logical range encompasses an infinity of discrete possibilities – negative discount rates, and positive rates to infinity; unbounded ranges of parameter values; a large or infinite variety of model specifications; and so on. Instead, the economist must judge which are the economically meaningful alternatives, and consider the implications of them in their constrained variety. The economist ought also to see whether there are general conclusions that may be drawn from the meaningful set of alternatives as a whole.

Few economists or policy makers would agree with Frank Ramsey that any discount rate above zero simply shows a want of imagination. On the other hand, few or no economists would suggest that the public discount rate should be higher than the real private discount rate for projects with the same risk. These considerations should provide agreed boundaries for the appropriate discount rate.

These are some specific findings:

(1) In all sets of runs, the present value of higher population growth is higher at low rates of discount or when it is zero, and up to quite substantial discount rates – 5 per cent at a minimum – even with parameters that are unreasonably unfavourable to this outcome. This finding may be contrasted with the conclusion of main-stream growth theory that lower population growth is better across the board, and even that negative population growth is better than a stationary population. This suggests that – putting aside both the other positive and negative effects of population growth such as transfer payments to retired persons, environmental adjustment costs, public child services and the like – higher population growth is a good thing in developed countries, given the value judgements about the discount rate that are implicit in our other social decisions.

When examining table 8.2, it should be noted that the appropriate comparison is between the two 'warranted' rates of population growth and saving, $\dot{L} = 0.01$, $s = 0.02$ and $\dot{L} = 0.02$, $s = 0.04$. The combination of $\dot{L} = 0.01$, $s = 0.04$ is included to show that at higher rates of saving, a given rate of population growth can produce better results than at the warranted savings rate. Results not shown here suggest that at higher and closer-to-optimal savings rates, the advantage of higher rates of population growth is even more marked, in the sense of producing higher present values at even higher rates of discount.

(2) In all sets of runs with functions that are theoretically reasonable, higher rates of population growth have lower present values at *some* rate of discount – starting somewhere between 5 and 10 per cent. But no matter how high the discount rate, the advantage of lower population growth over higher population growth is either negligible or non-existent. This is because the consumption advantage resulting from less capital dilution that lower population growth yields in the early years is a very slight advantage at best. This implies that there is no meaningful risk argument against higher population growth, in the context of this model.

(3) Together, the advantage of higher population growth at low discount rates, and the absence of disadvantage at high discount rates, suggests that a strategy of higher population growth dominates a strategy of lower population growth.

III.   DISCUSSION

The reader may well wonder whether one or more influences left out of the formal analysis qualify or reverse the findings stated above. For example, at the end of a paper that finds that population growth is positively related to welfare through a 'chain letter' retirement transfer-payment mechanism, Samuelson (1975) suddenly reverses course and says:

> Ultimately, positive exponential population growth will presumably bring back into importance the scarcity of natural resources ignored by the model.... For several generations people may benefit on a lifetime basis by having numerous children to support them well in their old ages, out of filial piety or by means of social security. And yet until the end of

time their increases in population will cause the law of diminishing returns to be brought into play to leave all subsequent generations in a worsened situation. To the degree that childhood dependency is intrinsically less costly relative to old-age dependency, this dyshygienic temptation becomes all the more dangerous.

We may first examine the issue in the steady-state context. Consider equation (6.6) again. If natural resources will be increasingly scarce and therefore rising in price, this can be interpreted as implying diminishing returns in the Cobb–Douglas production function, as indicated by the sum of exponents $\alpha + \beta$ adding to less than unity. If the exponents of labour and the stock of technology μ and Δ in equation (6.5a) were approaching zero, and if the production-function exponents $\alpha + \beta$ add to less than unity, then a faster growing labour force implies slower growth of consumption, but this is simply growth theory without technology being regarded as endogenous. If $\mu + \Delta$, or even just μ, is positive, then $\alpha + \beta$ would have to be considerably smaller than unity for the result to be reversed, that is, for faster population growth not to imply faster growth of consumption. (The possibility that the exponent of Y is so large as to make the right-hand side of the equation negative is sufficiently implausible that we need not consider it.) For illustration, in Phelps's special case, the exponents would need to be little more than half their size in constant returns for the result to continue to hold,[3] and hence the possibility may be assumed to be implausible in the steady-state context.

In the context of policy making and a horizon of between, say, half a century and three centuries, there is still plenty of time for the effects of population growth to be felt upon availability of natural resources, and hence that possibility should be discussed. Just as soon as we do not make the logical assumption that resources are finite and therefore necessarily diminishing in availability as we use some of them – an assumption that I argue is neither sound nor useful[4] – then there is no longer an entailed negative effect, and the question becomes an empirical one. This question boils down to whether the effect of additional population in depleting resources dominates their effect in creating new resources (by discovery, invention and substitution) or whether the latter dominates the former. The appendix presents extensive data in the tradition of Barnett and Morse (1963) showing that the long-run historical course of the prices of all raw materials is downwards, that is, there has been greater rather than less availability with the passage of time and the growth of population. There seems to be no reason to believe that this has happened *despite* the growth in population, but rather it seems more plausible to believe that it has occurred *because* of the growth of population, for the very reason given in the supply-and-demand analysis earlier; in essence, natural resources are similar to other capital in this respect. And it is, therefore, unnecessary to inquire how an increasing shortage of natural resources would qualify the central conclusion of this chapter.

IV. SUMMARY AND CONCLUSIONS

Steady-state equilibrium analysis is not appropriate for policy decisions, because if a nation chooses one or another population growth rate, it begins with the same endowment of capital and people and techniques no matter what the population growth rate chosen. Therefore, the appropriate analysis is one which compares the result of two or more growth rates beginning from that initial position. And the logical decision criterion is a present-value comparison of streams of consumption per head.

This chapter simulates the effects of various rates of population growth with variations in specifications and parameters. The chief result is that with virtually every variant, faster population growth shows better consumption results with real discount rates up to 5 to 10 per cent, a level which is far above the long-run adjusted riskless rate; at higher discount rates, lower (or negative) population growth rates have higher present values. And even at very high discount rates, lower population growth rates imply present values only a bit above those for higher population growth rates. The advantage is overwhelmingly with higher population growth in this analysis.

NOTES

1 Enke's (e.g. 1966) focus is quite different than that of this chapter, being on the evaluation of the present worth of a single person or cohort, rather than the long run of growth theory. (Also, Enke's work is internally inconsistent; see Simon, 1969; 1977, chapter 20.)

2 Some knowledge becomes less useful as it gets older. But it is most unlikely that knowledge obsolesces enough to matter in this context.

3 In the special case of the Phelps equation without constant returns

$$\left(\frac{\dot{Y}}{L}\right) = \left(\frac{2\beta + \alpha - 1}{1 - \alpha}\right)\dot{L}$$

The text statement's 'stylized' assumptions are $\beta = 0.67$, $\alpha = 0.33$.

4 Incredible as it may seem at first, the term 'finite' is not only inappropriate but is downright misleading in the context of natural resources, from both the practical and the philosophical points of view. As with so many of the important arguments in this world, this one is 'just semantic'. Yet the semantics of resource scarcity muddle public discussion and bring about wrong-headed policy decisions.

A definition of resource quantity must be operational to be useful. It must tell us how the quantity of the resource that might be available in the future could be calculated. But the future quantities of a natural resource such as copper cannot be calculated even in principle, because of new lodes, new methods of mining copper and variations in grades of copper lodes; because copper can be made from other metals; and because of the vagueness of the boundaries within which copper might be found – including the sea, and other planets. Even less possible is a reasonable calculation of the amount of future services of the sort we are now accustomed to get from copper, because of re-cycling and because of the substitution of other materials for copper, as in the case of the communications satellite.

Even the total weight of the earth is not a theoretical limit to the amount of copper that might be available in the future. Only the total weight of the universe – if that term has a useful meaning here – would be such a theoretical limit, and I do not think anyone would like to argue that the term 'finite' has a meaning in that context.

With respect to energy, it is particularly obvious that the earth does not bound the quantity available to us: our sun (and perhaps other suns) is our basic source of energy in the long run, from vegetation (including fossilized vegetation) as well as from solar energy. As to the practical finiteness and scarcity of resources – that brings us back to cost and price, and by these measures history shows progressively decreasing rather than increasing scarcity.

Why does the word 'finite' catch us up? That is an interesting question in psychology, education and philosophy; unfortunately there is no space to explore it here. (See Simon, 1981, pp. 47-50.)

9

The Overall Effect of Immigrants upon Natives' Incomes

I. INTRODUCTION

This chapter illustrates the use of the sort of model described in chapters 6 and 7 in the realistic context of policy decisions about immigration into the US. The two main elements that must be added to the basic macro-model with endogenous technical progress are: (a) special treatment of the returns to pre-existing capital obtained by the immigrants; and (b) transfers to the immigrants in the form of welfare payments and services, as well as transfers from the immigrants in the form of taxes. This chapter is intended to show how the basic model discussed in this book is relevant to actual social issues.

The model used here follows the simple line of the equation adapted from Phelps, rather than the richer model analysed in chapters 6, 7 and 8. This is because, in the context of immigration, the effects of education and *per capita* income and of the stock of knowledge can be assumed away because they will vary relatively little over the period under consideration.

The present value assessment has much in common with that in chapter 8, but here the treatment is more fully realistic.

Section II reviews the theory of the effect of the allocation of capital ownership, and sketches a new way of calculating that effect for the US. Section III discusses the inter-generational transfer effect. Section IV discusses the effect of immigrants upon productivity, and then combines all these elements into a simulation model that estimates the net on-balance effect of immigrants on the incomes of natives.

II.   THE CAPITAL-OWNERSHIP EFFECT

The prevailing theoretical approach from Malthus' time until recently – and still the prevailing popular view – is that immigrants lower the income of 'natives'[1] through capital dilution and diminishing returns. The given endowment of capital, combined with more workers, yields less output per average worker.

Borts and Stein (1964) and Berry and Soligo (1969) pointed out that if immigrants do not share in the returns to capital, and yet are paid their marginal product, the total returns to capital are increased by more than the sum by which natives' wages are lowered; hence immigrants increase the average income of natives under these conditions. This proposition is shown in figure 9.1, taken from Berry and Soligo, where the approximate-triangle X represents the gain to natives as a whole.[2]

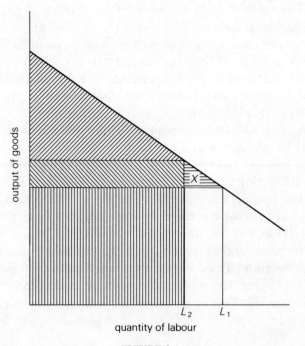

FIGURE 9.1

Berry and Soligo made it clear that immigrants' impact upon natives' average income depends upon whether immigrants obtain rights to the returns to the existing capital. But Usher suggested that the gain to natives from the 'triangle' X is small compared to the loss to natives if immigrants capture part of the returns to capital, a demonstration I also made quantitatively in an analysis of the effect of Russian immigrants upon 'veteran' Israelis' incomes (Simon, 1976). The task, then, is to estimate the proportion of the return to capital that goes to immigrants. And this is not a simple or straightforward task.

Usher's approach was to estimate the value of the capital stock. This method is necessarily fraught with all the well-known difficulties of valuing existing industrial capital, plus the special difficulties of valuing the physical and organizational capital of government, and of farms and other land whose market price depends largely upon the value of product rather than the cost of producing the capital. Usher's calculation of effective public ownership was therefore quite delicate and judgemental. Nevertheless, Usher made a back-of-the-envelope calculation that 58 per cent of the capital in the UK is in effect publicly owned. If this were the appropriate figure, the loss to natives from immigrants would indeed be very large relative to the 'triangle' gain that would result if effective public-capital ownership by immigrants was zero.

Working with the streams of payments to capital owners and to labour would avoid some of the difficulties of valuing capital that arise in Usher's method, and I tried to do this earlier. But both this and Usher's method now seem to me misdirected for illuminating the particular problem at hand. The reasoning is as follows.

Recall that the aim here is to determine the effect of immigrants *upon natives' incomes*. A calculation of the sort that Usher made (based on the concept that I, too, used in my 1976 paper), or the sort of calculation that I made working with streams of payments for an earlier version of this chapter may reveal something about the benefits obtained from the capital *by the immigrants themselves*. But the benefits to the immigrant are not the obverse of costs to natives.

Consider Usher's central statement: 'When a man migrates from one country to another, he abandons his share of public property – the use of roads and schools, the rights to a share of revenue from minerals in the public domain and so on – in the former country and acquires a share of public property in the latter, conferring a benefit upon the remaining residents of the country from which he comes and imposing a cost upon the original residents of the country to which he goes' (1977, p. 1001). This assertion by Usher, to which I also subscribed earlier (1976), no longer seems correct to me. The most obvious defect is that there are economies of scale in true public goods. For example, the benefit the immigrant receives when he or she sees the Statue of Liberty is not balanced by a corresponding cost to natives, even before or after the immigrant becomes a citizen and a part owner of the Statue. And to a greater or lesser extent the same is true of roads, public television transmitters, museums, military real estate and wilderness. Furthermore, there is no clear correspondence between the contemporary market value, or the original cost of such public capital, and the benefits derived from it. Therefore we need a method that directly estimates the effect *upon natives* rather than an indirect estimate by way of the benefits obtained by immigrants. And more specifically, we want to know the effects upon natives' money incomes, because estimating the costs or benefits to them of changes in the physical and cultural environment caused by immigrants is not presently possible.

A satisfactory analysis is a bit complex, and the solution arrived at will not compel agreement in every reader. Rather than try to state the case in full length and over-full detail here (where the subject is only tangential), I shall only mention the key elements in it, refer the reader to a full treatment (Simon and Heins, 1985) and employ an adjustment factor which surely overstates the magnitude of the effect in such a fashion as to make the accounting less favourable to the admission of immigrants; as we shall see, however, other aspects of the analysis combine to make the on-balance conclusion favourable to the admission of immigrants, nevertheless. The two main elements of the capital-dilution analysis are: (a) In their roles as producers, only those immigrants who work for the government receive any of the returns to the capital they work with; workers in private industry receive no such returns, and they may be assumed to receive only their marginal product. Taxes paid by businesses are no different in this respect than expenditures for imported raw materials, say. Therefore, the proportion of immigrants that work for government allows us to estimate this component fairly readily. (b) Allowance must be made for public capital such as schools and hospitals for which the quantity needed is affected by the number of persons. This allowance is quite tricky. It depends upon the cost of additional construction per immigrant, the proportion funded by sinking bonds, the rate of depreciation and the payout period in the sinking bonds.

The analysis uses an adjustment that implies immigrants receive their numerical proportion of the returns to capital from 35 per cent of the capital, assuming they own none. This surely overstates the matter by a great deal, the analysis by Simon and Heins arriving at an estimate of 8 per cent. But because the aim of the analysis is to illustrate the usefulness of the theory rather than to arrive at policy-relevant estimates and because of the desire to weight the argument 'conservatively' against the admission of more immigrants, this stylistic mode of discussion should suffice.

The importance for natives' incomes of the extent of capital returns captured by immigrants can be derived from a Cobb–Douglas model to be developed later. This partial effect corresponds to the proportion of the average immigrant's income that is transferred to or from the immigrant on one or another assumption of capital-returns capture. If the immigrant were to capture none of the returns to capital, the immediate effect[3] on natives' incomes would be very slightly positive (equal to 0.1 per cent of the immigrant's income). If the immigrant were to capture *all* the returns, there would be a first-year negative effect equal to 32 per cent of the immigrant's income. For other capital-capture proportions, the effects on natives as proportions of the immigrant's first-year income are, respectively: 10 per cent, −4 per cent; 20 per cent, −8 per cent; 30 per cent, −12 per cent. At the 35 per cent-capture rate the effect is a transfer to the immigrant equal to 14 per cent of the immigrant's income.[4]

These calculations agree with Usher's conclusion that the triangle of benefit to natives in the absence of returns to existing capital captured by immigrants is small relative to the capital dilution cost to natives at even small proportions of capital-returns capture. But as we shall see, this effect is soon swamped by the other effects.

III.   THE INTER-GENERATIONAL TRANSFER EFFECT

Modigliani (1966) and Samuelson (1975) have shown in a different context that an additional person – and more generally, a positive population growth rate – will have a positive partial effect on incomes by way of existing patterns of life-cycle saving and con- sumption. This argument has not previously been applied to immi- grants, but in fact it applies even more strongly to immigrants than to native births because the childhood public-consumption portion of the life cycle is not present with immigrants, as we shall see later in the data on the age distribution of immigrants.

Though Modigliani and Samuelson talk about the saving of an additional person that makes him or her increase the incomes of others, we must notice that *pure* saving is not meant here, but rather a retirement system based on transfer payments. If you immigrate, build a barn with your own hands (saving and investment) and then sell milk from it, no one benefits from the saving other than you. Or if you build the barn and rent it to me, no one else's income is raised more than if you did the same construction work on salary for a construction company. It is your immigrating and then *giving 10 per cent of your salary* to the already-fixed number of native retirees that increases the average income of your age cohort (by decreasing their contributions to the retirees), and therefore the incomes of the natives as a group.

The existence of this benefit from immigration depends on two assumptions:

(a) The public consumption patterns of children, adults and retirees are such that an additional complete native family with a larger number of children than retirees – a family typical of popula- tion growth – transfers more to the rest of the economy in social security payments in a given year than it consumes in public expendi- tures on children plus transfers to retirees; this is very marked in the United States (Clark and Spengler, 1979), though somewhat less so in European countries where child-support transfers are relatively larger than in the US.

(b) The age distribution of immigrants when they arrive has more workers and fewer dependants than the age distribution of the native population. These are the most important reasons why this second assumption is overwhelmingly true: (i) even those retirees who do come with immigrant families are not entitled to old-age benefits; (ii) the age distribution of immigrants is much more heavily concen- trated in the prime working ages than is the native population, as may be seen in table 9.1. On average, it is the young, strong and

TABLE 9.1
Distributions by age of legal immigrants at entry, and US population

Age	US population, 1970 (Social Indicators, 1976, p. 32)	Legal immigrants to US, 1967–1973 (INS data from Keely and Kraly, 1978)
0–19	38.0	35.5
20–39	25.6	46.4
40–59	22.2	13.8
60+	14.2	4.3

single who migrate. [This is especially true of illegals; mostly male, mostly single (among Mexicans, most of the married men leave their wives and children in Mexico, for example), and mostly youthful; for details, see Simon, forthcoming, chapter 3 and passim.]

(c) Labour-force participation among immigrants in various age and sex cohorts tends to be higher than among natives, and unemployment among immigrants is not relatively high (Simon, 1985, chapter 11).

(d) The distribution of education and skills among immigrants is favourable relative to the native labour force, and hence earnings and taxes are relatively high (Simon, 1985, chapters 3 and 11.)

These data imply that immigrants constitute a class which, on net balance, contributes to natives by age-and-youth transfer payments. Section VI will discuss whether there are off-setting negative transfer effects of immigrants through other social-welfare channels.

One may wonder whether the net flow of transfers caused by the immigrant cohort tends to balance out when the immigrants get older. This seems so if one looks only at the immigrants themselves rather than at the whole sequence of events caused by the entry of the immigrants, which includes their children who then grow up into productive workers. When the immigrants get older, the immigrants' own offspring more than supply the necessary retirement transfers ['more' rather than 'equal to' because of the effect in (a) above]. Were this system to be considered in an equilibrium context, this would not seem to be true. But it is in the very nature of the entry of each immigrant that it is a one-time disequilibrium event, and it is the gains from the difference between it and an otherwise comparable equilibrium – that is, the system without the immigrant – that constitute the transfers captured by the natives.

Perhaps a hypothetical example will clarify this important but elusive point. Imagine that a 'native' family consists of my spouse and me, both now aged 35, our 3-year-old twins, and my retired grandfather. Your immigrant family consists of your spouse and you, both aged 25. Both families pay 20 per cent of our $20,000 yearly incomes in taxes. Our family now receives a government pension for the grandfather (and some minor support for the twins) whereas your family receives no such payments, so on balance I gain from you now. After a few years the balance will become slightly more even as your spouse and you also have two children, and 40 years later the yearly balance will become roughly equal after your spouse and you retire and collect a government pension. But since my family was the net gainer in the early years – the years which weigh heaviest in a present-value calculation of the 'investment' value to natives of admitting your family as immigrants, a calculation properly made at the time of the admission decision – the calculation is influenced positively by the pension effect (and to a much smaller extent, by the child welfare programmes). And the calculation for this one immigrant family is in no way altered by the fact that other immigrants may or may not enter in future years.

In passing, it is interesting to notice that the immigrant-saving effect is the opposite of the negative child-dependency effect that has been the mainspring of the Coale–Hoover (1958) argument against population growth in less-developed countries. And the life-cycle facts may well be such that, even in LDCs, over its lifetime an additional child has a positive net transfer effect on the income of others.

The actual magnitude of the life-cycle saving effect is roughly equal to the proportion of an immigrant's salary that goes to fund social security and other federal old-age programmes. At present this is around 14 per cent of the average salary (*Social Security Bulletin, Annual Statistical Supplement*, 1983, p. 61; 10 per cent instead of 14 per cent is used in the model to be 'conservative'), and the social-security percentage is almost sure to rise in the next few years. So we see that this positive effect is large, and of the same order of magnitude as the negative capital-returns-capture effect seen in section II.[5]

IV.   LONG-RUN PRODUCTIVITY AND THE INTEGRATED MODEL

Aside from their special characteristics as cultural newcomers and as non-owners of capital, immigrants represent additional people *as people*. The likely most important long-run effect of immigrants is the effect of the immigrants (in their role of additional workers and consumers) upon the productivity of the country of immigration, which is the central subject of this book. As we shall see, in a reasonably short span of time, this factor dwarfs all the others in the analysis of immigrants.

If an economist is to be worth his/her keep, he or she must take account of the *size* and *importance* of the various effects, and calculate the net effect. One can only obtain a satisfactory overall assessment of the effect of immigrants on the standard of living of citizens by constructing an integrated model of the economy, and then comparing the incomes produced by the economy under various conditions of immigration and population growth.[6]

For simplicity and clarity, the model deals with a single cohort of immigrants; a continuous analysis yields similar results, however. Also for simplicity, I sometimes talk of a representative family instead of the cohort as a whole.

The question is whether the native population – that is, the people living in the country *before* the immigrant family arrives – are better off or worse off economically if the immigrant comes or does not. In more precise terms, we wish to know if the lifetime income Z of the (average member of the) native population is higher or lower if the immigrant comes, that is, whether

$$Z_m > Z_n \quad \text{or} \quad Z_n > Z_m$$

Lifetime incomes with and without the immigration are, for our purposes here, functions of gross income G less taxes T discounted at d

$$Z_m = (G_{m, t=1} - T_{m, t=1}) + d(G_{m, t=2} - T_{m, t=2}) + \ldots \qquad (9.1)$$

and

$$Z_n = (G_{n, t=1} - T_{n, t=1}) + d(G_{n, t=2} - T_{n, t=2}) + \ldots \qquad (9.2)$$

Therefore, we must estimate the natives' yearly gross incomes and taxes if there are, and if there are not, immigrants.

The Effect of Immigration Upon Gross Incomes of Natives

We start with the effect of the immigrant on natives' incomes through the two major lines of influence: (a) the capital-dilution effect, and (b) the economies-of-scale-and-productivity effect. I have estimated the combined effect of these two forces in a macro-model similar to the set-up in chapter 8,[7] though using the simpler knowledge-production function

$$A_t - A_{t-1} = aA_{t-1}^{\Delta}L_{t-1}^{\gamma} \qquad \gamma, \Delta = 0.5 \tag{9.3}$$

The other equations and parameters of the model are:

$$Y_t = A_t L_t^{\beta} K_t^{\alpha} \tag{9.4}$$

$$K_t = sY_{t-1} + K_{t-1} \tag{9.5}$$

$$L_t = L_{t-1} + 0.02L_{t-1} \tag{9.6}$$

The initial values are $A_t = 1.0$, $K_t = 1\,000$, $Y_t = 500$, $\alpha = 0.67$, $\beta = 0.33$, $\gamma = 0.5$, $\Delta = 0.5$ and b is chosen so the initial rate of change of $A = 0.02$ yearly. The initial $L = 1\,000$ for the without-immigration case, and $1\,020$ for the with-immigration case.[8]

For the income-effect calculations the increment of immigrant workers in period $t = 1$ must be large enough so that the effects are not obscured by rounding error. It was therefore set equal to a 2 per cent increase in native labour force in year $t = 1$ (10 per cent in some runs to show that the size of the increment matters little). Then the difference in citizens' incomes in future years between the situations (a) if the immigrants do come in $t = 1$, and (b) if they do not come, are calculated. The final calculation is in terms of the effect of one additional immigrant.

Concerning the extent to which immigrants gain the returns from the capital with which they work, table 9.2 shows various calculations which should cover all possible values; 35 per cent is the value that I have continued to work with, for the following set of reasons:

TABLE 9.2

The effect of an immigrant upon the incomes of natives at various assumptions about the proportion of capital returns that go to immigrants (expressed as a percentage of the immigrant's earnings)

| Year | Assumptions about the capture of returns to capital | | | | | |
| | 20% | | | 35% | | |
	(1) Income effect, %	(2) Social security	(3) Total	(4) Income effect, %	(5) Social security	(6) Total
1	−7	+10	+3	−14	+10	−4
2	−7	+10	+3	−12	+10	−2
3	−5	+10	+5	−11	+10	−1
4	−4	+10	+6	−10	+10	0
5	−2	+10	+8	−8	+10	+2
6	−1	+10	+9	−7	+10	+3
7	1	+10	+11	−5	+10	+5
8	2	+10	+12	−4	+10	+6
9	4	+10	+14	−3	+10	+7
10	5	+10	+15	−1	+10	+9
11	7	+10	+17	0	+10	+10
12	8	+10	+18	+2	+10	+12
13	10	+10	+20	+3	+10	+13
14	11	+10	+21	+4	+10	+14
15	13	+10	+23	+6	+10	+16
16	14	+10	+24	+7	+10	+17
17	16	+10	+26	+8	+10	+18
18	17	+10	+27	+10	+10	+20
19	18	+10	+28	+11	+10	+21
20	20	+10	+30	+12	+10	+22
21	21	+10	+31	+14	+10	+24
22	23	+10	+33	+15	+10	+25
23	24	+10	+34	+16	+10	+26
24	25	+10	+35	+18	+10	+28
25	27	+10	+37	+19	+10	+29
26	28	+10	+38	+20	+10	+30
27	30	+10	+40	+21	+10	+31
28	31	+10	+41	+23	+10	+33
29	32	+10	+42	+24	+10	+34
30	34	+10	+44	+25	+10	+35

(a) though I do not regard the returns-to-capital approach as funda-mentally sound, for reasons given above, it probably is still the prevailing view. And 35 per cent surely is far above any reasonable value, if the returns-to-capital approach makes sense. (b) A sounder approach, in my view, is to add the demographic-capital effect (which might be about 2 per cent of income each year, one-fifth of the transfers-and-taxes effect), with the government-capital effect (which is another 2 per cent of each year's income, on reasoning given earlier) and then work backwards with a returns-to-capital framework to arrive at an estimate of roughly 10 per cent. This is much less than the 35 per cent figure used. Any lower value shows immigrants to be even more favourable for natives' incomes.[9]

On the 35 per cent assumption, the pre-tax effects on citizens' incomes amount to the percentages of the immigrant's net income shown in column 4. Those figures may be interpreted as follows: in year 1, citizens' incomes are (in the aggregate) lower by 14 per cent of the income of the average immigrant, aside from taxes (though the effect on individual natives is very small because of the small proportion of immigrants relative to natives). By year 12, citizens' net incomes are higher than they would otherwise be, because of the immigrants. By year 19, citizens' incomes are higher by an amount equal to 10 per cent of the income of each immigrant who arrives in year 0.

Now we must take account of the immigrants' saving-and-transfer effect as discussed in section III. Social security is the main issue. Immigrants collect no social security, both because of age distribu-tion and because of not being entitled to any benefits in the present. The immigrant family's contributions are assumed to be roughly 10 per cent of earnings (in reality 14 per cent as of 1982; see p. 158). This makes the overall accounts positive in year 5 and thereafter, and just *slightly* negative in years 1–4, as seen in column 6.

The stream of negative and positive effects may be evaluated just like any other investment with negative outgoings at the beginning and positive incomes later on. On a capital-returns assumption of 35 per cent, the rate of return on the 'investment' decision to bring in an immigrant is 9.3 per cent per annum without the social security effect, and 19.3 per cent with it, an excellent investment by any standard.[10]

The results of a variety of other specifications of the basic model with respect to savings rate, initial rate of technical progress, propor-

TABLE 9.3

Rates of return on investment in immigrants for a variety of models (increment of immigrants equal to 2 per cent of labour force in $t = 1$)

				Rates of return per annum in per cents	
b	s	γ, Δ	Capital capture %	Without social security	With social security
0.02	0.04	0.5	0.2	18.4	28.4
0.02	0.04	0.5	0.35	9.3	19.3
0.02	0.07	0.5	0.35	12.2	22.2
0.02	0.10	0.5	0.35	14.8	24.8

tion of returns to capital captured by immigrants and exponents of the technical progress function are shown in table 9.3. The very lowest rate of return for any reasonable set of parameters is 0 per cent (not a negative rate, however) for the results *without* the transfer-payment effect, and 10 per cent with it. So immigrants are an excellent 10 per cent-return-per-annum investment even under these most 'conservative' of parameters.

V.   DISCUSSION

In discussions of the economic impact of immigrants on natives' standard of living, transfer payments and social welfare programmes (other than social security) are often suggested as a negative offset to the positive effects of the immigrants. In fact, however, immigrants seem to have an overall *positive* effect through these other transfers. One reason, in the case of the US, is the simple kind of economies of scale with respect to the defense budget; it is likely to be invariant to the number of immigrants, and therefore immigrants reduce defense expenditures per citizen.

As to whether immigrants are disproportionate gainers from transfers because of having low income, Chiswick (1978) has shown that only a few years after entry into the US immigrants typically approach or equal natives in income, at which time their taxes should be roughly equal to natives'. And preliminary findings from my analysis of the 1976 Survey of Income and Education show that the difference between other welfare payments to immigrants and to natives is small compared to the difference in social security payments.

Concerning illegals, North and Houston (1976) found that 73 per cent of illegal aliens had Federal income tax withheld, and 77 per cent paid social security tax – even though they can never collect on it. On the other hand, the proportions who use welfare services are small: medical, 27 per cent; unemployment insurance, 4 per cent; child schooling, 4 per cent; federal job training, 1 per cent; food stamps, 1 per cent; welfare payments, 1 per cent. (See Simon, 1985, for a more complete survey of the relevant evidence.) And practically no illegals or Cubans or Indo-Chinese are in a position to avail themselves of the most expensive welfare programmes of all: social security and other aid to the elderly.

The reader may wonder whether a person need live in the United States in order that the US obtain the benefit of the person's impact on productivity. The answer differs somewhat depending on the person's origin, whether from a more-developed or a less-developed country. The answer may also depend on the person's education and occupation, but the former is more clear-cut and probably much more important.

Recall that a person may influence technical progress through both his/her demand for goods and his/her supply of knowledge. Let us consider each of these separately beginning with the more problematic case, that of the person who already lives in a more-developed country such as Sweden or Japan.

It is indeed true that there is international trade, and a Swede's demand for goods may be satisfied in the US. But it is also true, and more relevant, that only a small proportion of US goods are sold abroad. It is more likely that an increment of US-made cars or newspapers or smoke detectors will be sold if a given person chooses to reside this year in the US rather than in Sweden. This should be enough to make the point. But an even more conclusive argument comes from a more general view of trade: if a person comes to the US and still imports a Swedish car, Sweden's imports (directly or indirectly) from the US will rise by the amount of other goods equal in value to the auto. Therefore, total production in the US will rise by the amount of the immigrant's output and income, along with an effect through learning-by-doing and other demand-induced productivity-increasing mechanisms.

We must also consider, however, whether the flow of technology among developed countries is so free that it does not matter in which country the technical progress is first made. By now there seems to be consensus among students of the subject that it does matter, for a variety of reasons. For one thing, there is a time lag in the transfer of technology. Second, much technical progress is a matter of local adaptation, such as new agricultural varieties and techniques that depend on particular soil and climatic conditions; this is why even individual states within the US can get a high return on R&D in agriculture (Griliches, 1958; Evenson, 1968).

If a person goes from a poor country where little new technology is being created, to a rich country where much technology is being created, the argument above is obviously even stronger. Here the US benefits not merely by the person contributing to technology that will be differentially helpful to the US, but also by the absolute increment of technology that the person creates. The more technically advanced (relative to the state of the art) is the industry a person works in, the greater the opportunity for that person to advance the state of the art, it would seem.

It is not a contradiction to this line of thought that the rate of economic growth *per capita* has been as high or higher in the poorer countries as in the US in the post-Second World War period. The poorer countries can take advantage of the technological progress in the richer countries much more than the reverse.

In brief, on reasonable assumptions immigrants have a positive discounted effect on citizens' incomes, starting almost immediately and getting large quite rapidly.

VI.   SUMMARY AND CONCLUSIONS

The subject of this chapter is the effect of an additional immigrant upon the incomes of 'natives' of a country like the US. In the past, the capital-dilution aspect of the subject has been approached with the concept of 'returns to capital'; the extent of the negative capital-dilution effect was measured by the putative extent of the capture of these returns by natives. But this concept does not hold up upon inspection; the only returns to capital obtained by immigrants are the returns captured by those immigrants working for government. There is also a capital cost to natives of immigrants' use of 'demographic capital'. But because these complexities are outside the scope of this book, the capital-returns concept is used as an operational proxy for all capital effects. And the parameter used here is far larger than any conceivable actual capital costs to natives.

Transfer payments and taxes are very important effects of immigration, bestowing a large net benefit upon natives. This effect is also included in the model.

The effect of the immigrant upon productivity – the sum of learning-by-doing, creation of new knowledge and economies of scale of various sorts – is also embodied in the model. Within a few years, the productivity effect comes to dominate the results and dwarf the capital-dilution and saving-and-transfer effects.

Overall, the model shows a very high rate of return to natives on 'investment' in immigrants, on any reasonable parameters.

NOTES

1   By 'native' I mean those residing in the country prior to the arrival of the immigrant in question. There is no good term in English to cover this concept. Israeli writers on immigration use 'veteran', but this sounds unfamiliar in English. 'Citizen' focuses attention on legal rather than residential status. 'Native' seems to exclude prior immigrants, which I do not intend to do, but it seems to be the best term nevertheless.

2   This line of reasoning implicitly assumes that there is only one wage-earning occupation in the economy. If this assumption is relaxed, the analysis is more complex. If there are a variety of occupations and the immigrants come with the same distribution of skills as the natives, then the result is the same as it would be if there was only one occupation. But if the immigrants come with a different distribution of skills, then there are the same sorts of overall gains to trade that occur in international trade of goods. On the other hand, the occupations that are disproportionately represented by the immigrants suffer worse wage declines than average. The Vietnamese immigrants of the late 1970s and the Cuban immigrants of 1980 seem to have a broad spectrum of occupations, whereas the Mexicans seem to be largely semi-skilled labourers, so both sorts of cases seem to be important. The general question of an effect analogous to gains to trade was raised in

conversation by Mark Rosenzweig, and to my knowledge has not been analysed. Hence I have no feeling for how important it may be. But to the extent that it operates, it has a beneficial effect on the average native's income.

3 The longer run effects in years after entrance, and as the immigrant grows older, will be analysed later.

4 These calculations arise from runs of the model with a 4 per cent savings rate. At a more realistic higher savings rate, the capital-dilution effect on natives is less over the years.

5 No mention is made here of other taxes and transfers with respect to immigrants. For citizens as a whole, these flows balance out. Because of the 'favourable' age distribution of immigrants and their high rate of employment, the net effect is almost surely that immigrants pay more in taxes than the cost of the other services they use. [See Simon (1984) for more details.]

A traditional but fallacious related argument in favour of immigration must be dealt with here. It has been alleged at least since Francis Walker, the first president of the American Economic Association, that immigrants are a better 'buy' than additional children because immigrants arrive with the publicly financed portion of their educations already paid for by another country's public (or in more modern arguments, at a lower cost). This argument may be appropriate and relevant when historians (e.g. Neal and Uselding, 1972) look backward, assume some substitution between additional children and additional immigrants and reckon the advantage to having had immigrants. But the argument is not relevant when the discussion is forward-looking (e.g. Blitz, 1977), and the native fertility of the country of immigration is assumed invariant to immigration; it is then not reasonable to calculate apparent savings on the education of immigrants, because sunk costs are sunk for decision-making purposes; the only question for policy purposes is whether the *future* native incomes and outgoings will be on balance more positive or negative with the immigrant's presence than without it. Of course an immigrant's education and human capital have an effect through the gains to capital discussed earlier, as well as through possible gains to trade (see endnote 2, this chapter). But these effects cannot be estimated by valuing the cost of the immigrant's education or the cost of the same education in the country of immigration.

6 After finishing this chapter I discovered an interesting model by Ekberg (1977) which also makes technical progress endogenous in a migration context. Ekberg uses a Kaldor-like function, where the increment to technical progress depends upon the percentage change in the stock of capital, which I elsewhere argue is not very appropriate for a study of this sort. My 1976 article on Russian immigration into Israel is the only other study of the sort I know of.

7 The exponents are those that fit the requirement that the function be homogeneous of degree one, and Phelps's assumption that 'if the technology level should double we would require exactly twice the amount of research to double the absolute time rate of increase of the technology' (1966, p. 135). The assumption of the steady-state savings rate is also 'conservative' in the sense that it is less advantageous to a larger population (and hence to immigrants) than would be a higher savings rate; this is reasonably clear upon inspection, and is verified in other work by this writer. The coefficient a is that complement of the initial values chosen for A and L which starts the simulation smoothly into motion and which corresponds to the steady-state rate of change of A in the non-immigrant case, which is equal to the rate of growth of the labour force in Phelps's model; it is kept the same in the plus-immigrants case so as to hold all initial conditions exactly the same in the two cases except the growth of the labour force; this, too, is a 'conservative' assumption in the sense explained above.

An iterative programme is used to make investment approximately a function of current-period income rather than prior-period income, so that the computer model would approximate the steady-state analytic model; the results are much the same with and without this refinement, however.

8 There would appear to be no danger here that the choice of production function forces the outcome, as in some studies of distributive shares. The cohort of immigrants whose effect is analysed is small relative to the native population, and hence its effect upon the overall distribution between capital and labour.

Additionally, Ekberg (1977) experimented with a constant elasticity of substitution (CES) function and obtained the same results as with a Cobb–Douglas model.

9 The reader may wonder about how the representative immigrant's share of capital, and the returns to it, changes with years of residence in the US, and whether this is reflected in the model. With time, the immigrant's share rises to 100 per cent, of course. But this is counter-balanced by purchase payments by immigrants which are necessarily financed by higher-than-average saving. Hence the result should be the same whether this is explicitly shown in the model, or implicitly as in the present model.

10 11.1 per cent and 21.1 per cent for the larger increment of immigrants.

10
Summary and Conclusions

Summarizing this book is easy. The standard theoretical analyses of both Malthusian statics and growth-theoretic dynamics conclude that additional people have negative effects upon the standard of living. The operative mechanism is capital dilution, plain and simple, in both those sorts of analyses. But when various feedbacks of population size are brought into the models – especially the creation of new technology in response to increased demand, and as a result of there being more knowledge creators – the conclusions are altered radically. Additional people are then seen to have a positive effect in the long run.

In the short run, however, before the system has time to adjust, more people do cause a lowering of the standard of living. The key welfare-economics question is whether the overall effect should be judged as positive or negative, given a particular discount factor and the pattern of negative and positive effects over time.[1] The analysis carried out here suggests that using reasonable discount factors, the overall effect is likely to be evaluated as positive, when the main forces are taken into account.

The highly aggregated theoretical analyses that form the main part of the book are buttressed by micro-economic theoretical analysis of the processes of invention and adoption of innovations, and also by empirical data on the relationship of population size to various measures of technology creation and productivity, and to the availability of natural resources. This material also jibes with the historical record. For example, the standard analysis suggests that the economy should be improved across the board by the Black Death. But though some farmers and labourers may have benefited, the economy as a whole suffered badly from depression as an aftermath of that catastrophe.

The material presented in this book also fits together with the empirical data presented in the first part of my 1977 book concerning the relationship of population to other key elements of the economic mechanism, for example, health, the amounts of farm and non-farm capital per person and the amounts of work people do, though the main emphasis of that book was on less-developed countries whereas the main emphasis of this book is on the modern technology-creating regions and industries of the world considered as a single sector.

In 1970 I concluded a book on the economics of advertising – a subject to which I had devoted all my best energies for several years – by saying that the topic did *not* warrant additional research, in my judgement. The key economic issues with respect to advertising are not subject to serious question or public debate, except at their fringes, and the important public questions about advertising all relate to public taste and ethics rather than to economics. I mention this to establish my credentials as a person who does not automatically call for more research.

It is quite different with the economics of population, however. People are the *only* important element in an economy, not only because they are the key productive factor but also because their welfare is the central object of economic endeavour. (Some would say it is the *only* object, while others include in their social welfare functions the welfare of animal and plant life, and of natural conditions.) And the number of persons is affected by government policies and private views – for example, immigration laws everywhere, and natality policies in China and Singapore and Eastern Europe – that are based in important part upon judgements about the economic effects of more or fewer people. Therefore it behoves us to do more and better research on this topic. Considering the importance of the topic, extraordinarily little research has been done in the past or is being done at present, in part because funding of research in economic demography has almost all gone to the study of the determinants of demographic changes rather than to study of the consequences, and to research on the consequences among animals rather than in human society. It is my hope (though I confess not my expectation) that it will be different in the future.

Yet, research or no, people almost surely will prevail in the future, as they have prevailed in the past. There will continue to be more people in the very long run, despite possible plateaus and declines, even as people sensibly evaluate their costs. And there will be a higher standard of living, at first despite the greater numbers and then later because of them. On that confident note I happily end.

NOTES

1 Alfred Marshall, in his *Principles*, says that Time (with a capital T) is the chief difficulty in understanding economic processes. Nowhere is this more true than in the evaluation of the effects of population size and growth.

APPENDIX A

A Constant Long-run K/Y Ratio is a Meaningless Observation

I. INTRODUCTION

Received growth theory is about steady states. A steady state is characterized by a constant capital–output ratio. And one of the key putative 'stylized facts' upon which growth theory builds, and against which it tests its propositions, is – in Solow's words – that 'the ratio of capital to output shows no systematic trend' (1970, p. 2).

This appendix argues, however, that this 'stylized fact' has no economic meaning. The observed monetized capital–output ratio is not an appropriate comparison with the physical growth-theoretic results. And to the relevant extent that it is meaningful to discuss changes in the physical capital–output ratio, it probably has been falling, as theory leads us to expect. The appendix reconciles these ideas, showing how the monetized K/Y ratio can be constant or nearly constant, even if the relevant physical ratio is falling.

The basic idea seems odd at first reading; indeed the entire matter seemed very odd to the writer when first coming upon it, simply because the conclusion is at odds with all conventional practice. But it is hoped that the reader will not be put off by this unconventionality.

Notation

L = labour force
Y_j^i = total output in market i during period j
K = stock of capital
$v = Y/K$ = reciprocal of capital–output ratio
w = the wage rate
r = rate of return on capital
c, α, β = constants

II. THE ARGUMENT

Typical citations showing a constant K/Y ratio are Denison's data for the US and eight European countries for 1950–1962; Barger's for 1950–1964; Mathews' and Feinstein's UK data for 1856–present (all cited by Solow, 1970, pp. 5–7); and the CED–Denison data for the US from 1909 to 1958 (US Department of Commerce, p. 189). Eltis (1973, p. 266) cites estimates by Kendrick and Sato (1963) and Klein and Kosobud (1961) as showing that the K/Y ratio has fallen in the US in the twentieth century. But Kuznets (1973, pp. 121–64) concluded that we do not know whether the monetary K/Y ratio was higher than at present even in pre-modern times (say 1688 in England). But as we shall see shortly, this argument is not relevant here, because it is not meaningful.[1]

These data on the K/Y ratio all purport to show that two independent entities – K and Y – remain in a constant relationship. In all cases the estimates of output are in monetized valuations from national income accounts, and the estimates of capital come from various surveys of assets measured in money. These modes of measurement are of the utmost importance for the argument.

In the long run, however, the money values of output and capital are not, and *cannot be*, in a very different ratio than is observed because of *market forces inherent in competitive markets*. That is to say, the K/Y ratio does not indicate a constant *physical* relationship between capital and output. (And please keep in mind that a production function is basically a physical-technological construct.) The reason is this: in a competitive market, the price of output is determined only by the total cost of inputs; if the price of bulldozers falls, the price of bulldozing will fall. Hence if the money cost of the capital or labour input falls due to technological change, the money value per unit of output in that market must fall also. The rest of the argument is an elaboration of this simple observation, and a straightforward proof that, using quite realistic assumptions, the two quantities change by the same proportion. This is the cause of the observed constant K/Y ratio.

A word about the valuation and measurement of capital: the estimates of the capital shares of a given country made by government organizations and individual scholars are, of course, subject to a large number of difficulties. Ideally one would measure the current market value of the various chunks of capital, thereby reflecting current technology and capital condition. But the actual published estimates derive largely from (a) estimates of depreciation, which are not likely to come very close to market facts, together with (b) original purchase prices, whose meaning is much affected by technological change and inflation. These difficulties are among the many which muddy the meaning of a capital-stock estimate. But in the long run these errors of estimation must tend to wash out and leave some rough correspondence between the book value and the market value of a country's capital, as is assumed by those who estimate capital stocks; this is all that is required for discussion here. Furthermore, to the extent that there is indeed relative constancy of the K/Y ratio, as is claimed for that stylized fact, it is itself evidence that the book-value estimates bear some stable relationship to market value.

There are also the enormous conceptual difficulties concerning the notion of an aggregate production function which are associated with the Cambridge controversy. But these issues need not detain us here because the aim is not to elucidate the meaning of the capital term in the K/Y ratio, or to discuss the meaning of aggregate production functions, but rather only to explain why the monetized K/Y ratio is likely to remain unchanged with time.

Before stating the argument more precisely, it is illuminating to look at a related situation where capital and output also remain in a constant ratio. In agriculture, the market value of a unit of land is roughly four times the market value of the output of that unit of land, in countries ranging from China to Australia, in all the years for which data are available.[2] The explanation of this constancy is that when the value of output changes, the price that is bid for land changes in response. Therefore, the ratio of land capital in money to farm output in money tells nothing whatever about the physical facts of production, but only about capital markets and portfolio behaviour.

Land may not seem perfectly analogous to industrial capital because the overall amounts in acres vary less from year to year than do physical measures of capital. But as with industrial capital, land's market price is influenced both by the demand for it as well as by the supply-side cost of clearing new land and of improving old farmland with irrigation and drainage. Perhaps the main difference between land and industrial capital is that the market in farmland is mostly in old farmland where the costs have been sunk long ago, whereas most industrial capital transactions are in new capital.[3]

Now let us return to the industrial K/Y ratio. Assume that labour's share of output is β; we do not fully understand why β should be near-constant over time and similar in various countries, but that it is indeed such a near-constant is a fact that we can safely build upon;[4] figure A.1 shows some relevant data graphed by Brems. They suggest that labour's share is reasonably constant over time in the US, and among Denison's sample of nine Western countries. Of course these data do not *prove* constancy, nor could any data, but the hypothesis of a trend in the US, or meaningful differences among the nine countries, certainly cannot be confirmed with tests of statistical significance. This should accord to this constancy of labour's share a status as a stylized fact at least as secure as the constancy of the monetized K/Y ratio. Hence this should not be a sticking point in the argument.[5]

There are many theories of this constancy in labour's share, but none of them use the capital–output ratio as an argument, and hence the argument of this appendix is not affected by which theory of this constancy the reader prefers. Therefore, let us simply say that, one way or another, labour always negotiates or fights or competes itself into share β of total output.

We can also take as a reasonable stylized fact that the rate of return on capital has no trend; US data supporting this assumption are shown in figure A.2 (Brems, 1980); the comments made above about the data on labour's share also apply to these data.

We can now write

$$Y = wL + rK \tag{A.1}$$

and

$$wL = \beta Y \tag{A.2}$$

Hence

$$rK = \alpha Y \tag{A.3}$$

since $Y = \alpha Y + \beta Y$.

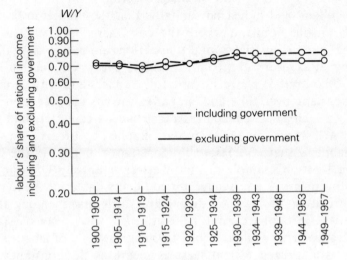

Kravis I B 'Relative Income Shares in Fact and Theory', *Am. Econ. Rev.* Dec. 1959, *49*, 919 and 928.

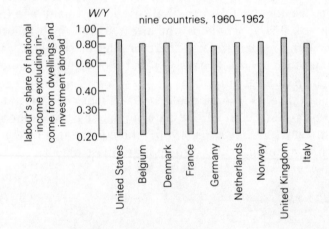

Denison E F *Accounting for United States Economic Growth 1929–1969*, Washington, D.C., 1974, 260.

Denison E F *Why Growth Rates Differ, Postwar Experience in Nine Western Countries*, Washington, D.C., 1967, 42.

FIGURE A.1   Labour's share *W/Y* US, 1900–57 and nine countries 1960–2
(*Source:* Brems, 1980, pp. 43, 44)

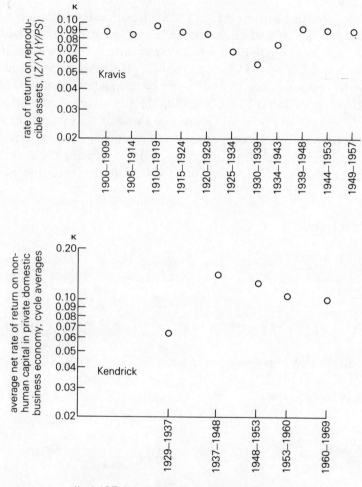

Kravis I B 'Relative Income Shares in Fact and Theory', *Am. Econ. Rev.* Dec. 1959, *49*, 938.

Kendrick J W assisted by Lethem Y, Rowley J *The Formation and Stocks of Total Capital*, New York 1976, 124.

FIGURE A.2   Rate of return on capital *x*, US, 1900–69
(*Source:* Brems, 1980, p. 40)

Assume that these relationships hold in representative market 1, in period 1. Let us further suppose that (where market is the super-script, and period the subscript) in market 1 the amount of capital needed to produce output Y_1^1 falls sharply, because either labour or capital becomes more efficient. To fix the imagination, let us visualize an example cited by IBM: 'A set of computations that cost $1.26 on an IBM computer in 1952 costs only 7/10ths of a cent today.'[6] Assume for convenience that demand is completely inelastic. If so, the value of the capital in use will fall sharply to some cK_1^1, where c is some constant less than unity, and the value of output will *also* fall until the new price of computing services equals the new cost. We can figure the new value of output as follows (writing the argument in an algebraically extended form as an aid to the intuition in this counter-intuitive matter):

By assumption

$$(wL)_2^1 = \beta Y_2^1 \tag{A.4}$$

and

$$Y_2^1 = (wL)_2^1 + rK_2^1 \tag{A.5}$$

By definition and previous assumption

$$rK_2^1 = \alpha Y_2^1 = rcK_1^1 \tag{A.6}$$

and

$$rK_1^1 = \alpha Y_1^1 \tag{A.7}$$

Divide (A.7) by (A.6)

$$\frac{rK_1^1}{rcK_1^1} = \frac{\alpha Y_1^1}{\alpha Y_2^1} \tag{A.8}$$

cancel and rearrange

$$Y_2^1 = cY_1^1 \tag{A.9}$$

By definition

$$v_1^1 = \frac{Y_1^1}{K_1^1}, \quad \text{and} \quad v_2^1 = \frac{Y_2^1}{K_2^1} \tag{A.10}$$

and hence by definition and cancellation

$$v_2^1 = \frac{cY_1^1}{cK_1^1} = v_1^1 \tag{A.11}$$

So we see that the capital–output ratio in market-value terms remains constant when there is an increase in productivity. It would be more complex to extend the analysis to the economy as a whole, but the matter would seem sufficiently obvious intuitively so that such a demonstration is not necessary.[7]

III. THE ACTUAL COURSE OF THE PHYSICAL K/Y RATIO

Now that we have seen that there is no empirical reason in the observed monetary K/Y ratios to believe that the physical K/Y ratio is constant, we are free to theorize about the course of the physical K/Y ratio as economic development proceeds. One may choose not to engage in this speculation at all, a position that is perfectly consistent with one implication of this appendix, that is, that a growth model may imply a decreasing K/Y ratio; one can simply ignore the K/Y ratio completely. But it seems to me that such speculation is at least interesting even if it has no implication, because it illuminates the process of economic development.

A falling physical capital–output ratio seems to me to be an obvious technological fact – or at least it is obvious once we put behind us the idea of a capital–output ratio in value terms. To show this we must proceed in step-by-step fashion, making only those comparisons that can legitimately be made, and not making illegitimate comparisons. This means that we cannot compare entire capital stocks, largely because new consumer products are introduced with the passage of time.

Let us begin with identical tools used to make identical products at different moments in history. Consider the important example of farmland. A given acre of Illinois land produces – even after other physical inputs are allowed for – a much larger amount of corn now than in earlier years. And if an Amish farmer chooses to work with horses, the horses together with the Illinois land produce more output per acre and per horse (with equal or fewer man hours) than in previous years. And there is no reason not to attribute this increased output–capital ratio to labour-augmenting technological progress – better calendars, better knowledge of hybrid seeds, information about optimal planting depths, improvements in motive power and so on. Or take the homely example of the claw hammer, which has changed little in form for many years; the amount of fastening that a carpenter does in a day with a claw hammer has risen considerably over the years because of improvements in nails, materials to be fastened, materials transportation and so on. And still other examples: with the same endowment of human legs we get faster miles run, higher heights jumped and longer distances leaped, due to better knowledge of track techniques and training methods (but hopefully not because of new drugs). With the same ox or baby we now get more lifetime days of work due to better knowledge of nutrition and disease prevention. We build the same house with less stone, due to advanced civil engineering knowledge of stresses.

The same must be true of almost every tool that we now use, unchanged from earlier years, to produce the same output. And for most of these tools additional uses have been discovered over the years, which can only be interpreted as a reduction in the capital-output ratio.

If one were to consider tools for the same purpose that have *improved* over the years – diesel locomotives compared to steam locomotives or horses – the comparison is more strained, yet it suggests even more strongly an increased technological output–capital ratio. If a farmer replaces a team of horses with a tractor that uses the same number of man hours, then implicit in the replacement decision is that the new capital dominates the old, in the Pareto sense of having a higher output–capital ratio, and for this farmer the price of output may be taken as constant with respect to this decision. Unless the decision also improves a drop in man hours (which then embroils us in relative prices) the shift to the tractor may be seen immediately as a reduction in the capital-output ratio. For much of our capital stock the choice does involve relative cost valuations of labour and capital, and much other of our capital produces goods and services that were not produced in the past. Hence pairwise technological comparisons are not possible for much of our capital stock, and therefore no time-series comparison of the K/Y ratio can be made for that portion of our capital. But that in no way vitiates the obvious conclusion that where comparisons *are* reasonable and fair, the technological capital–output ratio (the K/Y ratio that everyone agrees is relevant, rather than the monetized ratio) shows a decline with the increase in per worker output and income. Therefore it is most natural and reasonable to accept as a stylized fact a decreased capital–output ratio with the passage of time.

If, however, the reader does not find the discussion in this section congenial, it may be disregarded completely. It has no bearing on the main point of this appendix.

IV. SUMMARY AND CONCLUSIONS

Standard growth models, including growth models such as Kaldor's and Arrow's that make technical progress endogenous, rely for support on their results being in accord with the observed fact of a roughly constant capital–output ratio. This appendix argues that the idea of a constant K/Y ratio is (a) fundamentally wrong in a physical-technical sense, and (b) meaningless in an economic sense, because a roughly constant K/Y ratio is a necessary outcome of an economy with roughly constant distributive shares, as is the observed fact. Capital and output measured in value terms maintain a constant relationship because the price of output is a function only of the cost of inputs in competitive markets. The appropriate capital and output concepts for a growth model are technological rather than value measures, and substitution of the latter for the former (due to difficulty of measuring the former) results in confusion, wrong-headed theory and unsound conclusions.

NOTES

1 One must be careful about concluding that the K/Y ratio is constant on the basis of studies using the Cobb–Douglas production function, which con-

strains the distributive shares to be constant, and thereby biases the K/Y ratio estimate. But there is enough evidence from other types of studies to support a conclusion that the K/Y ratio is more-or-less constant. Most important here, however, is not whether or not the ratio is constant, but that theorists *assume* it to be constant and build models in consonance with that assumption.

2 In China in 1921–25, the K/Y ratio in Chinese dollars for the average farm acre (excluding livestock and supplies) was $\$1736/\$376 = 4.6$; for land alone, it was $\$1374/\$376 = 3.7$. In Orissa, India, 1958–59, the average investment per acre was Rs.535, and in land alone it was Rs.474, whereas output there was Rs.125 per acre, a K/Y of 4.3. In the Punjab, 1955–56, the value of land averaged Rs.840 per acre, where the value of output per acre was Rs.193, giving a K/Y of about 4.3. In Andhra Pradesh in 1959–60, the K/Y ratio (land plus all other capital) was 6.4. In the years 1910–16, the ratio of land value to output ranged from 3.05 to 3.56 in Australia, Canada, France, Russia, Switzerland and the United States – countries in which land was surely a smaller proportion of total capital than in India or China. The US Midwest is the only major exception; land prices there continue to confound all analysts. (Paragraph largely drawn from Simon, 1977, p. 257, with references given therein.)

Since this paragraph was written and published, the ratio rose even higher in the US, peaking around 1980. But then it began a precipitous fall that is still continuing at the time of this writing (October 1985), and there is considerable reason to think that the process could continue until the ratio reaches 3.5 or 4. I have let the original paragraph stand because I think it illustrates the validity of the long-run historical experience in the case of this ratio (as also in the cases of other dimensions of economies) even when the experience of a few years or even decades seems to falsify it.

3 Some would question whether land should even be considered capital in this context, making the argument that land is a natural endowment and the returns to it are a rent to the descendants (natural or financial) of the person who simply affixed a mark to it. But this argument simply will not work. First, if the land were simply used and used, it would soon be useless for agriculture. Land must constantly be maintained, and this maintenance is gross investment. Second, when it was originally claimed, the land had to be cleared and made useful for agriculture. And as we know from contemporary land-clearing projects in Siberia, Brazil, Africa and elsewhere, the cost of land clearance is not far from the market value of comparable land presently in use – as one may expect. Costs per acre (2.471 acres equal one hectare) among a sample of land-development projects were: Guatemala, $32 and $91; Nigeria, $118; Sudan, $218; Ceylon, $307; Morocco, $307; United States, $612; Kenya, $973. The weighted average of a world sample of projects in settled

areas was $400 per acre. More recently, a considerably lower estimate has been made by the FAO: 'to add 5–7 million hectares to food production would cost between $137 and $312 per hectare'. For irrigation alone, on presently cultivated lands in India, the estimate is $250–$300 per acre. The weighted average cost for a variety of world projects was $325 per acre, and omitting one large project it was $581 per acre. And though some land may be cheaper to clear than others (e.g. the US Midwest was cheaper than the Brazilian jungle) even the cheapest-to-clear land was far from the 'free gift' that some historians speak of. The costs of disease, danger from Indians, isolation, lack of markets and so forth, were very substantial. Proof is found in eighteenth-century New England where people remained even though population grew to the point at which it was considered 'overcrowded' and land prices rose, because the perceived cost of opening the new land was greater. Additional evidence is the relationship of the cost of purchasing underdeveloped land to the cost of readying it for farming. In the eighteenth century a representative 40-acre US field cost $50, but fencing, clearing and cabin-building cost $250. (Footnote largely from Simon, 1977, p. 240. References given therein.)

4 If labour's share has increased, it is consistent with diminishing inequality, which certainly has *some* political–historical roots that may be considered exogenous here.

5 I regret that the data shown here are not up-to-the-minute. But they are the best product of a recent search of the literature by my colleague Hans Brems (1980).

6 Advertisement in *New York Times Magazine*, 11 November 1978, p. 63.

7 Brems (1973, p. 171) also noticed the discrepancy between the money and physical concepts of the capital coefficient, and he suggests a reconciliation by way of the rise in the prices of producer goods relative to consumer goods. This explanation is not at all incompatible with the explanation suggested above. But my inspection of the data suggests that the prices of producer and consumer goods are not likely to explain much of the effect under discussion here.

Are Natural Resources an Increasing Constraint upon Growth?

I. INTRODUCTION

Writers on economic growth from Jevons (1865) to Kaldor (1957) to Samuelson (1975) have mostly regarded natural resources[1] as a special kind of brake on economic growth. And in the case of economists such as Kaldor and Samuelson, resources have been seen as a qualification to the proposition that growth might continue forever in a benign fashion. Yet – curious behaviour for economists – this argument has not been formalized or even compared to the historical record, but has only been offered as an *ex cathedra* truism.[2]

Examined more closely, however, the proposition that natural resources are a special kind of brake on growth is far from obvious or unarguable. As many writers have pointed out, natural resources have had progressively decreasing importance in the global budget (Barnett and Morse, 1963) and in influencing the fates of particular countries, for example, Japan and Hong Kong (Bauer, 1981). This fact is not easily consistent with the conventional idea that the resource situation grows worse rather than better with increasing use of resources as history unfolds. And even casual inspection of the historical record shows that resource costs have not been rising, no matter what measurement you look at.[3] Yet more needs to be said on the subject to make the point convincing.

This appendix tackles the question as follows. After some clarification of concepts, the historical record is examined. We see long-term trends of falling cost of raw materials as far back as there is data (to 2500 BC in some cases). And we also have evidence on elasticity of substitution between raw materials and other productive inputs that makes sense of the falling costs. But there is no logical necessity that the future will see a continuation of this trend, just as there can never be such a logical necessity for any prediction. And many persons interested in this topic have opined – usually based on the assumption of fixity or finitude of resources plus Malthusian diminishing returns – that these benign trends will reverse in the future. Though a very long observed trend might itself be basis enough for a prudent forecaster to prefer its evidence to contrary theoretical speculation, the argument for a continued trend of cost reduction in natural resources would be stronger if there is also plausible theoretical reason for such a trend. Therefore, this appendix continues with a criticism of the standard argument for long-run increasing scarcity. It then proceeds to offer a theoretical framework which suggests that continuation of cost reduction is not impossible or implausible. This theoretical discussion begins with physical principles and then continues with economic arguments built upon those physical principles. The reader anxious to get to the new idea may skip the review section and jump to the end.

A central issue is how to characterize resources, of which copper and land and oil will serve as examples of different types. Resources clearly are a kind of capital upon which we draw. Natural resources *seem* different from factories and dams, however. And this is the nub of the seeming difference: we are accustomed to thinking that we augment our stock of non-resource capital by diverting some production from consumption to savings. But we do not usually think of augmenting our stocks of copper, land and oil in the same fashion; this seems to fly in the face of apparently commonsensical physical facts. I do not think that the appropriate physical interpretation of this apparent difference is as common sense has it, though.[4] I shall try to show that an economic interpretation leads to thinking of natural resources as quite analogous to other capital in respect to their stocks being augmentable, at a cost not greater than other capital, and at a cost that is not increasing with time but rather is decreasing. If this is so, then natural resources do not require special attention in the context of discussions of growth theory.

II.   ABOUT THE CONCEPTS OF SCARCITY AND COST[5]

Before beginning on the main work, a few comments on key concepts seem needed, beginning with 'scarcity'. It is more congenial for economists than for physical scientists to consider cost – outgo in physical or money terms, relative to some other quantity – as the appropriate measure of scarcity, rather than an actual or hypothetical estimate of physical quantities. But not all economists are satisfied with such a cost concept. Nor is the appropriate cost index always obvious. Therefore, some discussion of cost and scarcity is needed.

Ask yourself: if copper – or oil or any other good – were much scarcer today than it actually is, what would be the evidence of this economic scarcity. That is, what are the signs – the criteria – of a raw material being in short supply? Upon reflection perhaps you will agree that a complete absence of the material will not be a sign of scarcity. We will not reach up to the shelf and suddenly find that it is completely bare. It is obvious that the scarcity of any raw material would only gradually increase. Long before the shelf would be bare, individuals and firms, the latter operating purely out of the self-interested drive to make future profits, would be taking steps to hoard supplies for future resale so that the shelf would never be completely bare. Of course the price of the hoarded material would be high, but there still would be some quantities to be found at some price, just as there always has been some small amount of food for sale even in the midst of the very worst famines.

The preceding observation points to a key sign of what we generally mean by increasing scarcity: a price that has persistently risen. More generally, cost and price will be our basic measures of scarcity. But there is often reason to question which measure of cost or price is more relevant in a discusion of resource scarcity.

In some situations market prices can mislead us. The price of a scarce material may not rise high enough to 'clear the market' – that is, to discourage enough potential buyers so that supply and demand come to be equal as they ultimately will come to be in a free market (or even in a satisfactorily adjusted socialist system). If the price is deliberately held down by the seller or by the government, there may be waiting lines or rationing, which may also be taken as signs of scarcity. But though lines and rationing may be efficient and fair ways of allocating scarce materials in the short run, in the longer run they are so wasteful that every sort of society tends to prevent them by letting the price rise enough to clear the market. Therefore we are not likely to see lines and rationing if there is a long-run (as contrasted to a temporary) scarcity of a raw material.

In general, then, if the scarcity of a raw material increases, its price will rise. But the converse need not be true; the price may rise even without a 'true' increase in scarcity. For example, a strong cartel may successfully raise prices, as OPEC did in 1973 even though the cost of producing oil remained unchanged. This suggests that the price in the market is not always the best measure of scarcity, and therefore we should also consider other measures.

Production costs come quickly to mind as an index of scarcity. We may measure the cost of a ton of copper by measuring the amount of workers' time necessary to produce it. But there are obvious difficulties with this approach. Capital equipment may be substituted for labour in order to economize on the use of workers' time; no allowance for the cost of the equipment is made in this approach. And some workers' time is more expensive that others'; an hour of a college-trained technician's time is worth more in the market than an hour of a pick-and-shovel man. Production costs measured in labour hours rather than in money may also be difficult to interpret because of changes in wage.

Another possible cost index is unit cost measured in payments for labour plus payments for capital. Barnett and Morse (1963) showed that, by this measure from 1870 to 1957 raw-material cost fell in much the same manner as do the other indices, but faster than in most indices. But this measurement also is not easy to make.

A more conventional approach is to compare the unit market price of, say, copper to the unit market price of some other good that seems to be unchanging – say, grain. But the cost of producing grain (and most other things) has also been changing over the years owing to changes in seeds, fertilizers, technology and so on. So if the cost of grain has been falling, then the cost of copper would be falling even if the relationship between the two prices – the terms of trade – has remained the same over the years.

A wrinkle on the terms-of-trade approach is to compare the price of copper to the price of a good whose production technology has changed little for a long time – say, a haircut. But the wages of barbers have gone up over the years, as can be seen from the fact that a barber in the US now has a much higher standard of living than did a US barber 100 years ago, because the wages of people in other occupations have risen owing to gains in technology and education. So this comparison, too, does not give us a 'true' or 'absolute' measure of changes in the price of copper.

Yet another approach is to examine the price trend of the source of the raw material – for example, the price of farmland instead of the price of grain, or the price of copper mines instead of the price of copper – relative to some other goods. But the price of the resource will rise if there is a technological improvement in production methods even if there is no change in the 'scarcity' of the product; the price of good farmland in the US rises when crop yields go up or when new machinery is introduced (though the price of poor farmland falls because it is no longer profitable to use such land at all).

And as yet we have said nothing about inflation. But allowing for price changes in a commodity due to changes in the general price level also raises a host of difficult questions.

How to choose among this welter of measures of public cost and price? We must accept the inevitable: there can be no 'true' or 'absolute' public measure of cost or price. Rather, different measures of cost give different sorts of information, useful for different purposes. But this we can say with assurance: the average cost of all consumer goods taken together – an index of consumer prices – has fallen over the years in more-developed countries, measured in terms of what an unskilled worker can buy; this is shown by the long-run increase in the standard of living. Therefore, if a raw material has remained at least level in price compared to the average of all (or of consumer) goods, its 'real' cost has fallen. And in fact the price of mineral natural resources has declined even more sharply than has the average price of other commodities, as we shall see shortly. Furthermore, all other measures of mineral costs have also declined over the long run. (See the next section. Also see Barnett and Morse, 1963; Simon, 1981. One may wish to compare Smith, 1979, though I do not feel that his work calls Barnett's conclusions in the same book into question at all.) Hence we can be quite sure that the cost of mineral natural resources has declined substantially, by any reasonable test.

A more personal – but often relevant – test of scarcity is whether you and I (and other people) feel that we can afford to buy the material. That is, the relationship between price and income may matter. If the price of food remains constant but income falls sharply, then we feel that food is more scarce. By a similar test, if our wages rise while the price of oil remains constant, our fuller pockets lead us to feel that oil is getting less scarce.

A related test of scarcity is the importance of the material in one's budget. One is not likely to say nowadays that salt has become appreciably more scarce even if its price doubles, because salt accounts for an insignificant share of our expenditures. (Once, though, salt was a precious commodity, which itself illustrates the process being described here.)

To restate the main theme: price, together with related measures such as production cost and share of income, is the appropriate test of scarcity at any given moment. What matters to us as consumers is how much we have to pay to obtain goods that give us particular services; from this standpoint, it couldn't matter less how much iron or oil there 'really' is in some natural 'stockpile'. Therefore, to understand the economics of natural resources, it is crucial to understand that the most appropriate economic measure of scarcity is the price of a natural resource compared to some relevant benchmark. Future scarcity is our interest. Our task, then, is to forecast future prices of raw materials.

III.   RESOURCES AND THE SERVICES THEY PROVIDE

It is not capital itself – and the stock of natural resources clearly should be thought of as capital – that is of interest to us, but rather the services that we get from capital. For example, it is not the computer itself, but rather the computing services we get from it, and then the use of those computing services in the production of other goods, that affects us. Similarly, it is not copper or land or oil that matters to us, but rather the services that they render in the creation of final products. Therefore the relevant measure of the stock of capital is the cost of the services that we get from the capital. The market price of new pieces of capital is an upper-bound estimate on this cost of services because of progressive increases in productivity of capital, for example, the cost of computing services has fallen sharply over the years.

If it can be shown that the cost of the services we get from raw materials has fallen as fast as the cost of producer-good capital services, then it would seem reasonable to conclude that raw materials have not been an increasing bottleneck to the production of final goods. And if there has not been a trend toward greater bottleneck constraint in the past due to raw materials, then – in the absence of reason to believe that we are now at a structural turning point, a matter dealt with in section VIII – there is at least a *prima facie* case that raw materials will not constitute a greater constraint in the future than in the past. So, given that standard series of trends in capital prices do not show much difference from trends in final goods prices, and given that raw material prices have tended to fall at least as fast as prices of final goods, the evidence suggests that the economic element that supplies services on a continuing basis – that is, capital – is increasing as satisfactorily when we consider natural resource 'capital' as when we think about other capital. Of course this notion of capital is counter-intuitive, because one cannot easily imagine looking at an increasing stock of copper or energy the way one can look at an increasing number of trucks. But when we reflect how fuzzy are our economic notions about the nature of *any* capital, this notion of natural resource capital may seem easier to accept.

To (forgive me) ground the argument a bit more, let us consider farmland. As discussed in the footnote on p. 182 of appendix A, the valuation of farmland in the market is a neat function of the land's output, about 3.5 : 1 throughout history and geography (see Clark, 1957, pp. 637–51). And we shall see that the price of farm output has been falling throughout history relative to other goods. This suggests that there has not been an increasing scarcity of farmland. And given that total agricultural output has been expanding and price has been falling, there is no basis for thinking that the underlying land-related mechanism – the stock of agricultural land capital – has not been increasing its capacity as fast as other capital.

Or consider land for housing: the price of quality-adjusted housing has not been going up over the years, and floor space is the central service that we seek from housing and from land for housing. Of course the price of a housing acre in Manhattan has been going up, just as has a farm acre's price in central Illinois, but this by itself says nothing about the mechanism yielding land services.

So far nothing has been said about *why* the cost of raw materials has not been rising, or whether there is theoretical reason to believe that raw material costs may continue to fall in the future. These theoretical issues will be addressed in a later section.

IV.   OBSERVED TRENDS IN RAW-MATERIAL SCARCITY

This section first considers trends in various indices of the cost of raw materials as materials, focusing on minerals. Then we shall dig a bit deeper into the trends in the cost of the services we get from raw materials in production. And last, we shall mention studies of natural resources in a production function to see how substitutable they are for other capital.

The historical cost record of raw materials is easy to summarize. Following on Barnett and Morse (1963), I have written about natural resources at length (1981), so I will be brief here: scarcity – as measured by the economically meaningful indicator of cost or price – has been *decreasing* rather than increasing in the long run for all raw materials except lumber and oil. Figures B.1 and B.2 show this effect for copper, which is representative of all the metals. And this trend of falling prices of copper has been going on a very long time.[6] The price of copper in labour time in the year AD 1 was about 120 times as great as it is in 1982 in the US. The price of iron was about 240 times as great then as now, and in 800 BC it was 360 times as great, while in 1800 BC it was 1620 times as great (calculated from data in Clark, 3rd edition, 1957, excursus, p. 652ff and Childe, 1942/1964).

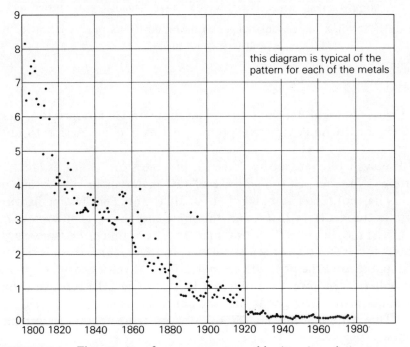

this diagram is typical of the pattern for each of the metals

FIGURE B.1   The scarcity of copper as measured by its price relative to wages

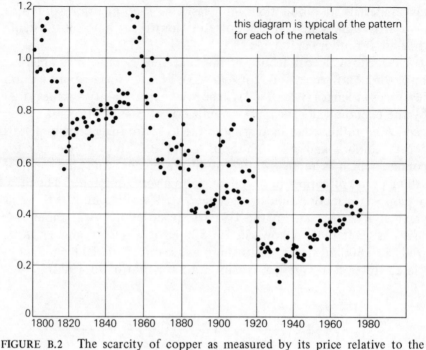

FIGURE B.2   The scarcity of copper as measured by its price relative to the
consumer price index

Figures B.3 and B.4 show the trends for materials grouped together, in relation to non-extractive product prices and in relation to unit costs.

The available data are for the US, but the story is not essentially different for the LDCs. The price of raw materials in labour time in LDCs has not fallen as markedly as in MDCs, because income has not risen as markedly in LDCs, but the price surely has fallen *somewhat* in LDCs, too, because the world market price is much the same everywhere and income has risen somewhat in LDCs. And there is reason to suppose that the price of raw materials relative to consumer prices has fallen even more sharply in LDCs than in MDCs because the production of other goods has not improved as sharply in LDCs as in MDCs (though the matter of services tempers this judgement somewhat).

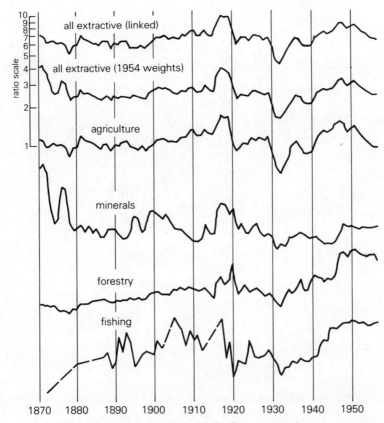

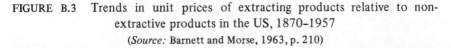

Note: solid lines connect points in annual series; dashed lines connect points over a year apart.

FIGURE B.3   Trends in unit prices of extracting products relative to non-
extractive products in the US, 1870–1957
(*Source:* Barnett and Morse, 1963, p. 210)

Food is an especially important resource, and the evidence is especially strong that we are on a benign trend despite rising population. The long-run price of food relative to wages, and even relative to consumer products, is shown in figures B.5, B.6 and B.7. Famine deaths have decreased even in absolute terms, let alone relative to population, in the past century, a matter which pertains particularly to the poor countries. *Per capita* food consumption is up over the last 30 years (figure B.8). And there are no data showing that the

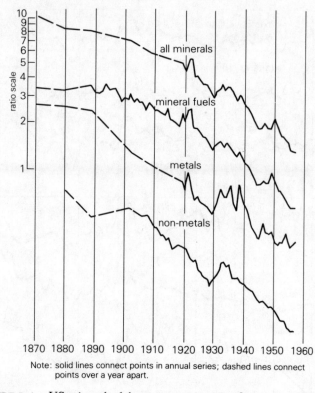

Note: solid lines connect points in annual series; dashed lines connect
points over a year apart.

FIGURE B.4　　US minerals: labour costs per unit of output, 1870–1957
(*Source:* Barnett and Morse, 1963, p. 181)

bottom of the income scale is faring worse, or even has failed to
share in the general improvement, as the average has improved. Given
the observed increase in mean income in the poor countries since the
Second World War, and given also the observed lack of widening of
the income distributions, there is *prima facie* reason to think that the
bottom of the income scale is faring better with respect to food as
well as other goods. Africa's food production *per capita* is down, but
no informed person thinks that has anything to do with physical
conditions; instead, it rather clearly stems from governmental and
other social conditions.

There is now an empirical literature of considerable size estimating
the substitution of natural resources and other input factors under

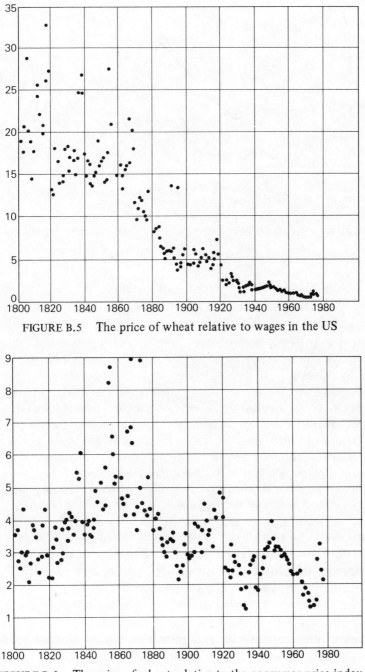

FIGURE B.5   The price of wheat relative to wages in the US

FIGURE B.6   The price of wheat relative to the consumer price index

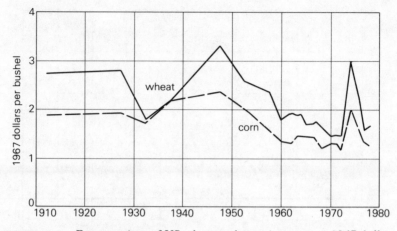

FIGURE B.7   Export prices of US wheat and corn in constant 1967 dollars

various conditions. (For a sample of recent work, see Berndt and
Field, 1981, including the introductory review by Field and Berndt.)
This literature is not directly relevant to the question at hand, however, because it does not relate such factors as population and
income changes to the substitution process. As Field and Berndt
(1981, p. 13) say:

> Finally, there is the issue of modeling technical change. In *Scarcity and
> Growth* Barnett and Morse list technological progress as the most important
> determinant of the secular decline in natural resource extraction costs and
> prices. Regrettably very little is known about factors altering the rate and
> bias of technological change. Although the theoretical literature on
> induced innovation is substantial, to the best of our knowledge this type
> of framework has not yet been amenable to empirical implementation.

Perhaps even more important, the more detailed these studies are, the
less room there is for the appearance of the effect of invention and
development of wholly new substitutes in response to price changes
of existing possibilities.

Of the studies in this tradition, one that at least tries to come close
to our interest here is that of Nordhaus and Tobin, and hence it
deserves a few more words and may serve as an illustration of the
genre. Nordhaus and Tobin experimented with a variety of three-

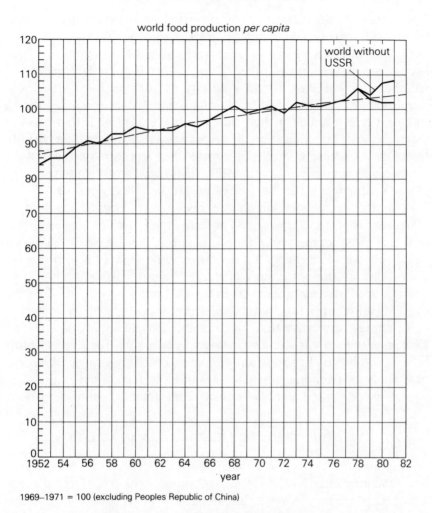

world food production *per capita*

1969–1971 = 100 (excluding Peoples Republic of China)

FIGURE B.8   World food production *per capita*
(*Source:* William J. Hudson, private communication)

factor (labour, capital, natural resources) production functions to find those that seem to explain best changes in the national product over time. Using a 'best fit' function, they estimated the elasticity of substitution between (a) natural resources and (b) a composite of labour and physical capital, regressing the ratio of the distributive shares on a function of the ratio of the inputs. The result was interpreted as an 'elasticity of substitution between neo-classical factors and resources of about 2 . . .' (1972, pp. 63–70). Also consistent with the observed facts is that technological change is natural-resource-saving relative to other factors of production. Irrespective of whether this latter or a high elasticity of substitution is the more important influence, however, Nordhaus and Tobin concluded that if 'the past is any guide for the future, there seems to be little reason to worry about the exhaustion of resources which the market already treats as economic goods'. (Of course some goods may not now be treated as economic, and therefore may have inappropriate prices placed on them. This is also true of pollution in many cases.)

A useful perspective on future raw-material scarcity is that of worst-case analysis. Singer (1981) offers rough calculations suggesting that: (a) given a reasonable time for transition – 100–200 years – we could rely on solar energy for all our energy needs at no worse than a doubling of present energy costs; (b) energy costs are now three-fourths of all raw material costs in the US; and (c) given our capacity to find substitutes for all the important non-energy raw materials in other raw materials that are available in vast quantities by any time measure, raw materials (including those used for energy) must be a bearably small proportion of our incomes even if (on his worst-case analysis assuming no major advances in technology) the prices of non-energy raw materials level off considerably higher than now.

V. SOME THEORY OF RESOURCE AVAILABILITY

In response to the suggestion that the facts of resource price trends are fundamental, Hardin (1982) responds, 'No, the facts are not fundamental. The theory is fundamental.' The 'theory' Hardin refers to is the Malthusian concept of diminishing returns. But that concept has two defects for our purposes here. First, if the concept is given content by specifying a period of the order of a human life expectation, give or take an expected length of life, that 'theory' fails completely in its predictive record; the trends have been downward throughout history despite forecasters having made dire predictions implicitly based on that concept since the beginning of recorded history and surely before.

Second, if instead of testing the 'theory' on the past they look to the future, Hardin and colleagues do not – as is their wont –

specify any observable (or even identifiable) time period during which prices will rise permanently to levels above what they are now, but simply say increased scarcity will happen 'sometime', then their theory is meaningless scientifically, according to the standard canon of scientific meaning, because a theory about 'sometime' cannot be tested, even in principle.

Hardin and similar thinkers certainly are correct, however, when they say that there is never logical entailment that past trends will continue their direction. Therefore we seek some structural knowledge of raw material scarcity. The matter will be considered first from a physical point of view, and then from an economic point of view. We shall not arrive at a theory supporting a uni-directional prediction for future trends. But I believe that we can safely conclude that there is no reason why past trends *cannot* continue.

The question that we wish to address theoretically must be kept firmly in mind: must the cost of one or more important raw materials rise in the long run? The doomsayers assert that there is theoretical reason to answer the question in the affirmative, that there is no escaping a rise in raw material cost in some very long run. Their reasoning is as follows: the reservoir of some raw material X is fixed, meaning that the reservoir cannot be increased just as the reservoir of authentic *Mona Lisa* paintings cannot be increased. (They have in mind, however, generic materials such as, say, copper and land and energy rather than one-of-a-kinds such as the *Mona Lisa* or Julius Erving; about those one-of-a-kinds there is no dispute.) Assume that the demand for the use of the material will (a) increase due to population growth or income growth or both, or (b) the reservoir will decline due to some of it being lost or otherwise unavailable, or (c) there will be both increased demand and decreased reservoir. Because (Hardin and like-minded writers assume) humankind first exploits the richest lodes and ores (that is, the lodes and ores cheapest to mine), successive mining operations will be successively more expensive; implicitly, those writers are assuming that eventually there will be either stationarity of technology or a growth in technology slower than the rate of decrease in richness of lode. Under those assumed conditions, cost must indeed increase.

Elsewhere (1981, chapters 1–3) I have said much more about the nature of technological forecasts and the variety in the forecasts made by various 'experts', so I will not repeat it here.

Certainly costs do increase during some periods, as reflected in real price rises at some times in history. And it is reasonable to suppose that during those periods the doomsday conditions hold (though price rises may sometimes be due to non-physical causes such as the formation of OPEC).

The optimistic cornucopian response to the pessimistic doomsayers is that technology to exploit the material will increase faster than the decline in richness of the reservoir. But whether this will be true or not is a matter of judgement; the history that it was so in the past is considered persuasive by the optimists but not persuasive by the pessimists. And there the matter has rested.

The only standard economic theory seemingly relevant has been Hotelling's theory of exploitation of particular exhaustible resources. That theory – which was originally intended to apply to a single mine rather than to a generic material – simply assumes the conclusion of exhaustibility and thereby formalizes the doomsday scenario sketched above. The ensuing body of theory has produced some lovely propositions which, however, are irrelevant if price will be falling rather than rising.

Stiglitz (1979) offered a theory in the neo-classical tradition which, on conventional assumptions, concludes there is no danger of resources being a brake upon economic development in the short term or intermediate term. Stiglitz's analysis is quite reasonable. It does, however, understate the optimistic outlook for raw materials because it concentrates on the substitution of capital for resources and gives short shrift to the substitution of one resource for another, the latter being the process which, in my view, is dominating, as we shall discuss shortly. It is perhaps for this reason that Stiglitz asserts that his analysis does not apply in the long run ('I am concerned here with the more immediate future', 1977, p. 37); that assertion provides a handhold which his critics can use to grapple with him.

Certainly it is correct, however, that there is never logical entailment that past trends will continue their direction. Therefore we will later seek some structural knowledge of raw-material scarcity.

Another sort of theory by economists is that of Georgescu-Roegen (1971) and Daly (1977), which expands on the assumption that energy is finite and that change in entropy should be taken into account in current economic decisions. The thrust of this theory, which they call 'neo-Malthusian', is to allocate the limited energy among generations and individuals in such fashion as to maximize a criterion of welfare which includes per-person income as well as moral well-being as measured by values specified by those writers.

It seems appropriate to illustrate the thinking of this school of thought because it is so different from the mainstream of economic thought. Unlike standard economic thought which takes tastes as given, these writers believe that the economist should choose goals for the society as well as provide intellectual machinery to help achieve goals. (Daly's book, *Steady State Economics*, is subtitled *The Economics of Biophysical Equilibrium and Moral Growth*.) As Daly puts it:

The temper of the modern age resists any discussion of the Ultimate End. Teleology and purpose, the dominant concepts of an earlier time, were banished from the mechanistic, reductionistic, positivistic mode of thought that came to be identified with the most recent phase of the evolution of science. Economics followed suit by reducing ethics to the level of personal tastes. No questions are asked about whether individual priorities are right or wrong, or even about how they are formed. The same goes for collective priorities. Whatever happens to interest the mass public is assumed to be in the public interest. Our modern refusal to reason about the Ultimate End merely assures the incoherence of our priorities, both individually and collectively. It leads to the tragedy of Herman Melville's Captain Ahab, whose means were all rational, but whose purpose was insane. The apparent purpose of growth economics is to seek to satisfy infinite wants by means of infinite production. This is about as wise as chasing a white whale, and the high rationality of the means employed cannot be used to justify the insanity of purpose. Rational means simply make insane purposes all the more dangerous. Among our presumed 'infinite' wants is there not the desire to be free from the tyranny of infinite wants? Is there not a desire for finite wants, for only good wants? If the assumption of infinite wants includes the desire for finite wants (and how could it be excluded except as a moral commandment that 'though shalt want more'?), then we have a kind of liar's paradox – one of our 'infinite' wants is the want for finite wants! And even if wants were infinite, it does not follow that infinite production, even if possible, would be capable of satisfying more than a finite subset of our 'infinite' wants. Some logical cracks thus appear in one of growth mania's cornerstones. (1977, pp. 76-7)

Georgescu-Roegen shares this viewpoint, as seen in his comment on the paper of Daly's from which the above quotation was taken:

This paper represents an improvement on Daly's earlier pleas. One new point deserves special attention: it is the map in which the hierarchy of ends and means is correlated with the categories of disciplines that keep the human mind continuously on the run. To have a single element by which everything is in the last analysis guided or judged has been a need felt by all truly philosophical schools. All great philosophers have imagined, if not a religious God, at least a philosophical one as the ultimate criterion, not for what ought to be, but for what must be. There is an indisputable need for an ultimate end by which we can judge which of our actions are 'good' and which are 'bad'. We always need a criterion of some sort or other. To take a simple but appropriate example: if the price ratio of coffee and meat is, say, 5 to 2, and I spend my budget at a point where my marginal rate of substitution between those commodities is 7 to 4, that is 'bad'. The criterion of maximum utility for my preference structure tells me so. But why should we not also ask the further question: are my preferences good or bad? Daly's point is that for this question we must turn to the ultimate end. This paper thus strengthens the impression emerging from his previous writings that the essence of Daly's conception is not economic or demographic, but, rather, ethical – a great merit in a period in which economics has been reduced to a timeless kinematics. As a befitting commandment for the ultimate end of a religion that should help mankind to survive and lead a decent life, I would suggest 'Love thy species as thyself.' Such a religion would certainly bring about the amiable community for which Daly fights untiringly. But as intimated earlier, the most challenging enterprise is to establish any religious faith, any faith in an ultimate end. (Georgescu-Roegen, pp. 102–3)

Explicit here is a turning-back on the notion of exchange value as the guiding principle of the economy, and a return to the use value concept. As Georgescu-Roegen puts it:

[I]n order to arrive at the 'true' cost of any material commodity, we must know the true values of natural resources *in situ*, which constitute the first cost item. Some economists trained in the neoclassical tradition have occasionally spoken of the 'true scarcity value' of natural resources *in situ*. Yet, to my knowledge, the determination of these values is a problem totally ignored by all tints of economic theory. (1977, p. 99)

Georgescu-Roegen rejects auction-based prices as inadequate because future generations cannot now bid on an asset such as the *Mona Lisa* or on current natural resource supplies.

The Roegen–Daly view – and also the view of the *Limits to Growth* group, Ehrlich and most 'ecologists' and popular writers on these subjects – rests squarely on the assumption of finitude. That concept, however, not only is not self-evident, but upon close examination turns out to be vacuous. A detailed examination of that matter now follows.

Whether the moral point of view of Georgescu-Roegen and Daly causes acceptance of a finite view of resources, or vice versa, or whether both are influenced by a common third element, is unknown to me. But this set of views does lead deductively to the conclusion that government must control the allocation of natural resources in a much more active fashion than is the case with the standard framework of economic thought which takes tastes as given, and (separately) which does not put the assumption of finitude of resources at the centre of the analysis. More specifically, Daly advocates government control of births with a license system, maximum limits on income and wealth, and government quotas on the extraction of natural resources (1977, pp. 53–63).

Implicit in the analysis of Daly, Georgescu-Roegen and other economic entropists is that additional people do not affect humankind's welfare or destiny except in their roles as consumers of resources. Given the fixed stock of energy, there is no place in their system for the production of new knowledge to affect long-run welfare. Of course these writers might have brought the production of new knowledge into their system by considering it as a way of using a given amount of energy more efficiently from a welfare point of view, but they do not do so; re-distribution among income classes and over time, and limitation of numbers of people, are the devices they suggest for improvement of the human lot (e.g. Daly, 1977, p. 151ff.) '[B]y focusing on ... the ability of new technologies to tap new resources, economists fall into the trap of ignoring the ultimate finitude of the common denominator of all useful things, low-entropy, matter-energy, which is scarce in an absolute sense' (Daly, 1977, p. 25).

Economists have long discussed the role of substitution of one raw material for another, though this mechanism is not part of the conventional pessimistic scenario[7] considered earlier in Hotelling's analysis. Barnett and Morse pushed this argument furthest and, backed by their showing of the historical record of declining costs, suggested that substitution takes place at a rate that will lead to continued declining costs (actually in combination with discoveries of new lodes and new methods of exploiting raw material).

Goeller and Weinberg dug into the physical facts that make more concrete our understanding of the possibilities of raw-material substitutions. By examination of the materials in current use in our world economy, and of the physical possibilities of substitution among them, they conclude that – aside from energy, phosphorous and traces of copper, zinc and cobalt for agriculture – materials that are acceptably cheap and in supplies so large that they may be considered to be on a cost plateau are available to substitute for all the raw materials we now use. 'Society would then be based upon glass, plastic, wood, cement, iron, aluminum, and magnesium' (1976/ 1978, p. 4).

This does *not* ensure that costs will decline starting *now*; just the opposite. The materials to be substituted for are now cheaper to obtain and use than are their potential substitutes, else they would not now be used. But it does promise that there is some point at which rising costs of the presently used materials might reach the plateau costs of the substitutes. And from then on, any technological advance would produce declining costs.

The Goeller–Weinberg analysis suggests that costs can decline almost indefinitely (that is, for many, many generations, beyond any foreseeable planning horizon), but on one additional assumption: energy costs that do not increase in the long run. In their thinking, this assumption is met by nuclear power. It is here the questions arise, because the argument cannot be made in either direction with as much surety as for the other raw materials. Can nuclear-fission plants be built so that they will be politically acceptable? And will nuclear fusion become economical? Though one can be very sure – as I am – that one or another or both will happen long before major substitution of other raw materials is necessary – surely in the next 50 or 100 years, if not in the next 20 years – this judgement is reached on general intuition rather than upon a few clearcut arguable propositions.

If one assumes to the contrary that no nuclear energy will become available, and also assumes that biomass fuels and solar power and wind power and wave power and heat from below the surface of the earth (in such forms as geothermal energy) can never be exploited sufficiently to alter the long-run picture, then fossil fuels[8] are the only option left. And one could then reasonably argue that within some sensible planning horizon, fossil fuels will be sufficiently depleted to produce rising costs of energy. If so, the costs of other raw materials might rise, too. But please notice that considerations of the total energy available within our system – however that system is defined – have no part in the discussion; the second law of thermodynamics and the concept of entropy can only be red herrings here. This conclusion emerges both from a practical look at the length of the sun's life (say a billion years) relative to the length of human history and the life span of one human, as well as from theoretical considerations of the possible boundaries to our system in a time frame comparable to the sun's life or less.

So where are we left with respect to our original question about the inevitability of increasing resource costs, and resources as a brake upon economic development? The answer now seems straightforwardly negative. From Goeller and Weinberg alone we can say: several possibilities of (in the original sense of the word) practically inexhaustible sources of energy exist. And if one or more of these possibilities pans out, then at some point there will start to be indefinitely declining costs of other raw materials. And this conclusion is perfectly compatible even with present technology in raw-material exploitation and substitution. Beyond this, increases in knowledge might by themselves produce declining raw-material costs indefinitely; indeed, just that has happened throughout all of human history.[9]

In brief, it is not *logically* erroneous to assert that raw-material costs *must* eventually rise. But any one of many plausible possibilities *could* lead to indefinitely decreasing costs: (a) If there is a master resource by means of which refined resource X can be produced without increasing cost of obtaining X in the unprocessed state, then the cost of X may decrease. This would hold for fresh water if the energy to desalinate water were cheap and decreasing. And this would therefore also hold for arable land for the very long time during which desalinated water would be used to irrigate deserts, and as cheap energy would make it cheap to transport the water. The case of aluminium (say) would not be very different from the case of water because the richness of ore would decrease very slowly no matter how much were to be used. (b) If the cost of energy is level indefinitely even though not near zero, as seems to be the case with nuclear fission, then for raw materials such as aluminium for which energy is the main additional input, costs will decline if there is technological advance greater than the decline in ore richness. This seems not at all implausible for aluminium, iron and other metals, including those found in sea water or at the bottom of the sea. (c) If the material can be substituted for by other materials embraced by possibilities (a) and (b) above, and if technological change can improve the efficiency of such substitution over time, then X's cost can fall. And according to the Goeller–Weinberg analysis, this includes almost all raw materials. (d) If the material can be grown – as with food and wood – the notion of finiteness is obviously irrelevant except in the view of those who worry about the running down of both the sun and all other sources of energy after millions or billions or trillions of years. And the earth's land also is not a theoretical limit to production for a variety of reasons. For these reasons, the *possibility* of decreasing cost for some materials – even if not the *likelihood* – would seem easy to agree upon. And here, as throughout this discussion, only non-increasing costs and not decreasing costs are necessary to confute pessimistic predictions. And that requires only cost plateaus for energy costs and for the materials that can provide for our basic needs, substituting for those in use now.

VI.   WHY HAVE MATERIALS PRICES FALLEN RELATIVE TO CONSUMER GOODS AND SERVICES?

The central notion of cost used until now in this appendix has been that of raw-material price relative to wages. There is no pure theoretical justification for this choice of definition but only a practical justification, to wit: if raw materials will be a decreasing proportional input (in value terms) into the mix of goods and services we use, and if wages in real terms will be going up (as we may expect them to, as long as there is technical advance and no constraint by natural resources), then, if raw-material prices will fall relative to wages, there is clearly no practical problem for consumers.

This section tries to go further, however, to speculate why raw-material availability has historically passed the much harder test of a fall in price of raw materials relative to consumer goods and services, the composite of which has itself been getting cheaper because of

more efficient production. To repeat, however, it should be understood that even if this question is of theoretical interest, and even if
it is of potential concern to investors in raw materials, it is not
relevant to the question of whether raw materials will exert a constraint upon future growth.

There seems to be no logical *necessity* for the price of raw materials
to fall relative to other goods. Without some other factor entering
the situation, we would expect natural resources to become relatively
more expensive due to exhaustion. And there is no reason to expect
technology – for deeper digging, cheaper transportation and the
like – to develop relatively more rapidly in natural resources than in
other sectors of the economy. Nor does it seem likely that the higher
degree of labour intensity (defined as the proportion of labour cost
to selling price) in consumer goods would explain the matter. The
following speculation, however, may be an explanation of the
observed empirical trends.

Assume a static economy with, say, three goods – perhaps one
consumer service, one good with a 20 per cent content of raw
material X_1 whose ore gets progressively less rich as more of it is
used, and the third with a 20 per cent content of X_2 whose ore
content remains of almost constant richness for now. There will
then be a progressive rise in the relative price of X_1 (and hence in the
average of all raw materials) as labour is shifted from the consumer
sector to the raw-material sector. Hence in a technologically stationary
economy, with no substitution, the terms of trade will be in favour
of raw materials; that is, raw-material prices will rise relative to
consumer goods.

Nor does the existence of technological advance imply that the
terms of trade must turn against raw materials. One might speculate
(though it is not a demonstrated fact, to my knowledge) that the
input of labour relative to capital is greater for consumer goods than
for raw materials. And one might further speculate that technical
advance works disproportionately in favour of goods whose labour
input is relatively low, in the sense that technical advance tends to
be capital-enhancing. But is the latter really true? The services of
writing, and singing, and doing arithmetic, have been made enorm-
ously cheaper over the years by the printing press, the phonograph
an radio, and the computer.[10] Therefore, without some closer and
more compelling analysis, technical advance as a general explanation

of the fall in raw-materials prices relative to consumer prices does not seem to hold water.

If technical advance is not a satisfactory explanation, then a difference in likelihood of substitution seems the most plausible candidate. And indeed, intuitively there seems to be an important difference in this respect between raw materials and consumer (or producer) goods: raw materials are simpler in what we want of them in that there are few dimensions (often only one or two) on which we perceive them to matter; there are usually more dimensions that matter to us with consumer goods. For example, in construction, dried mud's benefit to us – rigidity – may be supplied by wood or concrete or iron or aluminium or stone or even other apparently dissimilar materials including water as ice or snow.[11] But a car or a geisha has many dimensions that interest us: for the car – shape, speed, gadgets, amount of noise, starting time and so on; for the geisha – shape (but different shape than the car), sound, grace and so on. This multitude of relevant dimensions makes it more difficult for a totally new consumer product to replace an old one than for a new construction material to replace an old one, as it was not simple for the car (especially with complementary roads) to replace the horse.

To repeat, the key to substitutability may lie in the relative *simplicity* of raw materials. Generally we want a raw material for a single property – rigidity, conductivity and so on – whereas we typically demand several properties of a consumer good. And the smaller the number of characteristics in which you are interested, the easier it is to find a substitute that has that particular characteristic or characteristics. This is also true of simple producer goods relative to more complex producer goods. It would be easier to find close substitutes (in the sense that the substitution would be little noticed) for iron nails and cotton fabric than for airplanes and violins.

An important reason why there are more dimensions relevant for a consumer good is that the final form of the good is affected by consumers' tastes, and therefore is influenced by human physiology, psychology and learning, whereas raw materials are not so affected. Original raw inputs are constrained only by physical interchangeability. As discussed earlier, Goeller and Weinberg have shown how, with respect to raw materials, there are very few relevant characteristics that affect interchangeability. And of course an increasing stock of knowledge increases the possibility of interchangeability (e.g. the knowledge of how to work with iron increases the possibility of its substitution for copper), and thereby reduces the cost of substitution.[12] And knowledge of physics increases possibilities for substitutions for copper in communications uses.[13]

More generally, it is relatively easy to find materials to perform purely physical functions compared to those materials that satisfy a taste. Consider how easy it is to find objects in a room to prop open a door, but how hard it would be to find a satisfactory substitute for your cello.

This explanation of why substitution propensity may be the answer to the question before us certainly is neither precise nor compelling. But luckily a compelling answer to this question is not vital to the general argument of this book, it being enough that the price of raw materials falls relative to *wages*. If this section at least asks the question in a fashion that someone else can answer better, it will be worthwhile.

VII.   POPULATION GROWTH AND MATERIAL SCARCITY

So far the discussion in this appendix has proceeded without reference to various levels of population and rates of population growth, the very topic to which this book is addressed. It should be reasonably clear that population does not affect the qualitative discussion above about what will 'ultimately' happen in billions of years. But population certainly could affect the *timing* of changes in the direction of raw-material costs. It is this timing that we must consider.

The behavioural relationship between population (or more generally, demand) and resource cost is a key element. The relationship assuredly is not that which is suggested by the vulgar idea of a 'race' between them. More people certainly imply increased demand in the short run, and therefore higher costs than otherwise in the short run. But the long run is not just a sequence of short runs in this case, and hence it is fallacious to draw any conclusions from this short-run analysis. In the longer run, technology's advance comes from people, and technological advance is the sole factor responsible for the long-run declines in material cost.

The process by which increased demand due to more people and higher income causes advances in resource technology is only a special case of the general relationship between demand and technical advance analysed in chapter 14 of my 1981 book, where systematic empirical studies are presented. Here are some natural resource cases that illustrate the process:

(a) Tilton (1981) has reported studies analysing tin use in four applications – beer and soft drink containers, fruit and vegetable containers, solder applications and PVC plastic pipe. Though these studies do not address the question quantitatively, they suggest qualitatively that the price of tin affects technological change in tin-using industries (p. 14).

(b) Two historical vignettes: (i) Prices of copper and iron fell in early Babylonian history, as described earlier. (ii) Ivory used for billiard balls threatened to run out late in the nineteenth century. As a result of a prize offered for a replacement material, celluloid was developed, and that discovery led directly to the astonishing variety of plastics that now give us a cornucopia of products (including billiard balls) at a prices so low as to boggle the nineteenth-century mind.

(c) A contemporary example:

When Northrop Corp. cranks out fighter planes nowadays, something out of the ordinary rolls down the assembly line: airplane parts cut from wide bolts of shiny black cloth. To the uninitiated, that might seem to signal a serious decline in the nation's defense industry. But the cloth – a blend of carbon fibers and epoxy – represents a technological leap. Once baked, pressurized and cooled, it yields rustproof wing parts, fins and rudders. Each is about half the weight of a comparable aluminum part – yet as strong as steel.

The defense industry is not alone in its apparent fling with Seventh Avenue. In recent years corporations from coat to coast have dreamed up a dazzling array of new materials. (*Newsweek*, 1 February 1982, p. 56)

The cause of these advances in resources was evident to the writer of the story:

Spurred by the oil shortages of the 1970s and a drive to lessen America's dependence on imported minerals and metals, scientists have developed sophisticated new plastics, ceramics and metallic products – all aimed at increasing energy efficiency – and tapping domestic raw materials. (p. 56)

And the outcome is better resources than we had to start with:

> Now scientists are developing ceramic parts that can withstand those temperatures and whose toughness puts the stuff of toilet bowls to shame. One new process developed by Corning Glass Works modifies the molecular structure of ceramic powder so that it expands instead of cracking – even at temperatures of up to 5,000 degrees Fahrenheit. The technology is in its infancy, but scientists are enthusiastic. 'This industry is about to embark on what happened to metallurgy when melting was first discovered,' says Raymond Bratton, manager of ceramic sciences at Westinghouse. (p. 57)

(d) Another recent example is the development of mines to produce copper, uranium, iron, lead, zinc, coal and even diamonds in Canada's Arctic where the ore is of very high grade. A newspaper report says: '[W]ith resources depleting in more-moderate climes, industry is turning increasingly to the far north.' In the past, this was impossible.

> At one time it all seemed nearly unattainable because of the vast distances and hostile temperatures of this cold desert ... Developing just some of these resources will require great leaps in understanding. Companies will need to find better ways to move the products of earlier exploration through long distances and thick ice. They will need to find ways to feed and house large groups of workers. 'The technological fallout ... will be tremendous,' predicts Charles Heterington, president of Panarctic. (*Wall Street Journal*, 5 February 1982, p. 1)

So we are likely eventually to have resources from the Arctic cheaper than if the threat of increasing scarcity had not induced development in the Far North. This typifies the process of increased demand from population and income leading to new and cheaper resources.

(e) Bernal in *Science and Industry in the Nineteenth Century* (1953) provides case studies of steel; electricity, light and power; chemistry, bacteriology and biochemistry; and the theory of heat and energy in the nineteenth century showing that innovations respond to economic demand. In the case of electricity, for example, 'The barrier, or rather the absence of stimulus to advance, was economic. Electricity developed quickly when it paid, not a moment before' (p. 131). And a large population size and density imply higher total demand, *ceteris paribus*, which is why Edison's first street lighting was in New York City rather than in Montana. It is also clear that countries with more people produce more knowledge, assuming income is the same, for example, Sweden versus the US. And Bernal shows how the power of final demand works indirectly, too. 'Once electric distribution on a large scale was proved feasible and immensely profitable, then came a demand for large efficient power sources' (p. 129), leading to the development of turbines. And the development of light bulbs led to advances in creating vacua, after the subject 'had stagnated for about two hundred years ... Here was another clear case of the law of supply and demand in the development of science and technology' (p. 125).

On the related question of whether material well-being can be improved through there being more ordinary persons – not geniuses – who contribute to our knowledge in their everyday work, the story of electricity and power production is again illuminating. Bernal describes the 'stumbling progress of the first fifty years from 1831 to 1881 ... the effort put into the development (1831–1881) ... was small'. The people who made the necessary technical developments 'were not geniuses ... and others no more gifted could have hit upon these ideas earlier if the field had attracted enough workers' (pp. 130–1).

(f) Soichino Honda, the inventor and founder of the Japanese motorcycle and car firm bearing his name, urges on us this slogan: 'Where 100 people think, there are 100 powers; if 1,000 people think, there are 1,000 powers (*Wall Street Journal*, 1 February 1982, p. 15).

NOTES

1 'Natural resource' can be a confusing term standing for a confused concept. Several ways of thinking about this concept can be appropriate in one or another context. In the present context, 'natural resource' shall mean material used to make goods at the earliest identifiable stage of cooperation with labour. For example, copper ingots are used at an earlier stage than copper wire, copper ore at an earlier stage than ingots and the earth containing the ore at an earlier stage than the ore. Of course the identification of the 'first' stage must be arbitrary, but that is not likely to cause confusion. Another way to think about these stages is with reference to the amount of value that has been added to the material at the beginning of a given work stage. This sort of definition helps us make a qualitative distinction between a plastic computer disk made from petroleum, and oil in the barrel

at the well-head, or oil in the ground. In most contexts there is little question of what is meant by natural resources: copper, oil, land, air, water are likely to be included; wheat, and trees grown on tree farms, are likely to be excluded because we clearly grow more of them. I shall not refer to any particular resource as sustainable or non-sustainable, exhaustible or non-exhaustible, because I do not think any such qualities are inherent in the nature of a particular material, but rather they depend on circumstances. For example, at one rate of fishing, the supply of fish in a body of water will decrease in the near future, and therefore may be called non-sustainable, while at another rate of fishing (perhaps together with fish-farming practices) the annual rate may continue unabated.

2 Samuelson may serve as the illustration because of his eminence in the economic profession. In the very last lines of a paper entitled 'The Optimum Growth Rate for Population', which is devoted to the analysis of saving and whose central argument implies that higher population leads to higher income, Samuelson concludes:

Ultimately, positive exponential population growth will presumably bring back into importance the scarcity of natural resources ignored by the model .... For several generations people may benefit on a lifetime basis by having numerous children to support them well in their old ages, out of filial piety or by means of social security. And yet until the end of time their increases in population will cause the law of diminishing returns to be brought into play to leave all subsequent generations in a worsened situation. To the degree that childhood dependency is intrinsically less costly relative to old-age dependency, this dyshygienic temptation becomes all the more dangerous. (1975, p. 537)

The most interesting aspect of this quotation is that – following a long complex paper full of careful proofs – the assertion of resource drag is made without any reference to facts or theory, simply as if it is a known and accepted truth.

3 For the reader who may be wondering about the matter at this juncture, the recent technical literature and natural resource substitution (see, e.g. Berndt and Field, 1981) are mostly not relevant to the concerns of this chapter. More will be said about this later.

4 Popper's remark (1974/1976) is relevant: '[C]ommon sense, though often right (and especially in its realism), is not always right. And things get really interesting just when it is wrong'.

5 This section draws heavily upon my 1981 book.

6 Assume (a) income is measured by the amount (proportion) of time spent working for food; (b) food consumption is the same for all countries and periods with given proportion of population in agriculture; (c) 80 per cent

(it does not matter if the better estimate is 70 per cent or 90 per cent) of the population worked in agriculture in all ancient times; (d) the price of copper relative to wheat remained the same from 1800 BC to AD 1; (e) 10 per cent of US labour force was in agriculture in 1955 (6 449 000/62 171 000; *Historical Stats*, p. 127).

$$\frac{\text{price of copper in labour time in ancient times}}{\text{price of copper in labour time now}}$$

$$= \frac{\% \text{ in agric. then}}{\% \text{ in agric. now}} \times \frac{\text{copper price/wheat price then}}{\text{copper price/wheat price now}}$$

7 Even as unworried an economist as Stiglitz writes that 'it is obvious that continued exponential growth is impossible, if only because eventually, at a strictly positive growth rate, the mass of people would exceed the mass of the earth' (1979, p. 37). My noting this comment of Stiglitz's does not mean that I am here advocating any particular rate of growth. What I wish to point out is that Stiglitz considers some absolute limits as worth mentioning (though he may only be paying the idea lip service). This suggests that physical limits may be a more binding constraint in the future than now, rather than viewing scarcity at any moment in the future as being of the same nature and of less severity than now.

8 The term 'fossil fuels' may be a misnomer. Coal and oil may be the result of methane gas deep in the earth rather than of fossils (Steele, 1982). If so, there are possibilities of vast supplies of methane to be exploited.

9 It is true that energy costs have been mostly falling rather than rising throughout history. But in the recent past, energy costs have been a sufficiently small part of total cost for many raw materials so that even rising energy prices would not have altered this conclusion.

10 Even geishas may perform before groups whose size may be magnified by telecommunications. Prostitution is the example that comes to mind of the good or service that is least subject to technical change and cost reduction, because there seem few possibilities for substitution on many of the relevant dimensions of sexual encounters, with little possibility for reduction in real resources used as inputs to the process.

11 Not only do the Eskimos build homes of snow, but a recent article about mining firms in the Canadian arctic says that they build – with ice-water piped onto gravel, which then freezes – ship docks, which are much cheaper to build with ice than with cement which must be shipped in at high cost (*Wall Street Journal*, 5 February 1982, p. 1).

12 The concept of dimensions may at first seem vague and not operational. But the concept can be made operational if one thinks in terms of purchase

specifications. Consider, for example, the list of specifications a purchasing agent would write for the building material to be used for a functional (not decorative) lamp-post, and the list of specifications that he or she would write for a perfume or a spouse. The difference is illustrated by comparing how much easier it is to delegate acquiring building materials than acquiring a spouse.

13 The replacement of copper intercontinental telephone wires by satellites, which sharply reduces the price of those communications sources, may be a well-known example by now. Optical fibres are another recent dramatic development in the centuries-long process:

Gutenberg spent five years setting the Bible in type. Today the book, in electronic form, can be transmitted over ordinary copper telephone wires in less than an hour. The Bible can be sent in less than a second, however, through optical fibers, the very clear threads of glass that carry information as flashes of light instead of electric pulses.

And enough text to fill 16 Bibles could be transmitted in a single second through a new type of conduit that is emerging from laboratories, the monomode, or single-mode optical fiber. 'Potentially, single-mode fibers represent as much an improvement over the optical fibers of today as today's fibers did over copper wire,' says Paul Fleury, director of the Materials Research Laboratory at Bell Telephone Laboratories, the research branch of American Telephone & Telegraph Corp. 'At present, commercial-mode fibers can be made that are 10 to a hundred times better than ordinary glass fibers,' he says. 'In the research stage, the fibers are 1,000 times better.' . . .

Today's fibers are more expensive than copper, and monomode fibers are more costly still. But because of its higher capacity, glass is starting to supplant copper in long-distance communications and within major cities where the volume of telephone calls continues to swell but where the ducts that contain telephone wiring already are overcrowded with copper and cannot be enlarged.

For similar reasons, monomode fibers are likely to be adopted soon, despite their price, although prices should drop. Monomode fibers cost between $2.30 and $5.50 per yard. But within five years, the price will decline to about 23 cents per yard, according to projections by Lightwave Technologies Inc., a monomode maker in Van Nuys, Calif. At very high transmission rates, the cost of monomode fibers already is competitive, Lightwave officials say. (*The Wall Street Journal*, 23 July 1982, p. 13)

Bibliography

Abramovitz M *Resource and Output Trends in the US Since 1870* (NBER, 1956)

Alchian A A 'Costs and Outputs.' In: Abramovitz M *et al.* (eds) *The Allocation of Economic Resources* (Stanford: Stanford University Press, 1959)

Alchian A A 'Reliability of Progress Curves in Airframe Production.' *Econometrica*, XXXI, October 1963, 679-93

Alonso W 'The Economics of Urban Size.' In: Friedman J, Alonso W (eds) *Regional Policy Readings in Theory and Applications* (Cambridge: MIT Press, 1976)

Alonso W, Fajans M 'Cost of Living and Income by Urban Size.' Mimeograph, 1970

Armstrong J S *Long Range Forecasting* (New York: Wiley, 1978)

Arrow K J 'The Economic Implications of Learning by Doing.' *Review of Economic Studies*, XXIX (3), 80, June 1962, 155-73.

Asher H *Cost Quantity Relationships in the Airframe Industry* (Santa Monica, California: RAND Report No. R-291, July 1956)

Baloff N 'The Learning Curve – Some Controversial Issues.' *Journal of Industrial Economics*, XIV, July 1966, 275-83

Barkai H, Levhari D 'The Impact of Experience on Kibbutz Farming.' *The Review of Economics and Statistics*, LV, February 1973, 56-63

Barnett H J, Morse C *Scarcity and Growth: The Economics of Natural Resource Availability* (Baltimore: Johns Hopkins, 1963)

Bauer P T *Equality, the Thiird World and Economic Delusion* (Cambridge, Mass.: Harvard University Press, 1981)

Baumol W J *Economic Dynamics* (New York: Macmillan, 1951)

Becker G S 'A Theory of the Allocation of Time.' *Economic Journal*, 75, 1965, 493-517

Bernal J D *Science and Industry in the Nineteenth Century* (London: Routledge and Kegan Paul, 1953)

Berndt E A, Field B C *Modelling and Measuring National Resource Substitution* (Cambridge, Mass.: MIT, 1981)

Berry R A, Soligo R 'Some Welfare Aspects of International Migration.' *Journal of Political Economy*, 77, September/October 1969, 778-94.

Bethe H A 'The Necessity of Fission Power.' *Scientific American*, 234, No. 1, January 1976

Blakeslee A 'Which Foods Guilty in Cancer?' *Champaign-Urbana News-Gazette*, 21 June 1979, C-8

Blitz R C 'A Benefit-Cost Analysis of Foreign Workers in West Germany, 1957-1973.' *Kyklos*, 30, Fasc 3, 1977, 479-502

Bohning W R *The Migration of Workers in the United Kingdom and the European Community* (New York: Oxford, 1972)

Borts G H, Stein J L *Economic Growth in a Free Market* (New York: Columbia University Press, 1964) (Quoted by Usher, 1977)

Boserup E *The Conditions of Agricultural Growth* (London: George Allen and Unwin, 1965)

Brems H *Labor, Capital and Growth* (Lexington, Massachusetts: Lexington Books, 1973)

Brems H *Inflation, Interest, and Growth* (Lexington, Massachuseets: Lexington Books, 1980)

Browning M personal communication (1981)

Cassel G *The Theory of Social Economy*, 5th ed., trans. (New York: Harcourt Brace, 1932)

Chayanov A V *The Theory of Peasant Economy* (Homewood: Irwin, 1966). Edited by Thorner D, Kerblay B and Smith R E F

Chenery H B 'Patterns of Industrial Growth.' *American Economic Review*, 50, 1960, 624-54.

Chenery H B, Syrquin M *Patterns of Development, 1950-1970* (New York: Oxford, 1975)

Child V G *What Happened in History* (Baltimore: Penguin, 1942/1964)

Chiswick B R 'The Effect of Americanization on the Earnings of Foreign-Born Men.' *Journal of Political Economy*, 86, No. 5, 897-921

Clark C *Conditions of Economic Progress*, 3rd ed. (New York: Macmillan, 1957)

Clark R L, Spengler J J 'Dependency Ratios: Their Use in Economic Analysis.' In: Simon J L, DaVanzo J (eds) *Research in Population Growth*, Vol. II (Greenwich: JAI Press, 1979)

Coale A J, Hoover E M *Population Growth and Economic Development in Low-Income Countries* (Princeton: Princeton University Press, 1958)

Cohen M N *The Food Crisis in Prehistory* (New Haven: Yale, 1977)

Daly H E (ed.) *Toward a Steady-State Economy* (San Francisco: W H Freeman and Co., 1973)

Daly H E *Steady-State Economics* (San Francisco: Freeman, 1977)

Daly H E review of *The Ultimate Resource, The Bulletin of the Atomic Scientists*, January 1982, 39-42

David P *Technical Choice, Innovation, and Economic Growth* (New York: CUP, 1975)

de Solla Price D *Science Since Babylon* (New Haven: Yale, 1961)

de Solla Price D 'Nations Can Publish or Perish.' *Science and Technology*, 1967, 85-90

de Solla Price D 'Measuring the Size of Science.' *Israel Academy of Sciences and Humanities Proceedings*, 4, 6, 1971, 98-111

de Solla Price D 'Some Statistical Results for the Numbers of Authors in the States of the United States and the Nations of the World.' *Who is Publishing in Science* (Philadelphia: Institute for Scientific Information, 1975, 26-35)

Dixit A K *The Theory of Equilibrium Growth* (New York: Oxford University Press, 1976)

Ekberg J 'Long-term Effects of Immigration.' *Economy and Society*, XX:1, 1977, 3-22

Eltis W A *Growth and Distribution* (London: Macmillan, 1973)

Enke S 'The Economic Aspects of Slowing Population Growth.' *Economic Journal*, 76, March 1966, 44-56

Evenson R E *The Contribution of Agricultural Research and Extension to Agricultural Production* (PhD Thesis, University of Chicago, 1968) Summarized in Havami and Ruttan (1971, p. 289)

Everett A H *New Ideas on Population* (New York: August M Kelley, 1826/1970)

Fellner W 'Specific Interpretations of Learning by Doing.' *Journal of Economic Theory*, 1, 1969, 119-40

Fellner W 'Trends in the Activities Generating Technological Progress.' *American Economic Review*, 60, March 1970

Fischer C S 'Urban-to-Rural Diffusion of Opinions in Contemporary America.' *American Journal of Sociology*, 84, July 1978, 151-9

Fussler H H, Simon J L *Patterns of Use of Books in Large Research Libraries* (University of Chicago Press, 1969)

Georgescu-Roegen N *The Entropy Law and the Economic Process* (Harvard University Press, 1971)

Georgescu-Roegen N 'Comments on the Papers by Daly and Stiglitz.' In: Kerry Smith V (ed.) *Scarcity and Growth Revisited* (Baltimore: Johns Hopkins, 1979, 95-105)

Goeller H E, Weinberg A M 'The Age of Substitutability.' *Science*, 191, 1978, 663-89

Griliches Z 'Research Costs and Social Returns: Hybrid Corn and Related Innovation.' *Journal of Political Economy*, 66, October 1958, 419-31

Hagen E E *The Economics of Development* (Homewood: Irwin, 1975)

'Is the Era of Limits Running Out? A Conversation with Garrett Hardin and Julian Simon, *Public Opinion*, March 1982, 48-54

Haworth L T, Rasmussen D W 'Determinants of Metropolitan Cost of Living Variations.' *Southern Economic Journal*, 40, 1973, 183-92

Hayek F A *The Constitution of Liberty* (Chicago: University of Chicago Press, 1960)

Hayek F A 'The Theory of Complex Phenomena.' In: *Studies in Philosophy, Politics and Economics* (Chicago: University of Chicago Press, 1977)

Hayek F A 'The Changing Range and Content of Individual Responsibility.' Paper for the 5th International Humanistic Symposium, Portlavia, Greece, September 1981

Hayek F A 'From Common Concrete Aims to Common Abstract Rules.' Chapter 3 in *The Fatal Conceit* (forthcoming)

Heady E O 'Basic Economic and Welfare Aspects of Farm Technological Advance.' *Journal of Farm Economics*, 31, 1949, 293-316

Hicks J *The Theory of Wages* (London: Macmillan, 1932)

Higgs R 'American Inventiveness, 1870-1920.' *Journal of Political Economy*, 79, 1971, 661-7

Hirsch W Z 'Firm Progress Ratios.' *Econometrica*, 24, April 1956, 136-43

Hotelling H 'The Economics of Exhaustible Resources.' *Journal of Political Economy*, 39, April 1931, 137-75.

Hulten C R 'On the "Importance" of Productivity Change.' *The American Economic Review*, 69, March 1979, 126-36

Jevons W S *The Coal Question* (London: Macmillan, 1865)

Jones K, Smith A D *The Economic Impact of Commonwealth Immigration* (Cambridge: CUP, 1970)

Jorgensen D, Griliches Z 'The Explanation of Productivity Change.' *Review of Economic Studies*, 34, July 1967, 249-83

Kaldor N 'A Model of Economic Growth.' *Economic Journal*, LXVII, December 1957

Kaldor N, Mirrlees J A 'A New Model of Economic Growth.' *Review of Economic Studies*, 29, June 1962, 174-92. Reprinted in Mueller M (ed.) *Readings in Macroeconomics*, 2nd ed. (Hinsdale: Dryden, 1970, 306-22)

Keely C B, Kraly E P 'Recent Net Alien Immigration to the US: Its Impact on Population Growth and Native Fertility.' Talk to PAA, 1978

Kelley A C 'Scale Economies, Technical Change, and the Economics of American Population Growth.' *Explorations in Economic History*, 10, 1972, 35-52

Kendrick J W, Sato R 'Factor Prices, Productivity and Economic Growth.' *American Economic Review*, LIII, December 1963

Kennedy C 'Induced Bias in Innovation and the Theory of Distribution.' *Economic Journal*, 74, September 1964, 541-7

Kennedy K A *Productivity and Industrial Growth* (Oxford: OUP, 1971)

Kindleberger C P *Economic Development*, 2nd ed. (New York: McGraw-Hill, 1965)

Klein L R, Kosobud R F 'Some Econometrics of Growth: Great Ratios in Economics.' *Quarterly Journal of Economics*, LXXV, May 1961

Kuznets S 'Long Swings in the Growth of Population and in Related Economic

Variables.' *Proceedings of the American Philosophical Society*, 102, 1958, 25-52

Kuznets S 'Population Change and Aggregate Output.' In: Universities-National Bureau of Economic Research, *Demographic and Economic Change in Developed Countries* (Princeton: Princeton University Press, 1960)

Kuznets S *Population, Capital, and Growth* (New York: W W Norton, 1973)

Kuznets S 'Two Centuries of Economic Growth: Reflections on US Experience', *American Economic Review*, February 1977

Lee R B 'What Hunters do for a Living, or, How to Make Out on Scarce Resources.' In: Lee R B, Devore I (eds) *Man the Hunter* (Chicago: Aldine, 1968, 30-48)

Lee R D 'Economic Consequences of Population Size, Structure and Growth.' [International Union for the Scientific Study of Population]. *Newsletter*, 17 (January 1983), 43-59

Leontief W *Essays in Economics* (New York: Oxford, 1966)

Levhari D, Sheshinski E 'Experience and Productivity in the Israel Diamond Industry.' *Econometrica*, 41, March 1973, 239-54

Lindert P H *Fertility and Scarcity in America* (Princeton: Princeton University Press, 1978)

Love D 'City Sizes and Prices.' PhD Thesis, University of Illinois, 1978

Love D, Pashute L 'The Effect of Population Size and Concentration Upon Scientific Productivity.' In: Simon J L (ed.) *Research in Population Economics*, Vol. I (Greenwich: JAI Press, 1978)

Machlup F 'The Supply of Inventors and Inventions.' *Welwirtschaftliches Archiv*, Band 85, 1960, Heft 2, 210-54. A shortened version appears in Nelson R R (ed.) *The Rate and Direction of Inventive Activity* (Universities-Princeton University Press, 1962, 143-70)

McNeill W H *The Rise of the West* (New York: Mentor, 1963)

Meadows D H, Meadows D L, Randers J, Behrens W W III *The Limits to Growth* (New York: Potomac Association, 1972)

Meeks T J 'The Effect of Population Growth upon the Quantity of Education Children Receive: A Comment.' *Review of Economics and Statistics*, May 1982

Mellor J W 'The Use and Productivity of Farm Family Labor in Early Stages of Agricultural Growth.' *Journal of Farm Economics*, 45, 1963, 517-34

Miyashita H, Newbold P, Pilarski A, Simon J 'The Effect of Population Growth upon the Quantity of Education Children Receive: A Reply.' *Review of Economics and Statistics*, May 1982, 352-5.

Modigliani F 'The Life Cycle Hypothesis of Saving, the Demand for Wealth and the Supply of Capital.' *Social Research*, 33, 1966

Morawetz D 'Twenty-five Years of Economic Development.' *Finance and Development*, September 1977, 11

Morawetz D *Twenty-Five Years of Economic Development: 1950-1975*

(Baltimore: Johns Hopkins, 1978)

Neal L, Useldin P 'Immigration: A Neglected Source of American Economic Growth, 1790-1917.' *Oxford Economic Papers*, 24, 1972, 66-88

Nef J V *Cultural Foundations of Industrial Civilization* (Cambridge: Cambridge University Press, 1958; New York: Harper Torchbook edn, 1960)

Nef J V 'An Early Energy Crisis and Its Consequences.' *Scientific American*, May 1977, 140-51

Nelson R R (ed.) *The Rate and Direction of Inventive Activity* (Princeton: NBER-PUP, 1962). See also the longer version in *Weltwirtschaftliches Archiv*, Band 85, Heft, 1960, 210-54

Nelson R R 'Research on Productivity Growth and Differences.' *Journal of Economic Literature*, XIX, September 1981, 1029-64

Nordhaus W D *Invention, Growth, and Welfare* (Cambridge: MIT Press, 1969)

Nordhaus W D, Tobin J *Is Growth Obsolete?* (New York: NBER, 1972)

North D S, Houston M F *The Characteristics and Role of Illegal Aliens in the US Labor Market: An Exploratory Study* (Washington: Linton and Company, March 1976)

Petty W *Another Essay in Political Arithmetic* (1682) In: Hull C H (ed.) *The Economic Writings of Sir William Petty* (Cambridge: CUP, 1899)

Phelps E S 'Models of Technical Progress and the Golden Rule of Research.' *Review of Economic Studies*, April 1966, 133-45

Phelps E S 'Population Increase.' *Canadian Journal of Economics*, 1, 1968, 497-518

Phelps E S 'Some Macroeconomics of Population Leveling.' In: Morss E R, Reed R H (eds) *Economic Aspects of Population Change* (Washington: USGPO, 1972)

Piotrow P T *World Population Crisis: The United States Response* (New York: Praeger, 1973)

Pirenne H *Medieval Cities* (Princeton: Princeton University Press, 1925; paperback 1969)

Pitchford J D *Population and Economic Growth* (New York: North Holland, 1974)

Pollak R A Personal communication, October 1980

Popper K *Unended Quest* (La Salle, Illinois: Open Court Publishing Co., 1974/1976)

Ram R 'Population Growth and Educational Expenditures: Some Further Reflections and Evidence.' Mimeograph, October 1982.

Rescher N *Scientific Progress* (Pittsburgh: University of Pittsburgh Press, 1978)

Rosen S 'Learning by Experience as Joint Production.' *Quarterly Journal of Economics*, LXXXVI, August 1972, 336-82

Rosenberg N 'The Direction of Technological Change and Involvement Mechanisms and Focusing Devices.' *Economic Development and Cultural Change*, October 1969, 1-24

Rosenberg N 'Innovative Responses to Materials Shortages.' *American Economic Review*, LXIII, May 1973, 111–18.

Rosenberg N *Technology and American Economic Growth* (New York: Harper, 1972)

Rostas L *Comparative Productivity in British and American Industry*, Occasional Paper XIII, NIER, Cambridge, 1948

Royster V *Wall Street Journal*, 11 April 1979, 22.

Salehi-Isfahani D 'Ester Boserup Revisited: Population Growth and Intensification in Iranian Agriculture.' *IUSSP Paper No. 6 – Agrarian Change and Population Growth*, Liege, 1976

Samuelson P A 'A Theory of Induced Innovation along Kennedy, Weizsacker Lines.' *Review of Economics and Statistics*, 47, 1965, 343–56

Samuelson P A 'The Optimum Growth Rate for Population.' *International Economic Review*, 16, December 1975, 531–8

Scherer F H *Industrial Market Structures and Economic Performance* (Chicago: Rand McNally, 1970)

Schmookler J *Invention and Economic Growth* (Cambridge, Mass.: Harvard University Press, 1966)

Schmookler J *Patents, Inventions, and Economic Change* (Cambridge, Mass.: Harvard, 1973)

Segal D 'Are There Returns to Scale in City Size?' *Review of Economics and Statistics*, 58, 1976, 339–50

Sen A K 'Peasants and Dualism With or Without Surplus Labor.' *Journal of Political Economy*, 74, 1966, 425–50

Sheffer D 'Comparable Living Costs and Urban Size: A Statistical Analysis.' *American Institute of Planners Journal*, 36, 1970, 417–21

Shell K 'Toward a Theory of Inventive Activity and Capital Accumulation.' *American Economic Review*, LVI, May 1966, 62–68

Sheshinski E 'Tests of the Learning by Doing Hypothesis.' *Review of Economics and Statistics*, XLLX (November 1967), 568–78

Simon J L 'The Value of Avoided Births to Underdeveloped Countries.' *Population Studies*, 23, 1969, 61–68

Simon J L 'The Economic Effect of Russian Immigrants Upon the Veteran Israeli Population: A Cost-Benefit Analysis.' *The Economic Quarterly*, 23, August 1976, 244–52 (in Hebrew)

Simon J L *The Economics of Population Growth* (Princeton: Princeton University Press, 1977)

Simon J L *The Ultimate Resource* (Princeton: Princeton University Press, 1981)

Simon J L 'On the Evaluation of Progress and Technological Advance, Past and Future.' Xerox, 1984

Simon J L, Gobin R 'The Relationship between Population and Economic Growth in LDCs.' In: Simon J L, daVanzo J (eds) *Research in Population*

Economics, Vol. II, 1979

Simon J L, Heins A J 'The Effect of Immigrants on Natives' Income Through the Returns to Capital Captured by Immigrants.' *Journal of Development Economics* (forthcoming, 1985)

Simon J L, Pilarski A 'The Effect of Population Growth Upon the Quantity of Education Children Receive.' *Review of Economics and Statistics*, November 1979, 572-84

Simon J L, Steinmann G 'Population Growth and Phelps' Technical Progress Model.' In: Simon J L, Lindert P H (eds) *Research in Population Economics*, Vol. III, 1981, 239-54

Simon J L, Sullivan R 'Population Size, Knowledge Stock, and Other Determinants of Agricultural Publications and Patenting: England, 1541-1850.' Mimeograph, 1985

Singer M 'How the Scarcity Error Hurts America.' *Washington Quarterly*, Spring 1981

Slicher Van Bath B H *The Agrarian History of Western Europe, AD 500-1850* (London: Arnold, 1963)

Smith V K (ed.) *Scarcity and Growth Revisited* (Baltimore: Resources for the Future and Johns Hopkins University Press, 1979)

Solow R 'Technical Change and the Aggregate Production Function.' *The Review of Economics and Statistics*, 39, 1957, 312-20

Solow R *Growth Theory: An Exposition* (New York: Oxford University Press, 1970)

Sorokin P *Social and Cultural Dynamics* (Boston: Little Brown, 1937)

Spengler J J 'Agricultural Development is Not Enough.' In: Farnes R N *et al.* (eds) *World Population – The View Ahead* (Bloomington: Indiana University Press, 1968, 115)

Steele W 'The Methane Mystery.' *Mechanix Illustrated*, March 1982, 75-27, 136

Steinmann G, Simon J L 'Phelps' Technical Progress Function Generalized.' *Economic Letters*, 5, 1980

Stiglitz J E 'A Neo-classical Analysis of the Economics of Natural Resources.' Mimeograph, 1979

Stryker J D 'Optimum Population in Rural Areas: Empirical Evidence from the Franc Zone.' *The Quarterly Journal of Economics*, Vol. XCI, May 1977, No. 2, 177-93

Sullivan R *British Agriculture, 1500-1550: A Case Study of Long Run Technological Change*, PhD thesis, University of Illinois, 1983

Sveikauskas L 'The Productivity of Cities.' *Quarterly Journal of Economics*, 89, 1975, 393-413

Taylor E F, Wheeler J A *Spacetime Physics* (San Francisco: Freeman, 1966)

Tilton J E 'Prices, Innovation, and the Demand for Materials.' Mimeo, Penn State, 1981

Usher D 'Public Property and the Effects of Migration Upon Other Residents of the Migrants' Countries of Origin and Destination.' *Journal of Political Economy*, 85, 1977, 1001–26

Verdoorn P J 'Factors That Determine the Growth of Labor Productivity.' Translated by Thirlwall G and A P. In: Simon J L, daVanzo J (eds) *Research in Population Economics*, Vol. II (Greenwich: JAI Press, 1979) Originally in *L'Industria*, No. 1, 1949, 45–6

von Weiszacker C C 'Tentative Notes on a Two-Sector Model with Induced Technical Progress.' *The Review of Economic Studies*, 33, July 1966, 245–51

Wan Jr H Y *Economic Growth* (New York: Harcourt Brace Jovanovich, 1973)

Weinberg S *The First Three Minutes: A Modern View of the Origin of the Universe* (New York: Bantam, 1977)

West E C *Canada–United States Price and Productivity Differences in Manufacturing Industries, 1963* (Ottawa: Economic Council of Canada, 1971)

Winegarden C R 'Educational Expenditure and School Enrolments in Less-Developed Countries: A Simultaneous-Equation Method.' *Eastern Economic Journal*, 2, 1975, 77–87

Wright T P 'Factors Affecting the Cost of Airframes.' *Journal of the Aeronautical Sciences*, 3, February 1936, 112–18

Index

Index by Ann Barham